THE SAGA

THE BATTLE
OF KARBALA

FOREWORD BY
SAYYID HASSAN ALHAKEEM

EDITED BY
MOHAMED ALI ALBODAIRI

THE MAINSTAY
FOUNDATION

Foreword by: Sayyid Hassan al-Hakeem

Edited by: Mohamed Ali Albodairi

Printed in the United States.

ISBN: 978-1943393305

Contents

Foreword

On the tenth day of the month of Muharram, fifty years after the passing of the Holy Prophet Muhammad (s), Imam Hussain (a) and a small number of family members and companions were slaughtered at the hands of the Umayyad government. They made their stance on the land of Karbala with determination and resolve. They did not waiver in the face of an army of thousands. They made that stance in the hope that their memory will bring life to a Muslim nation which was spiraling fast down the road of deviance.

More than thirteen centuries have passed since. Yet every year, Muslims around the world continue to commemorate the tragedy and remember Imam Hussain's (a) great sacrifice. Devotees from around the globe flock to his grave in Karbala to visit and supplicate. They remember the events of that bloody massacre and the valor of Imam Hussain (a) and his companions. They recite verse and prose in commemoration of that stance.

Because of the great importance of the tragedy and the passion that it infused into the Muslim nation, Umayyad authorities did all they could to erase its memory. They forbade the mentioning of Imam Hussain (a), persecuted anyone who professed love to the Holy Prophet's (s) household, and spread false ideologies that absolved them of any culpability. Despite all this, Imam Hussain's (a) stance was engraved into the conscience of the Muslim nation. As Lady Zaynab proclaimed in the court of Yazid, "By God, you will never erase our remembrance or kill our inspiration."

As a fulfilment of Lady Zaynab's promise, Muslim historians were able to compile and record the events of the tragedy with great detail. Some scholars would even dedicate entire volumes to the tragedy. These books – known as the *Maqatil* (sing. *Maqtal*) – are now the chief sources for historical accounts in regards to Imam Hussain's (a) stance on the lands of Karbala.

Unfortunately, there has not been a comprehensive resource for this critical historic event in the English language. That is why the Mainstay Foundation has undertaken the task of compiling and publishing an encyclopedia of the history of the event. This volume, *The Saga: The Battle of Karbala*, is a compilation of the events that took place in the land of Karbala from the beginning of the battle on the 10th of Muharram to the martyrdom of Imam Hussain (a).

In compiling this encyclopedia, we were careful to ensure that all entries are properly referenced. Most entries are taken from the books of the *Maqatil* in which our scholars dedicated volumes to the memory of the battle of Karbala. Specifically, many entries are taken from:

- *Al-Saheeh min Maqtal Sayyid al-Shuhada (a)* by Muhammad al-Rayshahri,
- *Maqtal al-Hussain (a)* by Abdulrazzaq al-Muqarram,
- *Maqtal al-Hussain (a)* by al-Muwaffaq ibn Ahmad al-Khowarizmi,
- *Maqtal al-Hussain (a)* by Abu Mikhnaf,
- *Lawa'ij al-Ashjan* by Sayyid Muhsin al-Ameen, and
- *Mawsu'at Karbala* by Dr. Labeeb Beydoun.

We hope that this work is accepted by our beloved Imam Hussain (a) as a contribution to the preservation of his message and stance. We pray to God Almighty to accept our efforts and make them a means of growing closer to His service.

Finally, we want to take this opportunity to thank you for your support. As students of Islam and as compilers of this text, our greatest purpose is to please God by passing along this knowledge to others. By picking up this book, you have lent your crucial support to this endeavor. We hope that you will continue your support throughout the rest of this book, and we ask that you keep us in your prayers whenever you pick it up.

Sayyid Hassan al-Hakeem,

The Mainstay Foundation, London, UK

The Companions of the Imam

The Few Who Escaped the Slaughter

من المسلّم به أن كل من حضر مع الحسين من الأنصار قد استشهد، إلا نزرا معدودا من الأشخاص الذين لم يحرزوا شرف الشهادة لأسباب معينة، و هم:

It is undisputed that all of al-Hussain's (a) supporters present in Karbala were martyred, except for a handful of individuals who did not attain the honor of martyrdom for some specific reason. They are as follows;

من أهل البيت (عليهم السلام): ثلاثة من أولاد الإمام الحسن هم: زيد و عمرو و الحسن المثنّى، و قد كان الأخير جريحا فأخذه أسماء بن خارجة الفزاري قريب أمه، فداواه و عوفي. إضافة إلى الإمام زين العابدين علي بن الحسين (عليه السلام) الّذي كان مريضا يحتضر، ثم عافاه الله و نجّاه من القتل لعبرة لا تخفى.

From the Household [of the Prophet (s)], three of the children of Imam Hassan (a) survived and they are: Zayd, Amr, and al-Hassan II. The latter was wounded and taken and nursed by Asmaa ibn Kharija al-Fazari - a relative of his mother - until he recovered. This is in addition to Imam Zayn al-Abideen Ali ibn al-Hussain (a), who was fatally ill but was later cured by God, thus saving him from the massacre for an evident reason.

[أما الذي نجى] من الأصحاب ثلاثة هم:

From the companions, three survived. They are:

- الضحّاك بن عبد الله المشرقي: كان الضحّاك ذا عيال و دين، فقاتل مع الحسين (عليه السلام) على شرط، فوافقه الحسين (عليه السلام)

عليه، فلما أصبح (عليه السلام) فريدا أذن له بالانسلال من المعركة إلى أهله.

- Al-Dahhak ibn Abdullah al-Mashriqi [...] who faught with al-Hussain (a) on a condition [that he be allowed to leave if no one remained but him and al-Hussain (a)]. When [al-Hussain] (a) remained alone, he gave [al-Dahhak] permission to escape the battlefield and return to his family.

- عقبة بن سمعان: مولى الرباب زوجة الحسين (عليه السلام). و كان يخدم الحسين (عليه السلام) و قد صحبه في المعركة، فلما أخذ أسيرا إلى عبيد الله بن زياد و عرف أنه مولى للرباب، خلّى سبيله.

- Uqba ibn Sam'an, the servant of al-Rabab the wife of al-Hussain (a). He used to serve al-Hussain (a) and came with him to the battle. He was taken captive to Ubaydillah ibn Ziyad, who let him go when he heard that he is a servant of al-Rabab.

- علي بن عثمان بن الخطاب المغربي: من موالي أمير المؤمنين (عليه السلام) على ما رواه الشيخ الصدوق في (الإكمال).

- Ali ibn Othman ibn al-Khattab al-Maghribi, who was a servant of the Commander of the Faithful (a), as narrated by al-Shaykh al-Sadouq in al-Ikmaal.[1]

The Companions who Accompanied al-Hussain (a) from Mecca

حدّد أخطب خوارزم عدد الذين خرجوا مع الحسين (عليه السلام) من مكة،
فقال: «و فصل (عليه السلام) من مكة يوم الثلاثاء، يوم التروية، لثمان مضين
من ذي الحجة، و معه اثنان و ثمانون 82 رجلاً؛ من شيعته، و مواليه، و أهل
بيته.»

Akhtab Khawarizm listed the number of those who accompanied al-
Hussain (a) from Mecca as follows, "He (a) left Mecca on Thursday,
on the Day of Tarweyah, the 8th of Dhul Hijja, along with eighty two
men, including his followers, servants, and family members."

و في الطريق تبعه خلق كثير، فلما انتهى إلى (زبالة) بلغه مقتل مسلم بن عقيل
و هانئ بن عروة و عبد الله بن يقطر. فخطب في الناس مبيّنا مقاصده من
نهضته، فتفرق عنه الناس، حتى لم يبق معه إلا الذين خرجوا معه من مكة.
إذن فقد بقي معه رجال الثورة الحقيقيون وحدهم، بعد أن انجلى الموقف وتبيّن
المصير.

Along the way, many people joined him. When he reached Zubala and
the news of the martyrdom of Muslim ibn Aqeel, Hani ibn Urwa, and
Abdullah ibn Yaqtur reached him. He spoke to the people and
informed them of the ends for which he revolted. The people scattered
away from him so that no one remained except those who had came
with him from Mecca. Therefore, only those who were true to the
revolution remained with him when the position became clear and
their fate became evident.

و قد امتحن الإمام الحسين (عليه السلام) أصحابه مرة ثانية ليلة العاشر من المحرم، و طلب منهم الانصراف عنه، فأبوا و رفضوا، و آثروا البقاء معه حتى النهاية. و قد انضم إلى هذا العدد، قليل من الرجال الذين جاؤوا إليه فيما بعد.

Imam Hussain (a) tested his companions again on the eve of the 10th of Muharram. He asked them to leave him, but they refused and chose to remain with him to the end. In addition to these men [who accompanied him from the start] very few had joined later on.[2]

Those Who Joined al-Hussain (a) from Kufa

كانت الكوفة معقل الشيعة، فلما علم أهلها بمسير الحسين (عليه السلام) سعوا إليه، فبعضهم انضم إليه أثناء مسيره إلى كربلاء، و بعضهم انضم إليه في كربلاء، نعدّ منهم 21 شخصا [...].كما انضم إلى الحسين (عليه السلام): وهب بن عبد الله (حباب) الكلبي، الّذي كان نصرانيا فأسلم، و أسلمت معه زوجته، فقتلا في كربلاء [...].

Kufa was the capital of the Shia. When the Kufans heard of al-Hussain's (a) journey, they marched toward him. Some of them joined him before his arrival to Karbala, while others joined when he was in Karbala. We can list 21 such names [...]. In addition, Wahab ibn Abdullah al-Kalbi, who was a Christian and entered Islam along with his wife, joined Imam Hussain (a) and were martyred in Karbala. [...][3]

How Many were in the Camp of al-Hussain (a)?

نلاحظ ، قبل أن نذكر تقديرنا الخاص في المسألة ، أن عدد الاصحاب لم يكن ثابتا في جميع المراحل ، منذ الخروج من مكة إلى ما بعد ظهر اليوم العاشر من المحرم في كربلاء ، وإنما كان العدد متقلبا ،

We observe that, before we mention our own evaluation in this issue, the number of the Imam's (a) companions was not fixed throughout the stages of his journey. From the time he left Mecca to the afternoon of the 10th of Muharram in Karbala, the numbers changed.

بدأ عند الخروج من مكة بالعدد الذي ذكره الخوارزمي (اثنين وثمانين رجلا) ثم ازداد العدد كثيرا في الطريق ، ثم تقلص حتى عاد إلى العدد الاول ، وربما يكون قد نقص عنه قليلا ، ثم ازداد بنسبة صغيرة قبيل المعركة نتيجة لقدوم بعض الانصار ، وتحول بعض جنود الجيش الاموي إلى معسكر الحسين.

When he left Mecca the number started out with what Al-Khawarizmi mentioned (eighty-two men) and then increased on the road to Iraq. Then it decreased and dwindled down to the original number, and perhaps decreased beyond that. Then the number once again increased, but only nominally, right before or when the battle with some supporters coming forth. This was in addition to some of the Umayyad soldiers abandoning their posts and joining the camp of Imam Hussain (a).

وتقديرنا الخاص نتيجة لما انتهى بنا إليه البحث هو أن أصحاب الحسين الذين نقدر أنهم استشهدوا معه في كربلاء من العرب والموالي يقاربون مئة رجل أو يبلغونها وربما زادوا قليلا على المئة.

Our own particular assessment at the end of this study is that the number of companions that were martyred with Imam Hussain (a) in Karbala, including Arabs and non-Arabs, come out to be approximately a hundred men or perhaps a bit more.

ولا نستطيع أن نعين عددا بعينه ، لانه لا بد من افتراض نسبة من الخطأ تنشأ من تصحيف الاسماء ، ومن عدم دقة الرواة الذين نقلوا لاحداث وأسماء رجالها ، ولكن نسبة الخطأ المفترضة ليست كبيرة قطعا.

We are unable to pinpoint an exact number because undoubtedly there are possibilities of typographical errors in the names and the lack of precision on the part of narrators who related the course of events and the actual names of the companions. Nonetheless, the margin of error here is not a significant one.

وهذه النتيجة تتوافق إلى حد كبير مع الروايات التي تصور ما حدث في الحملة الاولى من القتال. قال الخوارزمي في روايته عن أبي مخنف :

The conclusion here is in agreement with the vast majority of the narrations that illustrate what took place in the first offensive of the battle of Karbala. Al-Khawarizmi says in his narration relating from Abu Mikhnif,

... فلما رموهم هذه الرمية قل أصحاب الحسين عليه السلام ، فبقي في هؤلاء القوم الذين يذكرون في المبارزة. وقد قتل ما ينيف على خمسين رجلا.

... and when the first offensive took place, the companions of Hussain (a) were lessened and those that remained are those mentioned in the duels that took place thereafter. A little more than fifty men were killed.

والذين ذكرهم ابن شهر اشوب يبلغون أربعين رجلا. فإذا لا حظنا إلى جانب هذا أن هؤلاء الذين يذكرون في المبارزة يبلغون أربعين رجلا تقريبا ، نكون قد قربنا من النتيجة التي أدى بنا إليها البحث.

Ibn Shahr Ashoub mentions that they were about forty men [that were martyred in the first offensive]. So if we add to this number the total number of companions that were mentioned in the duels – approximately forty men – we would have gotten closer to the conclusion that we have come to from this study.

وهنا ينبغي أن نعي أن التفاوت أمر مقبول ومعقول ، لان الرواة في جميع رواياتهم عن عدد أصحاب الحسين لم يتبعوا مبدأ الاحصاء وإنما اتبعوا طريقة التقدير المستند إلى الروية البصرية.

Here it is important to realize that the discrepancy in numbers between the narrators is both acceptable and reasonable. This is simply, as mentioned previously, because the narrators in all of their narrations on the number of Imam Hussain's (a) companions did not use statistics. They utilized the widely used method of approximation by mere eyesight.[4]

The Battle of Karbala

The Martyrs of Karbala are Like the Martyrs of Badr

في (منتخب كنز العمال) عن الطبراني في (المعجم الكبير) ما لفظه: عن شيبان

بن محرم، قال: إني لمع علي (عليه السلام) إذ أتى كربلاء، فقال: يقتل في هذا

الموضع شهداء ليس مثلهم شهداء إلا شهداء بدر.

In *Muntakhab Kanz al-Ummal* citing Al-Tabarani's *Al-Mu'jam Al-Kabeer*, Shayban ibn Muharram is recorded to have narrated, "I was with [Imam] Ali (a) when we arrived to Karbala. He said, 'There will be a murder in this land of martyrs unlike any but the martyrs of Badr.'"[5]

Salman Al-Muhammadi's opinion of the Martyrs of Karbala

قال هبيرة بن يريم: حدثني أبي قال: لقيت سلمان الفارسي فحدثته بهذا الحديث

[يقصد حديث كعب الأحبار عن مقتل الحسين (عليه السلام)] فقال سلمان:

لقد صدقك كعب ... و الذي نفس سلمان بيده، لو أني أدركت أيامه (عليه

السلام) لضربت بين يديه بالسيف، أو أقطّع بين يديه عضوا عضوا، فأسقط

بين يديه صريعا؛ فإن القتيل معه يعطى أجر سبعين شهيدا، كلهم كشهداء بدر

و أحد و حنين و خيبر.

Hubayra ibn Yaryam said, "My father once said, 'I met Salman Al-Farsi and relayed to him [the narration of Ka'b Al-Ahbar about the martyrdom of Imam Hussain (a)]. Salman said, "Ka'b has been honest with you... By Him who holds Salman's soul in His hand! If I were to live until that day, I would defend him with my sword until I an torn to pieces before him and fall while protecting him! Surely, those who die with him will be given the rewards of seventy martyrs like the martyrs of Badr, Uhud, Hunayn, and Khaybar!"'"[6]

The Martyrs alongside Imam Hussain (a) are Favored Over the Companions of the Holy Prophet (s) and Imam Ali (a)

قال الفاضل الدربندي ما ملخصه: لقد قال الإمام علي (عليه السلام) في وصف المستشهدين مع الحسين (عليه السلام) و مدحهم: «لم يسبقهم سابق، و لا يلحقهم لاحق». و إن هذا الكلام الشريف كالنور فوق الطور، تسطع منه أنوار كثيرة ...

The following is a synopsis of Al-Fadil Al-Darbandi's words: Imam Ali (a) has said in describing and praising the martyrs who died alongside Imam Hussain (a), "They have not been outdone by a forerunner, nor will they be overtaken by anyone after them." These blessed words are like a lantern atop a hill, illuminating a vast space.

فهل يحمل هذا الكلام الشريف على أنهم لا يفضل عليهم أحد بالنسبة إلى مقام الشهادة فقط. أم أن هذا يعني أنهم أفضل من حواريي رسول الله (ص) و حواريي أمير المؤمنين (عليه السلام) و حواريي الحسن (عليه السلام)؟

Do these blessed words mean that no one is favored over them when it comes to the status of martyrdom alone? Or does it mean that they are greater than the disciples of the Holy Prophet (s), Imam Ali (a), and Imam Hassan (a)?

فيجيب الفاضل الدربندي بأنه يفتي بأفضليتهم على كل هؤلاء. فإن كل من استشهد بين يدي الإمام المظلوم و هم حواريي الحسين (عليه السلام)، أفضل من حواريي رسول الله (ص) و هم سلمان و أبو ذر و المقداد،

Al-Fadil Al-Darbandi answers these questions with a declaration that the martyrs alongside Imam Hussain (a) are better than all of these disciples. Those who gave their lives and were martyred alongside the oppressed Imam (a) - the disciples of Imam Hussain (a) - are better than Salman, Abu Thar, and Al-Miqdad, the disciples of the Holy Prophet (s).

و من حواريي أمير المؤمنين (عليه السلام) و هم عمرو بن الحمق الخزاعي و أويس القرني و ميثم التمار و محمد بن أبي بكر، و من حواريي الحسن (عليه السلام) و هم سفيان بن أبي ليلى و حذيفة بن أسد،

They are better than Amr ibn Al-Hamaq Al-Khuzaei, Uwais Al-Qarani, Maytham Al-Tammar, and Muhammad ibn Abi Bakr, the disciples of Imam Ali (a). They are better than Sufyan ibn Abi Layla and Huthayfa ibn Asad, the disciples of Imam Hassan (a).

من غير استثناء أحد منهم إلا فيما خرج بالدليل؛ و ذلك كسلمان (عليه السلام)، فإنه لا استبعاد في تفضيله على المستشهدين من الأصحاب غير العترة الهاشمية النبوية.

There is no exception in this so long as there is no evidence to the contrary. For example, Salman is perhaps favored over the martyred non-hashimite companions.[7]

The Disparity in Ranks Amongst the Martyrs

ثم قال الفاضل الدربندي ما معناه: و قد ثبت أن المستشهدين من الآل في طبقة أعلى من بقية الأصحاب، و أفضلهم العباس و علي الأكبر و القاسم بن الحسن (عليه السلام). أما الأصحاب فهم متفاوتون في الفضل، و على رأسهم في الأفضلية: حبيب بن مظاهر و مسلم بن عوسجة و زهير بن القين و هلال بن نافع.

Al-Fadil Al-Darbandi said that after proving the martyrs of Karbala to be of a status higher than the disciples of the Holy Prophet (s) and the Imams (a), we should point out that the highest of the martyrs in status are Al-Abbas, Ali Al-Akbar, and Al-Qasim the son of Imam Hassan (a). As for the companions, they are of various ranks. The highest in status amongst them are Habib ibn Mudhahir, Muslim ibn Awsaja, Zuhair ibn Al-Qayn, and Hilal ibn Nafi'.

و أفضل هؤلاء حبيب بلا منازع، و هو من الذين علّمهم أمير المؤمنين (عليه السلام) علم المنايا و البلايا، و إنه لما قتل تبيّن الانكسار في وجه سيد الشهداء (عليه السلام)، و كان عمر حبيب نحو 75 سنة، و من جملة الكواشف الدالة على ذلك كون مدفنه في موضع مستقل عند باب الإذن.

The best amongst these is doubtlessly Habib who was taught by Imam Ali (a) the secrets of death and tribulations. When Habib was martyred, pain could be seen on the face of Imam Hussain (a). Habib was in his mid-seventies during the Battle of Karbala. One of the marks of his elevated status is the fact that he was given by the Imam (a) a grave separate from the remainder of the companions.

و يظهر التمايز بين فضيلة الأصحاب، بما نطقت به بعض الأخبار، بأنه لما تيقّن أصحاب سيد الشهداء (عليه السلام) القتل، كان معشر الخصّيصين منهم فرحين مسرورين، تتلألأ وجوههم و تشرق ألوانهم كالنجوم الزاهرة، و كان معشر غيرهم قد تغيّرت حالاتهم و اصفرت ألوانهم. و كان هؤلاء يتعجبون من عدم عروض الخشية و الخوف على الفرقة الأولى.

This disparity in rank between the companions can also be seen in one historical accounts that describes their condition before the battle. It says that when the companions came to the conclusion that they will surely die alongside Imam Hussain (a), a select number were seen delighted and joyful with their faces shining like bright stars, while others were worried and their faces were pale. The companions were astonished to see some amongst them who did not display any sign of fear or trepidation during a time like this.[8]

The Angels offer Aid to Imam Hussain (a)

عن أبان بن تغلب (قال) قال أبو عبد الله الصادق (عليه السلام): هبط أربعة
آلاف ملك يريدون القتال مع الحسين بن علي (عليه السلام)، فلم يؤذن لهم في
القتال، فرجعوا في الاستئذان. و هبطوا و قد قتل الحسين (عليه السلام)،
فهم عند قبره شعث غبر، يبكونه إلى يوم القيامة،

Aban ibn Taghlib narrates that Imam Sadiq (a) said, "Four thousand
angels descended seeking to join the battle alongside Hussain ibn Ali
(a). They were not granted permission. They ascended again to seek
permission [from God], but once they descended they found that
Hussain (a) had been killed. They remain by his grave unkempt and
covered in dust, mourning him until the Day of Resurrection.

و رئيسهم ملك يقال له: منصور. فلا يزوره زائر إلا استقبلوه، و لا يودّعه مودّع
إلا شيّعوه، و لا يمرض إلا عادوه، و لا يموت إلا صلّوا على جنازته، و استغفروا
له بعد موته. فكل هؤلاء في الأرض ينتظرون قيام القائم (عليه السلام).

They are led by an angel called Mansour. No visitor comes to him
except that they greet him. No [visitor] bids [the Imam (a)] farewell
except that they follow [and guard] him on his journey. If he falls ill,
they visit [and nurse] him. If he dies, they pray over his body and they
seek forgiveness for him after his passing. They are all on earth
awaiting the emergence of the Awaited One (a)."[9]

The Manifestation of Victory Descends Upon Imam Hussain (a)

ذكر أبو طاهر محمّد بن الحسين النرسي في كتاب (معالم الدين) أنه روي عن
مولانا الصادق (عليه السلام) أنه قال: سمعت أبي يقول: لما التقى الحسين (عليه
السلام) و عمر ابن سعد و قامت الحرب، أنزل الله تعالى النصر، حتى رفرف
على رأس الحسين (عليه السلام)، ثم خيّر بين النصر على أعدائه و بين لقاء
الله، فاختار لقاء الله.

Muhammad ibn Al-Hussain Al-Nirsi relays in his book "Ma'alim Al-Deen" a narration of Imam Sadiq (a) in which he says, "I heard my father say, 'When Imam Hussain (a) met Omar ibn Saad and the battle had begun, God Almighty sent down victory so that it fluttered over Al-Hussain's (a) head. He was given a choice between victory over his enemies and meeting God, so he chose to meet God.'"[10]

Some Prayed for Imam Hussain (a) but did not Aid Him

قال الدكتور علي الشلق في كتابه (الحسين إمام الشاهدين): و قد رأى الحصين بن نمير رجالا من أهل الكوفة على تل قريب ينظرون إلى الحسين (عليه السلام) و يبكون، و يدعون الله أن ينصر الحسين (عليه السلام). فصاح بهم: و يحكم!. انزلوا فقاتلوا، و وقّروا الدموع للأرامل و الأطفال.

Dr. Ali Al-Shalaq says in his book *Al-Hussain (a) Imam Al-Shahideen*, "Al-Husseyn ibn Numayr saw [during the battle of Karbala] some of the men of Kufa standing on a nearby hill looking upon Imam Hussain (a), weeping and praying to God to aid Imam Husssain (a). He cried out to them, 'Woe to you! Come down and fight. Leave the tears to the widows and the children.'"[11]

بينما قال الشيخ محمّد مهدي شمس الدين في كتابه (أنصار الحسين) ص 57 ط 2 عنهم: و هناك رجال تافهون، قال عنهم الحصين بن عبد الرحمن: إنهم كانوا وقوفا على التل يبكون، و يقولون: اللهم أنزل نصرك على الحسين (عليه السلام). ثم قال: و هذه رواية مشكوك فيها.

Sheikh Muhammad Mahdi Chamseddine in his book *Ansar Al-Hussain (a)*, "[There were] petty men that Al-Husseyn ibn Abdel-Rahman mentioned in his narration to be standing on the hilltop crying and saying, God bring down your victory!'" The Sheikh later stated that, "This narration is somewhat doubtful."[12]

The Armed Stance of Truth against Falsity

و نادى عمر بن سعد بأصحابه: ما تنتظرون بالحسين احملوا بأجمعكم، إنما هي أكلة واحدة ... فزحف عمر بن سعد ... ثم وضع سهمه في كبد قوسه، ثم رمى و قال: اشهدوا لي عند الأمير أني أول من رمى. فرمى أصحابه كلهم بأجمعهم في إثره رشقة واحدة فما بقي من أصحاب الحسين (عليه السلام) أحد إلا أصابه من رميتهم سهم.

Omar ibn Saad called out to his soldiers, "What are you waiting for! Advance at once against Al-Hussain (a), for it will be like a single meal..." Omar ibn Saad marched with his forces... and placed his arrow in his bow. He launched the arrow and said, "Be my witnesses at [the court of] the amir, that I was the first to launch an arrow." His soldiers followed, launching their arrows all at once in a single volley. None remained of the companions of Al-Hussain (a) except that he was hit by an arrow....

فلما رموهم هذه الرمية، قلّ أصحاب الحسين (عليه السلام) و قتل منهم ما ينوف على خمسين رجلا. و تسمى هذه (بالحملة الأولى).

When this volley of arrows was launched, the camp of Al-Hussain (a) was diminished. Approximately fifty men were killed. This is usually called "the first round."[13]

Imam Hussain (a) Grants His Companions Permission to Fight

فعندها ضرب الحسين (عليه السلام) بيده إلى لحيته، فقال:

Imam Hussain (a) then put his hand on his beard and said,

قوموا رحمكم الله إلى الموت الّذي لا بدّ منه، فإن هذه السهام رسل القوم إليكم.

Go forth - may God have mercy on you - and face inevitable death, for these arrows are the people's messengers to you.[14]

Imam Hussain (a) would not Begin the Battle

استعمل الحسين (عليه السلام) مختلف الوسائل الممكنة لهدي القوم و إرشادهم إلى الطريق الأقوم، و بذل جهده عسى أن يتجنّب القتال، لأنه صاحب دعوة خير و حبّ و سلام؛ دعوة الإسلام.

Imam Hussain (a) used all possible means to guide these people and lead them toward a righteous path. He exhausted his efforts in his attempts to avoid battle, as he was the carrier of a message of good, love, and peace - the message of Islam.

و كان (عليه السلام) يبغض القتل و القتال ما دام هناك طريقة بالتي هي أحسن، و لهذا كان يكره أن يبدأهم بقتال، كما قال (عليه السلام) لزهير و غيره من أصحابه في مواطن عديدة:

He hated to engage in battle and bloodshed so long as there was a way to guide by better means. That is why he would not be the one to initiate the battle. As he said to Zuhair and others of his companions on multiple occasions,

إني أكره أن أبدأهم بقتال.

I hate to initiate battle against them.

مقتديا بسيرة جده رسول الله (ص) و أبيه علي بن أبي طالب (عليه السلام) في دعوتهما إلى الله.

He was following the tradition of his grandfather, the Messenger of God (s), and his father, Ali ibn Abi Talib (a), in their call toward God.

24

و لكنه (عليه السلام) خاب ظنه فيهم، لأن الشيطان استحوذ عليهم فأنساهم ذكر الله العظيم، و ذلك عندما رشقوا معسكره بالسهام و كأنها المطر. فعندئذ لم يجد بدّا من قتالهم حتى يفيئوا إلى أمر الله. فأذن لأصحابه بالقتال، و قال لهم:

However, his hopes in these people were subverted. Satan had seized them, making them forget the remembrance of God Almighty. They launched their arrows, which rained down on the camp. At that point, he found no alternative to battle; perhaps they may then recant and come towards the path of God. He granted his companions leave to fight, saying to them,

قوموا رحمكم الله إلى الموت الّذي لا بدّ منه

Go forth - may God have mercy on you - to your inevitable deaths.[15]

Imam Hussain (a) Calling upon the People to Aid Him

ثم قال (عليه السلام):

Then [Imam Hussain (a)] said,

اشتدّ غضب الله على اليهود و النصارى إذ جعلوا له ولدا [و في رواية: اشتد غضب الله على اليهود إذ جعلوا له ولدا، و اشتدّ غضبه على النصارى إذ جعلوه ثالث ثلاثة]،

God's anger with the Jews and the Christians was exacerbated when they ascribed a son to Him. [And in another narration, "God's anger with the Jews was exacerbated when they ascribed a son to him, and His anger with the Christians exacerbated when they made him the third in a trinity."]

و اشتدّ غضب الله على المجوس إذ عبدت الشمس و القمر و النار من دونه، و اشتدّ غضب الله على قوم اتّفقت آراؤهم [أو في رواية: كلمتهم] على قتل ابن بنت نبيهم. و الله لا أجيبهم إلى شيء مما يريدونه أبدا، حتى ألقى الله و أنا مخضّب بدمي.

And God's anger with the Zoroastrians was exacerbated when they worshiped the sun, moon, and fire in His stead. And God's anger has been exacerbated against a people whose opinion [and in another narration, "whose word"] was united in slaying the son of their prophet's daughter. By God, I will never obey them in any of their demands till I reach God [with my beard] stained by my own blood.

ثم صاح (عليه السلام):

He then cried out,

ما من مغيث يغيثنا لوجه الله تعالى؟. أما من ذابّ يذبّ عن حرم
رسول الله؟

Is there not an aid who will aid us for the sake of God Almighty?
Is there no guardian who will protect the women of [the family of]
the Messenger of God (s)?

فبكت النساء و كثر صراخهن.

At that point the women began to cry and their wails grew louder.[16]

Imam Hussain's (a) Calls Awaken Some Good Souls

و سمع نفر من جيش العدوكلام الحسين (عليه السلام) و استغاثته، فاهتزّت مشاعرهم و تيقّظت ضمائرهم، فاندفعوا نحو الحسين (عليه السلام) ينصرونه و يدافعون عنه.

A group of enemy soldiers heard the cries of Al-Hussain (a) and his plea for aid. Their feelings were shaken and their conscience was awakened. They hurried toward Al-Hussain (a) in order to aid and protect him.

و سمع الأنصاريان سعد بن الحارث و أخوه أبو الحتوف استنصار الحسين (عليه السلام) و استغاثته و بكاء عياله- و كانا مع ابن سعد- فما لا بسيفيهما على أعداء الحسين (عليه السلام)، و قاتلا حتى قتلا.

The two Ansaris, Saad ibn Al-Harith and his brother Abu Al-Hutoof, who were in the ranks of Omar ibn Saad, heard the cries of Al-Hussain (a), his plea for aid, and the wails of his children. They turned their swords toward Al-Hussain's (a) enemies and fought until they were killed.[17]

Muslim ibn Awsaja and Nafi' ibn Hilal Enter the Battlefield

ثم خرج مسلم بن عوسجة الأسدي [...] ثم تابعه نافع بن هلال الجملي [...]

فخرج لنافع رجل من بني قطيعة، فقال لنافع: أنا على دين عثمان. فقال نافع: إذن

أنت على دين الشيطان، و حمل عليه فقتله. فأخذ نافع و مسلم يجولان في ميمنة

ابن سعد.

Then Muslim ibn Awsaja stepped forward [...] followed by Nafi' ibn Hilal al-Jamli [...]. A man from Bani Qutay'a came toward Nafi' and said, "I am on the religion of Othman." Nafi' replied, "Then you are on the religion of Satan." [Nafi'] charged towards him and killed him. Muslim and Nafi' continued to fight valiantly on the right flank of Ibn Saad's [army].[18]

Amr ibn Al-Hajjaj Recognizes the Bravery of the Companions of Imam Hussain (a)

و أخذ أصحاب الحسين (عليه السلام) بعد أن قلّ عددهم و بان النقص فيهم،
يبرز الرجل بعد الرجل، فأكثروا القتل في أهل الكوفة. فصاح عمرو بن الحجاج
بأصحابه: أتدرون من تقاتلون؟ تقاتلون فرسان المصر و أهل البصائر و قوما
مستميتين، لا يبرز إليهم أحد منكم إلا قتلوه على قلتهم. و الله لو لم ترموهم إلا
بالحجارة لقتلتموهم.

When the ranks of Al-Hussain's (a) companions dwindled and the
decrease in their numbers became evident, they began to go out one
after the other [to duel]. They killed many of the Kufans. Amr ibn Al-
Hajjaj called out to his companions, "Do you know who you are
fighting? You are fighting 'Fursan Al-Masr' [the knights of the realms],
'Ahl Al-Basaer' [the people of insight], and a [self-sacrificing] faction.
None of you will go out to duel them except that they will kill you,
despite their few numbers. By God, if you were only to pelt them with
stones you would kill them."

فقال عمر بن سعد: صدقت، الرأي ما رأيت. أرسل في الناس من يعزم عليهم
أن لا يبارزهم رجل منكم، و لو خرجتم إليهم وحدانا لأتوا عليكم.

Omar ibn Saad replied, "You are right; the correct opinion is yours.
Send to the people someone to tell them not to go out for duels
because if you go out one by one they will cut you down."[19]

Amr ibn Al-Hajjaj Advances Against Imam Hussain's (a) Right Flank

و حمل عمرو بن الحجاج على ميمنة أصحاب الحسين (عليه السلام) فيمن كان معه من أهل الكوفة. فلما دنا من أصحاب الحسين (عليه السلام) جثوا له على الرّكب، و أشرعوا بالرماح نحوهم، فلم تقدم خيلهم على الرماح، فذهبت الخيل لترجع، فرشقهم أصحاب الحسين (عليه السلام) بالنبل، فصرعوا منهم رجالا و جرحوا منهم آخرين.

Amr ibn Al-Hajjaj advanced along with his battalion of Kufans against the right flank of Al-Hussain's (a) camp. When he came near to Al-Hussain's (a) companions, they dropped to their knees and lifted their pikes. The horses did not charge the raised pikes and turned to retreat instead. Al-Hussain's (a) companions then pelted them with arrows, killing some and wounding others.

و كان عمرو بن الحجاج يقول لأصحابه: قاتلوا من مرق من الدين، و فارق الجماعة. فصاح الحسين (عليه السلام):

Amr ibn Al-Hajjaj would call on to his companions, "Fight those who have deviated from the religion and diverted away from unity." Al-Hussain (a) called in reply,

ويحك يا حجّاج أعليّ تحرّض الناس؟ أنحن مرقنا من الدين و أنت تقيم عليه؟!. ستعلمون إذا فارقت أرواحنا أجسادنا من أولى بصليّ النار!

Woe to you, O' Hajjaj! Do you rouse the people against me? Is it we who have deviated from the religion while you are its guardian? Surely, when our souls leave our bodies you will know who is truly deserving of dwelling in hellfire![20]

Amr ibn Al-Hajjaj Accuses Imam Hussain (a) of Deviating from the Religion

ثم دنا عمرو بن الحجاج من أصحاب الحسين (عليه السلام). ثم صاح بقومه: يا
أهل الكوفة الزموا طاعتكم و جماعتكم، و لا ترتابوا في قتل من مرق من الدين،
و خالف إمام المسلمين. فقال له الحسين (عليه السلام):

Amr ibn Al-Hajjaj drew near to the companions of Imam Hussain (a) and called out to his men, "O' People of Kufa, hold fast to obedience and unity. Do not hesitate to kill whoever deviates from the religion and goes against the imam of the Muslims." Al-Hussain (a) said to him,

يابن الحجاج أعلي تحرّض الناس؟ أنحن مرقنا من الدين و أنتم ثبّتم
عليه؟ والله لتعلمنّ أيّنا المارق من الدين، و من هو أولى بصليّ النار.

O' ibn Al-Hajjaj, do you provoke people against me? Did we deviate from the religion while you remained steadfast on it? By God, you will come to know which of us has deviated away from the faith and who truly deserves to dwell in hellfire![21]

The Martyrdom of Muslim ibn Awsaja

ثم حمل عمرو بن الحجاج من نحو الفرات فاقتتلوا ساعة، و فيها قاتل مسلم ابن عوسجة، فشدّ عليه مسلم بن عبد الله الضبابي و عبد الله بن خشكارة البجلي و ثارت لشدة الجلاد غبرة شديدة، و ما انجلت الغبرة إلا و مسلم صريعا و به رمق. فمشى إليه الحسين (عليه السلام) و معه حبيب بن مظاهر الأسدي، فقال له الحسين (عليه السلام):

Then Amr ibn Al-Hajjaj advanced from the direction of the Euphrates, where the parties clashed for some time. Muslim ibn Awsaja was amongst the warriors and he was faced by Muslim ibn Abdullah Al-Dababi and Abdullah ibn Khashkara Al-Balji. The battle grew so fierce that a thick cloud of dust was stirred. The dust did not settle until Muslim [ibn Awsaja] was felled, laying with some life in him. Al-Hussain (a) walked to him along with Habib ibn Mudhahir Al-Asadi. Al-Hussain (a) said to [Muslim],

رحمك الله يا مسلم فَمِنْهُمْ مَنْ قَضَى نَحْبَهُ وَ مِنْهُمْ مَنْ يَنْتَظِرُ وَ ما بَدَّلُوا تَبْدِيلًا

May God have mercy on you. 'There are some among them who have fulfilled their pledge, and some of them who still wait, and they have not changed in the least.' [The Holy Quran, 33:23]

و دنا منه حبيب و قال: عزّ عليّ مصرعك يا مسلم، أبشر بالجنة. فقال قولا ضعيفا: بشّرك الله بخير. قال حبيب: لو لم أعلم أني في الأثر لأحببت أن توصي إليّ بكل ما أهمّك. فقال له مسلم: بل أوصيك بهذا [و أشار إلى الحسين (عليه

السلام)] أن تموت دونه. فقال: أفعل و ربّ الكعبة فما أسرع من أن مات رضوان الله عليه.

Habib drew close to [Muslim] and said, "Your death has take a toll on me, O' Muslim. I give you glad tidings of paradise." [Muslim] replied faintly, "May God give you glad tidings of all that is good." Habib then said, "If I did not know that I am following in your footsteps I would have liked for you to instruct me in regards to everything that is of consequence [as a last will and testament]." Muslim replied, "My will is this man [and he pointed to Imam Hussain (a)] and that you die aiding him." [Habib] said, "By the Lord of the Ka'ba, I will." [Muslim] quickly perished, may God be content with him.[22]

Shimr Advances Against Imam Hussain's (a) Left Flank

ثم تراجع القوم إلى الحسين (عليه السلام)، فحمل شمر بن ذي الجوشن في الميسرة، على أهل الميسرة، فثبتوا له و طاعنوه. و حمل على الحسين (عليه السلام) و أصحابه من كل جانب. و قاتلهم أصحاب الحسين (عليه السلام) قتالا شديدا، فأخذت خيلهم تحمل، و إنما هي اثنان و ثلاثون فارسا، فلا تحمل على جانب من خيل الكوفة إلا كشفته.

Then Al-Hussain's (a) companions withdrew close to him. Shimr ibn Thiljawshan advanced against the left flank. They stood firmly and fought him. [The Umayyad army] advanced against Al-Hussain (a) from every direction. The companions of Al-Hussain (a) fought valiantly, advancing with their cavalry which consisted of thirty two horses. They advanced against the cavalry of Kufa and repelled [the Kufans] every time.[23]

Abdullah ibn Omair al-Kalbi Enters the Battlefield

كان عبد الله بن عمير الكلبي بالنّخيلة فرأى القوم يعرضون ليسرحوا إلى قتال الحسين (عليه السلام). فقال: و الله لقد كنت على جهاد أهل الشرك حريصا، و إني لأرجو ألا يكون جهاد هؤلاء الذين يغزون ابن بنت نبيهم أيسر ثوابا عند الله من ثوابه إياي في جهاد المشركين. فدخل إلى امرأته فأخبرها بما سمع، و أعلمها بما يريد.

Abdullah ibn Omair Al-Kalbi was in Nukhaila* when he saw the people getting ready to march towards and fight Al-Hussain (a).

He said, "By God, I have been thorough in my jihad against the polytheists. I hope that the reward of jihad of those who raid the son of their prophet's daughter is no less than the reward I have earned in my jihad against the polytheists." He went to his wife, told her of what he has heard, and informed her of his plan.

فقالت: أصبت أصاب الله بك أرشد أمورك، افعل و أخرجني معك. فخرج بها حتى أتى حسينا (عليه السلام) فأقام معه. فلما دنا عمر بن سعد و رمى بسهم ارتمى الناس. فخرج يسار مولى زياد بن أبي سفيان و سالم مولى عبيد الله بن زياد، فقالا: من يبارز؟ ليخرج إلينا بعضكم.

She said, "You have hit the mark, may God hit His mark through you [and] guide you in all matters. Do so and take me with you." He set out with her until they reached Al-Hussain (a) and settled in his camp. [On the day of Ashura] Omar ibn Saad shot the first arrow and the people

---

* Nukhaila: a town on the outskirts of modern-day Karbala.

followed suit. Then Yasar the servant of Ziyad ibn Abu Sufyan and Salim the servant of Ubaydillah ibn Ziyad stepped forth and [called for a duel].

فوثب حبيب بن مظاهر و برير بن خضير، فقال لهما حسين: اجلسا. فقام عبد الله ابن عمير هذا، فاستأذن الحسين بالخروج فأذن له، و كان رجلا آدم طويلا شديد الساعدين بعيد ما بين المنكبين. فخرج و قاتل قتالا مريرا. فلما برز له يسار: من أنت؟ فانتسب له. فقال له: لست أعرفك، ليخرج إليّ زهير بن القين أو حبيب بن مظاهر أو برير بن خضير.

Habib ibn Mudhahir and Burair ibn Khudair rose for battle, but Al-Hussain (a) [told them to hold off]. Abdullah ibn Omair rose and asked Al-Hussain (a) permission to enter battle, and he was granted permission. He was a tall man of a tan complexion, with stout forearms and broad shoulders. He set out and fought valiantly. When he stepped forward Yasar asked him, "Who are you?" [Abdullah] described his lineage, but [Yasar] replied, "I do not know you. Let Zuhair ibn Al-Qayn, Habib ibn Mudhahir, or Burair ibn Khudair step forward."

فقال له ابن عمير: يابن الفاعلة، و بك رغبة عن مبارزة أحد من الناس، و لا يبرز إليك أحد إلا و هو خير منك! ثم شدّ عليه فضربه بسيفه حتى برد، و هو أول من قتل من أصحاب ابن سعد. فإنه لمشتغل بضربه إذ شدّ عليه سالم مولى عبيد الله، فصاح به أصحابه: قد رهقك العبد، فلم يعبأ به حتى غشيه، فبدره بضربة اتّقاها ابن عمير بيده اليسرى فأطارت أصابع كفه، و مال عليه عبد الله فضربه حتى قتله. فرجع و قد قتلهما جميعا.

Ibn Omair said, "O' son of the doer [of ill, and in one narration: O' son of the adulteress], do you have a preference not to duel some men when there is no one who would step forth except that they are your better?" [Abdullah ibn Omair] then charged towards [Yasar] and struck him with his sword until he fell. He was the first man to fall from the camp of Omar ibn Saad. But while [Abdullah ibn Omair] was busy striking [Yasar], Salim the servant of Ubaydillah charged toward him. [Abdullah's] companions shouted, "The slave is drawing near you." But Abdullah did not seem to care about him until he got close. [Salim] quickly struck [Abdullah], but he shielded the blow with his left hand, severing his fingers. Abdullah turned toward [Salim] and struck him until he killed him. He returned to the camp having slain them both.[24]

The Martyrdom of Abdullah ibn Omair al-Kalbi and his Wife Umm Wahab

و حمل الشمر في جماعة من أصحابه على ميسرة الحسين فثبتوا لهم حتى كشفوهم، و فيها قاتل عبد الله بن عمير الكلبي [و هو عبد الله بن عمير بن عباس بن عبد قيس بن عليم بن جناب الكلبي العليمي أبو وهب] فقتل تسعة عشر فارسا و اثني عشر راجلا، و شدّ عليه هانئ بن ثبيت الحضرمي فقطع يده اليمنى، و قطع بكر بن حي ساقه، فأخذ أسيرا و قتل صبرا. و ذكر الطبري في تاريخه أنه كان القتيل الثاني من أصحاب الحسين (عليه السلام).

Al-Shimr and a number of his companions charged against al-Hussain's (a) left flank, but they remained perseverant until they repelled the advance. Abdullah ibn Omair al-Kalbi fought in that confrontation, killing nineteen cavalrymen and twelve infantrymen. Hani ibn Thubayt al-Hadrami charged at him and severed his right hand. Bakr ibn Hai severed his leg. He was taken captive and killed. Al-Tabari mentioned in his account that [Abdullah] was the second of al-Hussain's (a) companions to fall.

فمشت إليه زوجته أم وهب (بنت عبد الله من النمر بن قاسط) و جلست عند رأسه تمسح الدم عنه و تقول: هنيئا لك الجنة، أسأل الله الّذي رزقك الجنة أن يصحبني معك. فقال الشمر لغلامه رستم: اضرب رأسها بالعمود، فشدخه و ماتت و هي أول امرأة قتلت من أصحاب الحسين (عليه السلام).

His wife, Umm Wahab (bint Abdullah, from the family of al-Nimr ibn Qasit), came to him. She sat by his head, wiped his blood, and said, "May you enjoy paradise! I ask God who has granted you paradise to allow me to be with you." Al-Shimr said to his servant Rustum, "Strike her head with a pole." He bashed her head and killed her, making her the first female killed from the companions of al-Hussain (a).

و قطع رأس عبد الله و رمي به إلى جمة الحسين (عليه السلام)، فأخذته أمه و مسحت الدم عنه، ثم أخذت عمود خيمة و برزت إلى الأعداء، فردّها الحسين (عليه السلام) و قال:

Abdullah's head was severed and thrown toward al-Hussain (a). His mother took his head and wiped the blood off it. She took a pole from a tent and charged toward the enemy. Al-Hussain (a) stopped her, saying,

ارجعي رحمك الله، فقد وضع عنك الجهاد.

Return [back to the tent], may God have mercy on you, for fighting is not obligatory for you.

فرجعت و هي تقول: اللهم لا تقطع رجائي. فقال الحسين (عليه السلام):

She returned, saying, "O' God, do not crush my hopes!" Al-Hussain (a) said to her,

لا يقطع الله رجاءك.

God will not crush your hopes.[25]

Historical Confusion between Abdullah ibn Omair and Wahab ibn Abdullah

حصل خلط كبير عند المؤرخين بين اسمين هنا: عبد الله بن عمير بن جناب الكلبي، و بين وهب بن عبد الله بن حباب الكلبي، و ذلك للتشابه بين (جناب) و (حباب) من جهة، و لأن زوجة عبد الله بن عمير لقبها (أم وهب).

There has been much confusion amongst historians in regards to two individuals; Abdullah ibn Omair ibn Jonab al-Kalbi and Wahab ibn Abdullah ibn Hobab al-Kalbi. That is because of the similarity in their names (Jonab, Hobab) as well as the fact that Abdullah ibn Omair's wife's name was Umm Wahab.

و الذي أرجحه أن هناك شخصين مختلفين و كل واحد منهما استشهد على حدة؛ الأول خرج من الكوفة إلى (النّخيلة) إلى كربلاء، و هو عبد الله بن عمير، و الثاني كان نصرانيا فلقي الحسين (عليه السلام) في طريقه و أسلم، و صحبه إلى كربلاء، و هو وهب بن حباب.

I posit that these are two different individuals, each martyred at a different time. The first set out from Kufa to Nukhayla to Karbala, and he is Abdullah ibn Omair. The second, Wahab ibn Hobab, was a Christian who met al-Hussain (a) on the road, accepted Islam, and came to Karbala.

و الذي يقوّي رأيي هذا، أن هناك روايتين مختلفتين لاستشهاد (عبد الله) أو (وهب) و زوجته أو أمه (أم وهب). إحداهما تحكي أنه قتل و جاءت زوجته فجلست عند رأسه تمسح الدم عنه. و الثانية أن الأعداء احتوشوه فأخذوه

41

أسيرا، و قطعوا رأسه، ثم رموا به إلى عسكر الحسين (عليه السلام)، فأخذته
زوجته و ضربت به خيمة للأعداء فهدمتها.

What strengthens this position is that there are two narrations in regards to the martyrdom of Abdullah or Wahab and his wife or mother Umm Wahab. The first says that he was martyred and that his wife came to sit by him and wipe the blood off his head. The other says that the enemies captured him, severed his head, and threw it toward the camp of al-Hussain (a). His wife took his head and struck an enemy tent with it, collapsing it.

و الرواية الأولى تثبت أن زوجته (أم وهب) استشهدت بعده، حيث ضربها
أحدهم بعمود من حديد على رأسها. بينما تشير الثانية إلى أنها حاولت القتال، و
لكن الحسين (عليه السلام) ردّها إلى المخيم. وسوف تأتيك قصة استشهاد
وهب بن حباب الكلبي، الّذي أسلم مع أمه و زوجته، بعد قليل.

The first narration supports the fact that his wife Umm Wahab was martyred after him, when someone struck her with an iron pole on her head. The second said that she tried to fight but was stopped by al-Hussain (a), who returned her to the camp.

The story of Wahab ibn Hobab, who accepted Islam along with his wife and his mother, and how he was martyred will be recounted shortly.[26]

The World is the Prison of a Believer and the Paradise of a Disbeliever

روي عن أبي جعفر الثاني (الإمام محمّد الجواد (ع)) عن آبائه (قال) قال علي بن الحسين (عليه السلام):

It is narrated through Abu Jafar al-Thani (Imam Muhammad al-Jawad (a)), relaying on behalf of his forefathers, that Ali ibn al-Hussain (a) said,

لما اشتدّ الأمر بأبي الحسين (عليه السلام) نظر إليه من كان معه، فإذا هو بخلافهم، لأنهم كلما اشتد الأمر تغيّرت ألوانهم و ارتعدت فرائصهم و وجلت قلوبهم، و كان الحسين (عليه السلام) و بعض من معه من خصائصه تشرق ألوانهم، و تهدأ جوارحهم، و تسكن نفوسهم. فقال بعض لبعض: انظروا لا يبالي بالموت.

When my father al-Hussain's (a) situation looked dire, those around him looked at him and saw that [his demeanor was quite the opposite of theirs]. As the situation became more and more dire, their faces would become pale, their limbs would tremble, and their hearts would sink. Conversely, al-Hussain (a) and a few of his select companion's faces would brighten, their limbs would settle, and their souls would be tranquil. Some would say to others, 'Look! He does not fear death!' Al-Hussain (a) said to them:

فقال لهم الحسين (عليه السلام): صبرا بني الكرام، فما الموت إلا قنطرة تعبر بكم عن البؤس و الضراء إلى الجنان الواسعة و النعيم

43

الدائم. فأيكم يكره أن ينتقل من سجن [أي الدنيا] إلى قصر [أي الجنة]!

Be patient, O' sons of noble [forefathers]. Indeed, death is but a bridge that will allow you to cross from hardship and suffering towards an immense paradise and everlasting blessings. Who of you hates to be transported from a prison and into a palace?

و هي لأعدائكم إلا كمن ينتقل من قصر إلى سجن و عذاب. إن أبي حدثني عن رسول الله (ص): أن الدنيا سجن المؤمن و جنة الكافر، و الموت جسر هؤلاء إلى جناتهم، و جسر هؤلاء إلى جحيمهم. ما كذبت و لا كذّبت.

As for your enemies, it is a journey from a palace towards imprisonment and punishment. My father told me that the Messenger of God (s) said, 'Indeed, the world is the prison of a believer and the paradise of a disbeliever. Death is [the believers'] bridge toward their paradise, and [the disbelievers'] bridge towards their hellfire. Indeed, I have not lied nor will I be proven wrong!'[27]

Shabath ibn Rib'i Confesses to his Men's Wretchedness

و لما رأى عزرة بن قيس و هو على الخيل الوهن في أصحابه و الفشل كلما

يحملون، بعث إلى عمر بن سعد يستمده الرجال. فقال ابن سعد لشبث بن

ربعي: ألا تقدم إليهم؟ قال: سبحان الله، تكلف شيخ المصر، و عندك من

يجزي عنه؟

When Uzra ibn Qays who commanded [an Umayyad] cavalry [regiment] saw the weakness of his men and the failure of every charge, he sent a missive to Omar ibn Saad asking for backup. Ibn Saad said to Shabath ibn Rib'i, "Would you go to aid them?" [Shabath] replied, "Glory to God! You would command the master of these lands when there are others who would suffice?"

و لم يزل شبث بن ربعي كارها لقتال الحسين، و قد سمع يقول في إمارة مصعب:

قاتلنا مع علي بن أبي طالب و مع ابنه من بعده [يعني الحسن] آل أبي سفيان

خمس سنين، ثم عدونا على ولده و هو خير أهل الأرض، نقاتله مع آل معاوية

و ابن سمية الزانية؟! ضلال يا لك من ضلال. و الله لا يعطي الله أهل هذا

المصر خيرا أبدا، و لا يسددهم لرشد.

Shabath detested fighting al-Hussain (a) and was heard saying, "We fought alongside Ali ibn Abi Talib (a) and his son [al-Hassan (a)] after him against the family of Abu Sufyan for five years. Now we have turned against his son [al-Hussain (a)] who is the best of the people of the earth, siding against him with the family of Muawiya and the son of Sumayya the adulteress? Perversion! Oh the perversion! By God,

God will not give the people of this land any good nor support them with any foresight."

فمدّه بالحصين بن نمير في خمسمائة من الرماة.

[Omar ibn Saad] sent al-Hossayn ibn Numair to support [Uzra ibn Qays], along with five hundred archers.[28]

A Man Describes the Valor of al-Hussain (a) and His Companions

قيل لرجل شهد يوم الطف مع عمر بن سعد: ويحك، أقتلتم ذرية رسول اللّه (ص)! فقال: [...] إنك لو شهدت ما شهدنا لفعلت ما فعلنا!

A man who was amongst the army of Omar ibn Saad during the Battle of Karbala was told, "Woe to you! You have killed the progeny of the Messenger of God (s)!" He replied, "[...] If you would have seen what we saw, you would have done as we did!

ثارت علينا عصابة [يعني جماعة الحسين (عليه السلام)] أيديها في مقابض سيوفها، كالأسود الضارية، تختطم الفرسان يمينا و شمالا، و تلقي أنفسها على الموت، لا تقبل الأمان و لا ترغب في المال، و لا يحول حائل بينها و بين الورود على حياض المنية أو الاستيلاء على الملك، فلو كففنا عنها رويدا لأتت على نفوس العسكر بحذافيرها، فما كنا فاعلين لا أمّ لك!

A small group of men [meaning al-Hussain (a) and his companions] charged at us with their hands on the hilts of their swords. They were like raging lions, devouring our knights left and right. They rushed to death, neither accepting sanctuary nor seeking wealth. No one could stand between them and [their choice of either] death or seizing [the throne]. If we were to let up our attack for a moment, they would have taken the army from every direction. What else could we have done?"[29]

The Martyrdom of Abu al-Sha'tha' al-Kindi

و كان أبو الشعثاء الكندي- و هو يزيد بن زياد بن مهاصر الكندي- مع ابن

سعد، فلما ردّوا الشروط على الحسين (عليه السلام) صار معه. فقاتل بين

يديه، و جعل يرتجز [...] و كان راميا، فجثا على ركبتيه بين يدي الحسين (عليه

السلام) و رمى بمئة سهم ما أخطأ منها بخمسة أسهم، و الحسين (عليه السلام)

يقول:

Abu al-Sha'tha' al-Kindi (his name being Yazid ibn Ziyad ibn Muhasir al-Kindi) was in the ranks of Ibn Saad's army. When [the Umayyad army] rejected al-Hussain's (a) conditions, he joined his camp. He fought in al-Hussain's (a) ranks and [charged with chants of pride in his ancestry and dedication to al-Hussain (a)]. He was an archer, so he sat on his knees in al-Hussain's (a) camp and shot one hundred arrows - less than five of which missed their marks. All the while al-Hussain (a) would say,

اللهم سدّد رميته، و اجعل ثوابه الجنة.

O' God, guide his shots and reward him with paradise.

فلما نفدت سهامه قام و هو يقول: لقد تبيّن لي أني قتلت منهم خمسة. ثم حمل

على القوم فقتل تسعة نفر حتى قتل (رحمه الله).

When he ran out of arrows he stood up and said, "It seems that I have killed five of them." He then charged against the enemy and killed nine soldiers before being killed - may God have mercy on his soul.[30]

The Martyrdom of Burair ibn Khudair

ثم برز برير بن خضير الهمداني و هو [يرتجز] و كان برير من عباد الله الصالحين،
و كان زاهدا عابدا، و كان أقرأ أهل زمانه، و كان يقال له سيّد القرّاء، و كان
شيخا تابعيا، و له في الهمدانيين شرف و قدر.

Burair ibn Khudair al-Hamadani then stepped forward unto the
battlefield [reciting verses in praise of his ancestry]. Burair was a
righteous servant of God; an austere worshipper who was foremost
amongst reciters [of the Holy Quran] during his time. He used to be
called 'the Master of Reciters.' He was an elder and a Tabi'i [i.e. he was
not himself a companion of the Holy Prophet (s), but was a student of
Imam Ali (a) and the righteous companions], with great status and
honor amongst the Hamadanis.

فحمل و قاتل قتالا شديدا، و جعل ينادي فيهم: اقتربوا مني يا قتلة المؤمنين،
اقتربوا مني يا قتلة أولاد البدريين، اقتربوا مني يا قتلة عترة خير المرسلين. فبرز
إليه رجل يقال له يزيد بن معقل [و في رواية: يزيد بن المغفل].

He fought valiantly and would say during the battle, "Come at me, O'
slayers of the believers! Come at me, O' killers of the sons of the
warriors of Badr! Come at me, O' murderers of the family of the best
of Messengers (s)!" An enemy soldier by the name of Yazid ibn Ma'qil
[or, as in some narrations, Yazid ibn al-Mughfil], advance toward
[Burair].

و ذكر المقرّم هذا الكلام بشيء من التفصيل قال: و نادى يزيد بن معقل: يا
برير كيف ترى صنع الله بك؟ فقال: صنع الله بي خيرا و صنع بك شرا. فقال
يزيد: كذبت و قبل اليوم ما كنت كذّابا، أتذكر يوم كنت أماشيك في (بني

لوذان) و أنت تقول: كان معاوية ضالا و إن إمام الهدى علي بن أبي طالب؟

قال برير: بلى أشهد أن هذا رأيي.

Al-Mugarram recounted the event in some detail. He said, "Yazid ibn Ma'qil called out, 'O' Burair! How have you found what God has done to you?' [Burair] replied, 'God has done good by me and left you to your evil.' Yazid said, 'You lie, and you have never been a liar before! Do you remember when I was walking beside you in [the lands of] Bani Lawthan and you said, "Muawiya is misguided and the Imam of guidance is Ali ibn Abi Talib"?' Burair replied, 'Yes, I do attest that as my view!'

فقال يزيد: و أنا أشهد أنك من الضالين. فدعاه برير إلى المباهلة، فرفعا أيديهما إلى الله سبحانه يدعوانه أن يلعن الكاذب و يقتله. ثم تضاربا فضربه برير على رأسه ضربة قدّت المغفر و الدماغ، فخرّ كأنما هوى من شاهق، و سيف برير ثابت في رأسه.

Yazid said, 'I do attest that you are misguided!' Burair then called him to a *mubahala*,* each raising his hand and praying that God Almighty would curse the liar and lead him to his death. They charged at one another and fought until Burair struck [Yazid on the head] splitting his helmet and skull. He fell as if he was thrown off a cliff while Burair's sword was stuck in his skull.

---

* A *mubahala* is a type of debate where two sides of an issue pray to God for the damnation of the lying side. God says in the Holy Quran, "Should anyone argue with you concerning him, after the knowledge that has come to you, say, 'Come! Let us call our sons and your sons, our women and your women, our souls and your souls, then let us pray earnestly, and call down Allah's curse upon the liars.'" (The Holy Quran, 3:61)

و بينا هو يريد أن يُخرجه إذ حمل عليه (رضي بن منقذ العبدي) و اعتنق بريرا و اعتركا، فصرعه برير و جلس على صدره، فاستغاث رضي العبدي بأصحابه، فذهب كعب بن جابر الأزدي ليحمل على برير، فصاح به زهير بن أبي الأخنس: هذا برير بن خضير القارئ الّذي كان يقرئنا القرآن في جامع الكوفة،

And while Burair was attempting to extract his sword, Radi ibn Munqith al-Abdi attacked him, tackling him to the ground and wrestling him. Burair beat him and sat on his chest, so Radi al-Abdi called on his companions for help. Ka'b ibn Jabir al-Azdi charged at Burair while Zuhair ibn Abi al-Akhnas called out, 'That is Burair ibn Khudair, the reciter who used to recite the Quran to us in the Mosque of Kufa!'

فلم يلتفت إليه و طعن بريرا في ظهره، فبرك برير على رضي العبدي [...] و ألقاه كعب برمحه عنه و ضربه بسيفه فقتله (رضوان الله عليه). [...] و ذكر الخوارزمي أن الّذي قتله هو بحير بن أوس الضبّي.

But [Ka'b] did not heed his cry and stabbed Burair in the back. Burair fell on Radi al-Abdi [...]. Ka'b then used his spear to move Burair off and struck him with a sword, killing him. [...]"

Al-Khawarizmi recounts that his killer was actually Buhair ibn Aws al-Dabbi.[31]

Biographical Entry | Burair ibn Khudair

بنو مشرق بطن من همدان، قال الرواة: كان برير شيخا تابعيا ناسكا قارئا للقرآن
و من شيوخ القرّاء في الكوفة. و كان من أصحاب أمير المؤمنين (عليه السلام)،
و كان من أشراف أهل الكوفة من الهمدانيين. ذكر أرباب السير أن بريرا لما
بلغه امتناع الحسين (عليه السلام) من البيعة ليزيد الطاغية، خرج من الكوفة
حتى أتى مكة و صحب الحسين (عليه السلام) حتى استشهد معه (رضوان
الله عليه).

Burair ibn Khudair al-Hamadani al-Mashriqi. The Banu Mashriq are a
branch of the tribe of Hamadan. The narrators have said, "Burair was
a *Tabi'i** elder, a worshiper, and a reciter of the Holy Quran - rather, he
was amongst the senior reciters of Kufa." He was a companion of the
Commander of the Faithful (s) and a notable Kufan from the tribe of
Hamadan. Biographers say that when Burair heard that al-Hussain (a)
refused to pledge allegiance to the tyrant Yazid, he set out from Kufa
to meet al-Hussain (a) in Mecca. He remained with him until he was
martyred - may God bless his soul.[32]

---

* A *Tabi'i* is an individual who lived during the time of the Holy Prophet (s) or directly
afterwords but did not have the chance to meet him and listen to his words. Instead,
they learned directly from the companions who lived with the Holy Prophet (s).

Al-Hurr enters the Battlefield

ثم قال الحر للحسين (عليه السلام): يابن رسول الله، كنت أول خارج عليك
فاذن لي أن أكون أول قتيل بين يديك فلعلي أن أكون ممن يصافح جدك محمدا
(ص) غدا في القيامة. فقال له الحسين (عليه السلام):

Al-Hurr then said to al-Hussain (a), "O' son of the Messenger of God,
I was the first to set out against you, so give me permission to be the
first one to die in your support. Perhaps that would [grant me the
honor to] shake the hands of your grandfather Muhammad (s) on the
Day of Resurrection." Al-Hussain (a) replied,

إن شئت فأنت ممن تاب الله عليه، و هو التواب الرحيم.

*As you wish. You are of those whom God has [accepted their]
repentence, and He is the Ever Relenting, the All Merciful.*

فكان أول من تقدم إلى براز القوم و هو يرتجز [...]و خرج الحر بن يزيد الرياحي
و معه زهير بن القين يحمي ظهره، فكان إذا شدّ أحدهما و استلحم شدّ الآخر
و استنقذه، ففعلا ذلك ساعة.

He was the first to duel the enemy [reciting in verse his resolve to
protect al-Hussain (a)]. Al-Hurr set out with Zuhair ibn al-Qayn
guarding his back. If either of them found himself in trouble, the other
would charge to the rescue. They continued to fight for an hour or
so.[33]

Al-Hurr Battles Yazid ibn Sufyan

و روي عن أبي زهير العبسي أن الحر بن يزيد لما لحق بالحسين (عليه السلام)،
قال يزيد بن سفيان من بني شقرة و هم بنو الحارث بن تميم: أما و الله لو أني
رأيت الحر بن يزيد حين خرج لأتبعته السنان.

Abu Zuhair al-Absi narrates that when al-Hurr joined the camp of al-
Hussain (a), Yazid ibn Sufyan (of the Bani Shaqra, the sons of al-Harith
ibn Tameem) said, "By God, if I had seen al-Hurr ibn Yazid when he
left, I would have followed him with my spear [and killed him on the
spot]!"

قال: فبينا الناس يتجاولون و يقتتلون، و الحر بن يزيد يحمل على القوم مقدما،
و يتمثل بقول عنترة [...] و إن فرسه لمضروب على أذنيه و حاجبه، و إن دماءه
لتسيل. فقال الحصين ابن تميم- و كان على شرطة عبيد الله- ليزيد بن سفيان:
هذا الحر بن يزيد الّذي كنت تتمنى [قتله، فهل لك به]!

Men were engaged in heated battle as al-Hurr ibn Yazid charged
valiantly toward the enemy reciting the verses of Antarah [ibn Shaddad,
a pre-Islamic Arab warrior-poet]. His horse was wounded at the ear
and brows, with blood flowing [over its face]. Al-Hossayn ibn
Tameem, who was Ubaydillah's police captain, said to Yazid ibn
Sufyan, "This is al-Hurr ibn Yazid who you were hoping [to kill. Can
you take him on]!"

قال: نعم. فخرج إليه، فقال له: هل لك يا حر بن يزيد في المبارزة؟ قال: نعم قد
شئت، فبرز له. قال: فأنا سمعت الحصين بن تميم يقول: و الله لبرز له فكأنما

كانت نفسه في يده، فما لبّثه الحر حين خرج إليه أن قتله [و قتل أربعين فارسا و راجلا].

He said yes, set out towards [al-Hurr], and sid to him, "Do you, O' Hurr ibn Yazid, wish to duel?" He replied, "Yes, I do," and proceeded toward him. [The narrator, Abu Zuhair al-Absi,] said, "Then I heard Al-Hossayn ibn Tameem say, 'By God, [al-Hurr dueled] as if his soul is in his grasp [i.e. he fought with great valor, undawnted by certain death].' It was not long before [al-Hurr] finished off [his foe]."[34]

The Martyrdom of al-Hurr ibn Yazid al-Riyahi

ثم رمى أيوب بن مشرح الخيواني فرس الحر بسهم فعقره و شبّ به الفرس،
فوثب عنه كأنه ليث و بيده السيف. فقاتلهم راجلا قتالا شديدا و هو [يرتجز]
و جعل يضربهم بسيفه حتى قتل نيفا و أربعين رجلا.

Ayoub ibn Mashrah al-Khaywani then shot al-Hurr's horse [on the knee], hamstringing it. The horse fell, but he jumped off it like a lion with the sword in his hand. He fought valiantly on foot [while reciting verses of poetry taunting and intimidating his foes]. He fought them with his sword until he killed forty-some men.

ثم حملت الرجالة على الحر و تكاثروا عليه، فاشترك في قتله أيوب بن مشرح،
فاحتمله أصحاب الحسين (عليه السلام) حتى وضعوه أمام الفسطاط الّذي
يقاتلون دونه ... و هكذا كان يؤتى بكل قتيل إلى هذا الفسطاط، و الحسين
(عليه السلام) يقول:

The [Umayyad] infantry gathered against al-Hurr and overpowered him. [A group of enemy soldiers, including] Ayoub ibn Mashrah, collaborated in killing him. Al-Hussain's (a) companions carried him and placed him in front of the tent [at the forefront of the camp]. Whenever any of the martyrs was brought to the tent al-Hussain (a) would say,

قتلة مثل قتلة النبيين و آل النبيين.

A death like the deaths of the prophets and the families of the prophets.

ثم التفت الحسين (عليه السلام) إلى الحر و كان به رمق، فقال له و هو يمسح الدم عنه:

Al-Hussain (a) turned to al-Hurr while he still held his last breath. He wiped the blood off him and said,

أنت الحر كما سمّتك أمك، و أنت الحرّ في الدنيا و الآخرة.

You are al-Hurr [i.e. the free] like your mother named you! You are free in this world and the next!

و رثاه رجل من أصحاب الحسين (عليه السلام)، و قيل علي بن الحسين (عليه السلام)، و قيل إنها من إنشاء الإمام الحسين (عليه السلام) خاصة فقال:

One of the companions of al-Hussain (a) - with some historians saying that it was Ali ibn al-Hussain (a) or al-Hussain (a) himself - mourned him with the following verses,

لنعم الحرّ حرّ بني رياح * * * صبور عند مشتبك الرماح

و نعم الحر إذ نادى حسين * * * فجاد بنفسه عند الصباح

Glory to al-Hurr, the free-man of Bani Riyah

He was patient amidst the clashing of spears

Glory to al-Hurr, who heard the cry of Hussain (a)

And sacrificed himself that early morn!

و في (طبقات ابن سعد) أنه المتوكل الليثي.

In *Tabaqat ibn Saad*, [the poem is attributed to] al-Mutawakil al-Laithi.[35]

Biographical Entry | Al-Hurr ibn Yazid al-Riyahi

هو الّذي جعجع بالحسين (عليه السلام) و كان أول خارج عليه، ثم بعد ذلك أدركته السعادة و حظي بشرف الشهادة، فكان من أول المستشهدين بين يدي الحسين (عليه السلام) يوم الطف. و ذكر أرباب السير أنه لما استشهد الحر أخرج الحسين (عليه السلام) منديله و عصب به رأس الحر.

He is the [Umayyad commander] who blocked al-Hussain (a) [on his path to Kufa and pushed him towards Karbala] and so was the first to set out against him. He then [repented and was able to achieve eternal] happiness by gaining the honor of martyrdom, as he was amongst the first martyrs from the camp of al-Hussain (a) during the Battle of Karbala. Biographers recount that when al-Hurr was martyred, al-Hussain (a) took his kerchief and wrapped it around al-Hurr's head.

و ذكر الشيخ السماوي و مثله العلامة المظفر قال: و إنما دفنت بنو تميم الحر بن يزيد على نحو ميل من الحسين (عليه السلام) حيث قبره الآن اعتناء به. و لعل بنو تميم هم الذين تكتّلوا يوم الحادي عشر من المحرم و منعوا الناس من قطع رأس الحر و حمله، كما فعلوا ببقية الرؤوس، إذ قطعوها من الأبدان و حملوها على أطراف الرماح. و للحر بن يزيد الرياحي اليوم مشهد يزار خارج مدينة كربلاء، في الموضع الّذي كان قديما يدعى النواويس.

Al-Shaykh al-Samawi and al-Allama al-Mudhaffar say, "Banu Tameem buried al-Hurr ibn Yazid about a mile away from al-Hussain (a) out of respect for him. Perhaps it was Banu Tameem who gathered on the 11th of Muharram and stopped the severing and parading of al-Hurr's head - as all the other heads were severed from the bodies and hoisted atop spears. Today, there is a shrine atop al-Hurr's tomb on the outskirts of Karbala in the town that was previously called al-Nawawis.[36]

A Rebuttal to those who Accused al-Hurr of Apostacy

لقد حدثني جماعة من الثقاة أن الشاه إسماعيل الصفوي لما ملك بغداد، و أتى إلى مشهد الحسين (عليه السلام)، و سمع من بعض الناس الطعن على الحر بن يزيد؛ أتى إلى قبره، و أمر بنبشه، فرأوه نائمًا كهيئته لما قتل، و رأوا على رأسه عصابة مشدودا بها رأسه.

A number of trusted individuals have told me that when Shah Ismail al-Safawi occupied Baghdad and came to the shrine of al-Hussain (a), he heard some disparaging al-Hurr [saying that he was an apostate and that his repentance was not accepted]. He went to al-Hurr's tomb and commanded that his body be exhumed. They found his body as if he had just been killed [i.e. it had not decomposed] and found a kerchief wrapped around his head.

فأراد الشاه أخذ تلك العصابة، لما نقل في كتب السير أن تلك العصابة هي منديل الحسين (عليه السلام) شدّ به رأسه لما أصيب في تلك الواقعة، و دفن على تلك الهيئة. فلما حلّوا تلك العصابة جرى الدم من رأسه حتى امتلأ منه القبر، فلما شدّوا عليه تلك العصابة انقطع الدم. فأمر فبنى على قبره بناء، و عيّن له خادما يخدم قبره. و تبيّن له أن شهادته كانت على حقّ، و أنه معدود في الشهداء.

The Shah wanted to take that kerchief because biographers recount that the kerchief was actually al-Hussain's (a) and that he had wrapped it around his head when he was wounded in that battle. When they took the kerchief, blood flowed from his head until it filled the grave. When they wrapped it back around his head, the blood stopped. [Shah

60

Ismail al-Safawi] commanded that a shrine be built over his tomb and appointed a servant to maintain the shrine. Thus, it was clear that [al-Hurr] was martyred on the path of righteousness and that he is like all the other martyrs [of the Battle of Karbala].[37]

The Martyrdom of Wahab ibn Hobab al-Kalbi

ثم برز وهب بن حباب الكلبي، و يقال إنه كان نصرانيا فأسلم هو و أمه على
يد الحسين (عليه السلام)، و كانت معه أمه و زوجته. فقالت أمه: قم يا بني
فانصر ابن بنت رسول الله (ص). فقال: أفعل يا أمّاه و لا أقصّر ، فبرز و هو
[يرتجز].

Wahab ibn Hobab al-Kalbi then stepped forth unto the battle field. It
is said that he was a Christian who had accepted Islam along with his
mother because of al-Hussain (a). He was with his wife and mother
when his mother said, "Go, my son, and support the son of the
daughter of the Messenger of God (s)." He said, "I will, and I will not
fall short!" He charged into the battlefield reciting [verses touting his
strength and valor].

ثم حمل وهب و لم يزل يقاتل حتى قتل جماعة. ثم رجع إلى امرأته و أمه و قال:
يا أماه أرضيت ؟ فقالت: ما رضيت حتى تقتل بين يدي الحسين (عليه السلام)،
فقالت امرأته: بالله عليك لا تفجعني بنفسك.

Wahab charged and fought until he killed a number of enemy soldiers.
He then went back to his mother and his wife and said, "O mother,
are you pleased?" She replied, "I will not be pleased until you die in
support of al-Hussain!" His wife pleaded, "By God, don't grieve me by
your death!"

فقالت له أمه: يا بني اعزب عن قولها، و ارجع فقاتل بين يدي ابن بنت نبيك
تنل شفاعة جده يوم القيامة. فرجع فلم يزل يقاتل حتى قطعت يداه. و أخذت

امرأته عمودا و أقبلت نحوه و هي تقول: فداك أبي و أمي، قاتل دون الطيبين حرم رسول الله (ص). فأقبل كي يردّها إلى النساء، فأخذت بجانب ثوبه و قالت: لن أعود دون أن أموت معك.

His mother said to him, "Don't listen to her, my son. Go back and fight in support of the son of your Prophet's (s) daughter, and you will gain his grandfather's intercession of the Day of Resurrection." He returned to the battlefield and continued to fight until his arms were severed. His wife took a pole and ran toward him saying, "May my mother and father be sacrificed for you! Fight in protection of the righteous family of the Messenger of God (s)!" He went to take her back to the women, but she held on to his clothes and said, "I will not return, but will die alongside you."

فقال الحسين (عليه السلام): جزيتم من أهل بيت خيرا، ارجعي إلى النساء رحمك الله.

Al-Hussain (a) said to her, "May God reward you well as a family! Return to the women, may God bless you."

فانصرفت إليهن. و لم يزل الكلبي يقاتل حتى قتل (رضوان الله عليه).

She returned to the camp while al-Kalbi continued to fight until he was killed - may God bless his soul.[38]

Al-Shimr stabs the Tent and Tries to Burn the Camp

و حمل القوم بعضهم على بعض، و اشتد بينهم القتال. فصبر لهم الحسين (عليه السلام) و أصحابه، حتى انتصف النهار، و هم يقاتلون من جهة واحدة. فلما رأى ابن سعد ذلك أمر بإحراق الخيم.

The two sides charged at one another and the battle raged on between them. Al-Hussain (a) and his companions persevered until mid-day, while they were battling their foe from one direction. When Ibn Saad saw this, he gave orders to burn the tents [as they had stopped his troops from flanking al-Hussain (a) and his companions].

فقال الحسين (عليه السلام) لأصحابه: دعوهم فإنهم لن يصلوا إليكم.

Al-Hussain (a) said to his companions, "Let them be, for they will not reach you."

ثم حمل الشمر حتى طعن فسطاط الحسين، و نادى: عليّ بالنار لأحرق بيوت الظالمين (فصحن النساء و خرجن من الفسطاط). فحمل عليه أصحاب الحسين حتى كشفوه عن الخيمة. فناداه الحسين (عليه السلام):

Al-Shimr charged until he stabbed al-Hussain's (a) tent, calling, "Give me a fire so I can burn the tents of the oppressors." The women cried and ran out of the tent, until the companions of al-Hussain (a) charged at [al-Shimr] and repelled him from the camp. Al-Hussain then called out [to al-Shimr],

ويلك يا شمر تريد أن تحرق خيمة رسول الله؟!

Woe to you, Shimr. Do you wish to burn the tent of the Messenger of God?

قال: نعم. فرفع الحسين طرفه إلى السماء، و قال:

[Al-Shimr] replied, "Yes!" Al-Hussain (a) raised his eyes to the heavens and said,

اللهم لا يعجزك شمر أن تحرقه بالنار يوم القيامة.

O' God, Shimr will not stop you from burning him on the Day of Resurrection![39]

Hamid ibn Muslim Denounces Shimr's Action

و روي عن حميد بن مسلم (قال) قلت لشمر بن ذي الجوشن: سبحان الله،
إن هذا لا يصلح لك؛ أتريد أن تجمع على نفسك خصلتين: تعذّب بعذاب الله،
و تقتل الولدان و النساء؟! و الله إن في قتلك الرجال لما ترضي به أميرك.
(قال) فقال: من أنت؟ (قال) قلت: لا أخبرك من أنا. قال: و خشيت و الله
أن لو عرفني أن يضرني عند السلطان!

It is narrated that Hamid ibn Muslim said, "I said to Shimr ibn
Thiljawshan, 'Glory to God! That is unbecoming of you. Do you wish
to garner two traits; that you incur God's torment, and that you kill
women and children? By God, surely killing the men will be enough
please your master [Yazid].' He said to me, 'And who are you?' I
replied, 'I will not tell you who I am.' By God, I feared that if he knew
me, he would speak ill of me to those with authority."[40]

Shabath ibn Rib'i Disparages Shimr

قال: فجاءه رجل كان أطوع له مني (شبث بن ربعي) فقال له: ما رأيت مقالا
أسوأ من قولك، و لا موقفا أقبح من موقفك! أمرعبا للنساء صرت! قال: فأشهد
أنه استحيا فذهب لينصرف.

[Hamid ibn Muslim] said, "Then a man who he listened to more than
me - Shabath ibn Rib'i - came and said, 'I have not heard a statement
worse than yours, nor a stance worse than yours! Have you become a
terrorizer of women!' I swear that he was ashamed and left at once."[41]

Zuhair ibn al-Qayn Rescues the Tents

و حمل عليه زهير بن القين في رجال من أصحابه عشرة، فشدّ على شمر بن ذي الجوشن و أصحابه؛ فكشفهم عن البيوت، حتى ارتفعوا عنها.

Zuhair ibn al-Qayn took ten of his companions and charged against Shimr ibn Thiljawshan and his men. They repelled them from the camp and saved the tents.[42]

The Martyrdom of Amr ibn Khalid al-Azdi and His Son

و برز عمرو بن خالد الأزدي و هو [يرتجز] ثم قاتل حتى قتل رحمة الله عليه.
فتقدم ابنه خالد بن عمرو، و هو يرتجز [...]فلم يزل يقاتل حتى قتل رحمة الله
عليه.

Amr ibn Khalid al-Azdi charged into the battlefield [reciting verses of poetry in supplication to God Almighty]. He fought until he was killed - may God bless his soul. Then his son Khalid ibn Amr stepped forward, [reciting verses in glorification of God Almighty]. He fought until he was killed - may God bless his soul.[43]

Historical Confusion between Amr ibn Khalid al-Azdi and Amr ibn Khalid al-Saydawi

حصل خلط بين عمرو بن خالد الأزدي السابق، و بين عمرو بن خالد الصيداوي الّذي سيأتي ذكرُه في الفقرة التالية. و أغلب المصادر ذكرت الأخير (عمرو) ما عدا السيد الأمين في اللواعج الّذي ذكره (عمر). فالذي استُشهد في جماعة أربعة مع مولاه و صديقيه هو عمر بن خالد الصيداوي.

There has been some confusion amongst historians between Amr ibn Khalid al-Azdi, mentioned earlier, and Amr ibn Khalid al-Saydawi, who will be mentioned next. Most sources recount the name of the latter as "Amr," with the exception of al-Sayyid al-Ameen, who recounts his name as "Omar." The one who was martyred in a group of four, along with his servant and two friends, is Omar ibn Khalid al-Saydawi.

و قد ذكر السيد الأمين في (اللواعج) ص 132 شخصا ثالثا باسم مشابه و هو (عمرو بن خالد الصيداوي) و قد استُشهد بعد جون. قال: و برز عمرو بن خالد الصيداوي، فقال للحسين (عليه السلام): يا أبا عبد الله، قد هممت أن ألحق بأصحابي، و كرهت أن أتخلف و أراك وحيدا من أهلك قتيلا. فقال له الحسين (عليه السلام):

Al-Sayyid al-Ameen mentions in *al-Lawa'ij* (p. 132) a third individual by the name of Amr ibn Khalid al-Saydawi who was martyred after John.

[Al-Sayyid al-Ameen] said, "Amr ibn Khalid al-Saydawi stepped forward and said to al-Hussain (a), 'O' Abu Abdullah, I wish to join my companions and I would hate to survive long enough to see you murdered alone after the murder of your family.' Al-Hussain (a) said to him,

تقدّم فإنا لاحقون بك عن ساعة.

Go forth, for we shall join you soon.

فتقدم فقاتل حتى قتل.

He stepped forward and fought until he was killed."[44]

The Martyrdom of a Group of Companions

و أما عمرو بن خالد الصيداوي و سعد مولاه، و جابر بن الحارث السلماني و

مجمع بن عبد الله العائذي، فإنهم قاتلوا في أول القتال، فشدّوا مقدمين بأسيافهم

على أهل الكوفة، فلما أوغلوا فيهم عطف عليهم الناس و قطعوهم عن أصحابهم.

As for Amr ibn Khalid al-Saydawi and his servant Saad, Jabir ibn al-Harith al-Salmani, and Majma' ibn Abdullah al-'A'ethi, they had fought at the beginning of the battle, charging with their swords against the people of Kufa. When they charged deep inside enemy lines, the soldiers circled around them and cut them off from their companions.

فندب إليهم الحسين (عليه السلام) أخاه العباس (عليه السلام) فاستنقذهم

بسيفه و قد جرحوا بأجمعهم. و في أثناء الطريق اقترب منهم العدو فشدوا

بأسيافهم مع ما بهم من الجراح، و قاتلوا حتى قتلوا أول الأمر في مكان واحد.

Al-Hussain (a) sent al-Abbas to aid them, but they had already been wounded. While on the way back, they saw the enemy approaching and so they charged despite their wounds. They fought until they were killed together in the same spot.

و عاد العباس (عليه السلام) إلى أخيه و أخبرهم بخبرهم. و كان هؤلاء الأربعة

من مخلصي الشيعة في الكوفة، التحقوا بالحسين (عليه السلام) بالعذيب قبل

وصوله إلى كربلاء.

Al-Abbas returned to his brother and told him what had happened. These four were of the devout Shia of Kufa, having joined the caravan of al-Hussain (a) at the 'Atheeb al-Hijanat [on the outskirts of modern day Najaf] before he reached Karbala.[45]

Biographical Entry | Amr ibn Khalid al-Saydawi

كان عمرو من أشراف الكوفة، مخلص الولاء لأهل البيت (عليهم السلام). قام
مع مسلم بن عقيل، حتى إذا خانته الكوفة لم يسعه إلا الاختفاء. فلما سمع بمقتل
قيس بن مسهر، و أخبر أن الحسين (عليه السلام) صار بالحاجر، خرج إليه
مع سعد مولاه، و جابر بن الحارث السلماني و مجمع بن عبد الله العائذي، و
ابنه خالد.

Amr was amongst the notables of Kufa; a devout follower of the
Ahlulbayt. He was in the ranks of Muslim ibn Aqeel, but when they
were betrayed in Kufa, he could do nothing other than hide. When he
heard about the death of Qays ibn Moshir and was told that al-Hussain
(a) was in al-Haajir, he set out to meet him along with his servant Saad,
Jabir ibn al-Harith al-Salmani, and Majma ibn Abdullah al-'A'ethi and
his son Khalid.

و اتّبعهم غلام لنافع البجلي بفرسه المدعو (الكامل) فجنبوه. و أخذوا دليلا لهم
الطرماح بن عدي الطائي، و كان جاء إلى الكوفة يمتار لأهله طعاما. فخرج بهم
على طريق متنكبة، و سار سيرا عنيفا من الخوف، حتى انتهوا إلى الحسين
(عليه السلام) و هو بعذيب الهجانات، فاستقبلهم. و قال (عليه السلام):

They were followed by a servant of Nafi' [ibn Hilal] al-Bajali with a
horse of his called al-Kamil, so they took it along with them. They took
as a guide al-Tirimmah ibn Adi al-Taei, who had come to Kufa to
purchase food for his family. He took them through rugged terrain and
marched them restlessly due to fear [of being caught]. They met up

with al-Hussain (a) when he was in 'Atheeb al-Hijanat, who welcomed them and said,

أما و الله إني لأرجو أن يكون خيرا ما أراد الله بنا؛ قتلنا أو ظفرنا.

By God, I pray that what God intends for us is nothing but good, whether we are slain or are victorious.[46]

The Battle Continues Until Mid-day

و كان القتل يبين في أصحاب الحسين (عليه السلام) لقلة عددهم، و لا يبين في أصحاب عمر بن سعد لكثرتهم. و اشتدّ القتال و التحم، و كثر القتل و الجراح في أصحاب أبي عبد الله الحسين (عليه السلام) إلى أن زالت الشمس.

Each casualty seemed to show on al-Hussain's (a) camp; his companions were so few in the first place. On the other hand, the casualties of the day did not seem to show on the amry of Omar ibn Saad due to its massive numbers. The battle raged on and the number of martyrs and wounded continued to increase until the sun reached its zenith.[47]

Abu Thumama Remembers the Prayer

و رأى أبو ثمامة الصائدي زوال الشمس، فقال للحسين (عليه السلام): يا أبا عبد الله نفسي لك الفدا، أرى هؤلاء قد اقتربوا، و لا و الله لا تقتل حتى أقتل دونك، و أحب أن ألقى ربي و قد صليت هذه الصلاة التي دنا وقتها. فرفع الحسين (عليه السلام) رأسه إلى السماء و قال له:

Abu Thumama saw that the sun was approaching its zenith. He said to al-Hussain (a), "May my life be sacrificed for yuo, O' Abu Abdullah (a)! I see [the enemy] coming closer, and by God you will not be killed before I die protecting you. But I would love to meet my Lord after perfomring this prayer whose time is approaching." Al-Hussain (a) raised his eyes to the sky and said,

ذكرت الصلاة جعلك الله من المصلين، نعم هذا أول وقتها، سلوهم أن يكفّوا عنا حتى نصلي.

You have remembered prayer, may God make you amongst the worshipers [on the Day of Judgment]! Yes, this is the beginning of its time. Ask them to halt their advance so that we may pray.

فقال له الحصين بن نمير: إنها لا تقبل منك! فقال له حبيب بن مظاهر: لا تقبل الصلاة زعمت من آل رسول الله و تقبل منك يا ختّار !؟

[The companions did so, but] al-Hossayn ibn Numair replied, "It will not be accepted from you!" Habib ibn Mudhahir retorted, "You claim that it will not be accepted from the family of the Messenger of God (s) and that it will be accepted from a miscreant like you?!"

[...] فلما فرغ [أبو ثمامة] من الأذان نادى الحسين (عليه السلام):

[...] When [Abu Thumama] finished the Athan, al-Hussain (a) called out,

يا عمر بن سعد أنسيت شرائع الإسلام، ألا تكفّ عنا الحرب حتى نصلي؟!

O' Omar ibn Saad, have you forgotten the teachings of Islam! Would you stop your advance so that we may pray?

فلم يجبه عمر. فناداه الحصين بن نمير: يا حسين صلّ فإن صلاتك لا تقبل! فقال له حبيب بن مظاهر: ويلك لا تقبل صلاة الحسين و تقبل صلاتك يابن الخمّارة؟! فحمل عليه الحصين، فضرب حبيب وجه فرسه بالسيف فشبّت به و وقع عنها الحصين، فاحتوشه أصحابه فاستنقذوه.

Omar did not reply, but al-Hossayn ibn Numair said, "O'Hussain (a), pray for your prayer will not be accepted!"

"Woe to you! Al-Hussain's (a) prayer is not accepted, while yours is, O' son of a drunkard?!" replied Habib ibn Mudhahir. Al-Hossayn charged at him, but Habib struck his horse on its face with his sword. The horse threw al-Hossayn and he fell to the ground, but he was rescued by his men.[48]

The Martyrdom of Habib ibn Mudhahir

ثم خرج حبيب بن مظاهر و عمره ينوف على الخامسة و السبعين، و قاتل قتالا شديدا، فقتل على كبره اثنين و ستين رجلا، و هو [يرتجز] و حمل عليه بديل بن صريم فضربه بسيفه، و طعنه آخر من تميم برمحه، فسقط إلى الأرض.

Habib ibn Mudhahir then set out to the battlefield. He was an elder man, seventy five years of age. Yet he fought valiantly and killed 62 men despite his age, [reciting verses lauding the virtues of his companions as he swept the battlefield]. Badeel ibn Suraym charged at him and struck him with his sword. Another man from Tameem stabbed him with his spear, forcing him to the ground.

فذهب ليقوم و إذا الحصين بن نمير يضربه بالسيف على رأسه، فسقط لوجهه، و نزل إليه التميمي و احتزّ رأسه. فهدّ مقتله الحسين (عليه السلام) فقال:

He attempted to get up, but al-Hossayn ibn Numair struck him on his head with a sword. He fell to the ground again, [with al-Hossayn having dealt him his final blow]. The man from Tameem rushed to him and severed his head. Habib's martyrdom overwhelmed al-Husain (a), who would say,

عند الله أحتسب نفسي و حماة أصحابي.

It is in God that I place my hopes [of retribution for my murder and the murder of] my valiant companions.

و استرجع كثيرا. و في (مقتل الحسين المنسوب لأبي مخنف) ص 66: ثم قال الحسين (عليه السلام):

He continued to repeat [the Holy Verse, "Indeed we belong to God and to Him do we indeed return."] And in Abu Mikhnaf's *Maqtal* (p. 66), "Al-Hussain (a) then said,

لله درّك يا حبيب، لقد كنت فاضلا تختم القرآن في ليلة واحدة.

May God accept your work, O' Habib! You were a man of virtue, reciting the entire Quran in a single night."

و قيل: قتله بديل بن صريم.

It is also said that he was killed by Badeel ibn Suraym.[49]

Al-Qasim ibn Habib seeks Retribution for his Father's Murder

و قال الحصين التميمي (لبديل): أنا شريكك في قتله [أي قتل حبيب]. قال: لا
و الله. قال: أعطني الرأس أعلقه في عنق فرسي ليرى الناس أني شاركتك في
قتله، ثم خذه فلا حاجة لي فيما يعطيك ابن زياد! فأعطاه الرأس، فجال به في
الناس ثم ردّه إليه. فلما رجع إلى الكوفة علّقه في عنق فرسه.

Al-Hossayn al-Tameemi said to Badeel, "I am your partner in killing [Habib]!" Badeel replied, "By God, you were not!" Al-Hossayn said, "Give me the head and I will tie it to the neck of my horse so that the people could see that I helped you in killing him. You can then take it back, as I have no need for any prize you may get from Ibn Ziyad." Badeel gave al-Hossayn the head, which he paraded amongst the people then gave back. When they returned to Kufa, he tied it to the neck of his horse [and continued to parade it around the city].

و كان لحبيب ابن يسمى (القاسم) قد راهق، فجعل يتبع الفارس الّذي معه رأس
أبيه، فارتاب به. فقال: مالك تتبعني؟. قال: إن هذا الرأس الّذي معك رأس
أبي، فأعطني إياه حتى أدفنه. فقال: إن الأمير لا يرضى أن يدفن، و أرجو أن
يثيبني. فقال: لكن الله لا يثيبك إلا أسوأ الثواب، و بكى الغلام.

Habib had a son named al-Qasim who was then an adolescent. He [saw his father's head on the neck of the horse] and began to follow the horseman. The man noticed him and asked, "Why are you following me?" The boy replied, "This head you are carrying is my father's. Give it to me so I can bury it." The man said, "The governor does not wish it to be buried, and I wish to be given a prize for it." The boy wept and said, "Then God will not give you but the worst reprisal!"

ثم لم يزل يتبع أثر قاتل أبيه بعدما أدرك، حتى قتله و أخذ بثأر أبيه، و ذلك أنه كان في عسكر، فهجم عليه و هو في خيمة له نصف النهار، فقتله و أخذ رأسه.

[Al-Qasim] continued to follow his father's killer until he was able to kill him. He had followed the man to a barracks and attacked him in his tent in the middle of the day, killing him and taking his head.[50]

Biographical Entry | Habib ibn Mudhahir

هو حبيب بن مظاهر بن رئاب بن الأشتر الأسدي الكندي. إماميّ ثقة، و أدرك النبي (ص) و أمير المؤمنين و الحسن و الحسين (عليه السلام). و كان حافظا للقرآن من أوله إلى آخره. و سمع الحديث من رسول الله (ص) فهو صحابي.

Habib ibn Mudhahir ibn Ri'ab ibn al-Ashtar al-Asadi al-Kindi. A trusted Immami who was a companion of the Holy Prophet (s), the Commander of the Faithful, Imam Hassan (a), and Imam Hussain (a). He memorized the entirety of the Quran and relayed the narrations of the Holy Prophet (s).

قال أرباب التاريخ: إن حبيبا نزل الكوفة و صحب عليا (عليه السلام) في حروبه كلها. و كان من خاصته و حملة علومه [...]. و كان من جملة الذين كاتبوا الحسين (عليه السلام) و وفّى له.

Historians say that Habib had come to Kufa and served in all of the battles alongside Imam Ali (a). He was one of the Commander of the Faithful's (a) trusted companions and dedicated pupils [...]. He had writted letters to Imam Hussain (a) and fulfilled his promises to him.

و عند ورود مسلم بن عقيل الكوفة صار حبيب و مسلم بن عوسجة يأخذان البيعة للحسين (عليه السلام)، حتى إذا دخل عبيد الله بن زياد الكوفة و تخاذل أهل الكوفة عن سفير الحسين اختفيا، إلى أن ورد الحسين كربلاء، خرجا متخفيين و لحقا به و صارا من أصحابه.

When Muslim ibn Aqeel arrived to Kufa, Habib and Muslim ibn Awsaja began to gather the people and take their pledges to support al-Hussain (a). But when Ubaydillah ibn Ziyad came to Kufa and its people became reluctant to support al-Hussain's (a) messenger, they hid [from the persecution of the authorities]. When al-Hussain (a) came to Karbala, Habib and Muslim ibn Awsaja left Kufa in secrecy and joined his camp.

ثم كان حبيب على ميسرة الحسين (عليه السلام) يوم كربلاء، و عمره خمس و سبعون سنة. و هو واحد من سبعين بطلا استبسلوا في ذلك اليوم.

During the battle of Karbala, Habib commanded the left flank of al-Hussain's (a) army. He was a man of seventy five, one of the eldest of the seventy-some companions that fought alongside al-Hussain (a).[51]

Zuhair ibn al-Qayn Enters the Battlefield

لما قتل [...] حبيب بن مظاهر بان الانكسار في وجه الحسين (عليه السلام)
[...] فقام إليه زهير بن القين و قال: بأبي أنت و أمي يابن رسول الله ما هذا
الانكسار الّذي أراه في وجهك، ألست تعلم أنا على الحق؟ قال:

When [...] Habib had been martyred, al-Hussain (a) was overwhelmed
with grief [...]. Zuhair ibn al-Qayn stood close to al-Hussain (a) and
said, "May my mother and father be sacrificed for you, O' son of the
Messenger of God! What is the disheartenment I see in your face? Do
you not know that we are in the right?" Al-Hussain (a) replied,

بلى و إله الخلق، إني لأعلم علما يقينا أني و إياكم على الحق و الهدى.

Yes, I swear by the Lord of Creation! I know with absolute
certainty that you and I are on a path of truth and guidance!

فقال زهير: إذا لا نبالي و نحن نصير إلى الجنة و نعيمها. ثم تقدم أمام الحسين
فقال: يا مولاي أتأذن لي بالبراز؟ فقال:

Zuhair said, "Then we will not worry, as we will soon enter paradise
and enjoy its splendors!" He then stood in front of al-Hussain (a) and
said, "My lord, do you grant me leave to join the battle?" Al-Hussain
(a) said,

ابرز.

[Yes,] go out into the battlefield.

قال: ثم حمل على القوم، و لم يزل يقاتل حتى قتل خمسين فارسا، و خشي أن
تفوته الصلاة مع الحسين (عليه السلام) فرجع و قال: يا مولاي إني خشيت
أن تفوتني الصلاة فصلّ بنا.

He charged against the enemy and fought until he killed twenty knights. But he feared that he would miss the prayer alongside al-Hussain (a), so he returned and said, "My lord, I feared that I might miss prayer, so lead us [in this last prayer before our death]."[52]

Noon Prayer

فقال الحسين (عليه السلام) لزهير بن القين و سعيد بن عبد الله الحنفي:

Al-Hussain (a) said to Zuhair ibn al-Qayn and Saeed ibn Abdullah al-Hanafi,

تقدّما أمامي حتى أصلي الظهر.

Stand in front of me so that I can pray the noon prayers.

فتقدما أمامه في نحو من نصف أصحابه، حتى صلّى بهم صلاة الخوف. و يقال:
إنه صلى و أصحابه فرادى بالإيماء.

They stood in front of him along with about half of his companions so that he can pray *Salat al-Khawf.** It is also said that al-Hussain (a) and his companions prayed individually through gestures, [a form of *Salat al-Khawf* performed in times of extreme fear].[53]

---

* *Salat al-Khawf* is a special method of performing the obligatory daily prayers while in times of fear, especially during war.

Post noon

The Martyrdom of Saeed ibn Abdullah al-Hanafi

فوصل إلى الحسين (عليه السلام) سهم، فتقدم سعيد بن عبد الله و وقف

يقيه من النبال بنفسه، و ما زال يرمى بالنبل و لا تخطئ، فما أخذ النبل الحسين

(عليه السلام) يمينا و شمالا إلا قام بين يديه، فما زال يرمى حتى سقط إلى

الأرض، و هو يقول: اللهم العنهم لعن عاد و ثمود و أبلغ نبيك عني السلام، و

أبلغه ما لقيت من ألم الجراح، فإني أردت بذلك ثوابك في نصرة ذرية نبيك. و

التفت إلى الحسين (عليه السلام) قائلا: أوقّيت يابن رسول الله ؟

[While al-Hussain (a) was leading prayer], an arrow struck him. Saeed ibn Abdullah al-Hanafi stepped forward and began to shield al-Hussain (a) with his own body from a barrage of arrows. Whenever an arrow came toward al-Hussain (a) from left or right, Saeed lept to shield him. He continued to take arrows until he fell to the ground saying, "O' God, curse them like you cursed the people of 'Ad and Thamud. Send peace and blessings upon Your Prophet (s), and inform him of the wounds that I have taken. Surely, I only wanted Your reward by supporting the progeny of Your Prophet (s)." He turned to al-Hussain (a) and said, "Have I fulfilled my duty, O' son of the Messenger of God (s)?" Al-Hussain (a) replied,

قال: نعم أنت أمامي في الجنة.

Al-Hussain (a) replied, "Yes, and you shall walk in front of me into paradise."

(و في رواية) أنه قال: اللهم لا يعجزك شيء تريده، فأبلغ محمدا (ص) نصرتي و

دفعي عن الحسين (عليه السلام)، و ارزقني مرافقته في دار الخلود. ثم قضى

نحبه (رضوان الله عليه)، فوجد في جسمه ثلاثة عشر سهما، سوى ما به من

ضرب السيوف و طعن الرماح.

Another narration stated that Saeed said, "O' God, You are never
deterred against anything that You want! Inform Muhammad (s) of my
support and protection of al-Hussain (a) and grant me his company in
the Eternal Abode." After he passed away - may God bless his soul -
thirteen arrows were found on his body in addition to the cuts of the
swords and the stabs of the spears [that he suffered during battle].[54]

Biographical Entry | Saeed ibn Abdullah al-Hanafi

كان سعيد ممن استشهد مع الحسين (عليه السلام) يوم الطف. و كان من وجوه الشيعة بالكوفة، و ذوي الشجاعة و العبادة فيهم، و كان ممن حمل الكتب إلى الحسين (عليه السلام) من أهل الكوفة إلى مكة و الحسين (عليه السلام) فيها.

Saeed was amongst those martyred alongside al-Hussain (a) during the Battle of Karbala. He was one of the notables of Kufa, a man of valor and peity. He was one of the messengers who carried the letters of the Kufans to al-Hussain (a) while he was in Mecca.

و لما أراد الحسين (عليه السلام) أن يصلي الظهر يوم العاشر من المحرم، انتدبه ليقف أمامه ريثما يتمّ الصلاة، فوقف بين يديه يقيه السهام، طورا بوجهه و طورا بصدره و طورا بيديه و طورا بجبينه، حتى صار جسمه كالقنفذ، فسقط إلى الأرض صريعا، و قد وفّى ما عليه في نصرة سيد شباب أهل الجنة.

When al-Hussain (a) wanted to pray the noon prayer on the tenth of Muharram, he called Saeed to stand in front of him while he prayed. Saeed stood guarding him against the barrage of arrows with his own body until he became [covered in arrows] like a porcupine. He fell to the ground a martyr, having fulfilled his duty to the Master of the Youth of Paradise.[55]

Al-Hussain (a) Gives Glad Tidings to His Companions

فلمّا فرغ (عليه السلام) من صلاة الظهر قال لأصحابه:

After the prayer al-Hussain (a) said to his companions,

يا كرام هذه الجنة قد فتّحت أبوابها و اتصلت أنهارها و أينعت ثمارها و زيّنت قصورها و تؤلّفت ولدانها و حورها. و هذا رسول الله (ص) و الشهداء الذين قتلوا معه، و أبي و أمي، يتوقعون قدومكم عليهم، و يتباشرون بكم و هم مشتاقون إليكم.

O' most noble [companions]! This is paradise; its gates are open, its rivers are flowing, its fruits are ripe, its palaces are decorated, and its servants and maidens are delighted [for your arrival]! This is the Messenger of God (s) and the martyrs killed beside him, along with my father and mother, awaiting for your arrival! They joyously pass word of your coming and long for your arrival.

فحاموا عن دينكم و ذبّوا عن حرم رسول الله (ص) و عن إمامكم و ابن بنت نبيكم، فقد امتحنكم الله تعالى بنا، فأنتم في جوار جدنا و الكرام علينا و أهل مودتنا، فدافعوا بارك الله فيكم عنا.

So defend your faith and protect the family of the Messenger of God (s) and your Imam and the son of your Prophet's (s) daughter! God Almighty has tested you with us! You are in proximity of our grandfather [the Prophet (s)], honored by us, and the people of affection toward us! So defend us, may God bless you!

فلما سمعوا ضجوا بالبكاء و النحيب و قالوا: نفوسنا دون أنفسكم و دماؤنا دون
دمائكم و أرواحنا لكم الفداء. و الله لا يصل إليكم أحد بمكروه و فينا الحياة و
قد وهبنا للسيوف نفوسنا، و للطير أبداننا، فلعلنا نقيكم زحف الصفوف، و
نشرب دونكم الحتوف، فقد فاز من كسب اليوم خيرا، و كان لكم من المنون
مجيرا.

When they heard this, they began to wail and cry. They said, "Let our lives be taken rather than yours! Let our blood be spilled rather than yours! May our souls be sacrificed for you! By God, no one will reach you with any harm while we still live! We have pledged ourselves to the sword and our bodies to [scavenging] birds, so that perhaps we may protect you from the march of this army and taste death instead of you! Victorious is he who acts righteously today and protects you against impending death!"[56]

Omar ibn Saad Hamstrings al-Hussain's (a) Horses

ثم إن عمر بن سعد وجّه عمرو بن سعيد في جماعة من الرماة فرموا أصحاب الحسين (عليه السلام) حتى عقروا خيولهم و لم يبق مع الحسين فارس إلا الضحاك بن عبد الله المشرقي. يقول: لما رأيتُ خيل أصحابنا تعقر أقبلت بفرسي و أدخلتها فسطاطا لأصحابنا.

Omar ibn Saad directed Amr ibn Saeed along with a group of archers to pelt al-Hussain (a) and his companions until their horses were killed or hamstrung. No knight remained on his steed except for al-Dahhak ibn Abdullah al-Mashriqi who said, "When I saw my companions horses being hamstrung, I took my horse and stowed it in a tent."

و اقتتلوا أشد القتال. و كان كل من أراد الخروج، ودّع الحسين (عليه السلام) بقوله: السلام عليك يابن رسول الله، فيجيبه الحسين (عليه السلام):

[Al-Hussain's (a) companions] continued to fight valiantly. Whenever one of them wanted to set out into battle, he would bid farewell to al-Hussain (a) by saying, "Peace be upon you O' son of the Messenger of God (s)." Al-Hussain (a) would reply,

و عليك السلام و نحن خلفك، فَمِنْهُمْ مَنْ قَضَى نَحْبَهُ وَ مِنْهُمْ مَنْ يَنْتَظِرُ وَ ما بَدَّلُوا تَبْدِيلًا [الأحزاب: 23].

Peace be upon you, and we will follow you. 'There are some among them who have fulfilled their pledge, and some of them who still wait, and they have not changed in the least' (The Holy Quran, 33:23)[57]

The Martyrdom of Abu Thumama

و خرج أبو ثمامة الصائدي فقاتل حتى أثخن بالجراح. و كان مع عمر بن سعد ابن عم له يقال له قيس بن عبد الله بينهما عداوة، فشدّ عليه و قتله، رضوان الله عليه.

Abu Thumama al-Sa'edi stepped forth onto the battle field and faught until he was weakened by his wounds. He had a cousin named Qays ibn Abdullah in the army of Omar ibn Saad and there was some enmity between them. [Qays] charged at [Abu Thumama] and killed him - may God bless his soul.[58]

The Martyrdom of Zuhair ibn al-Qayn

ثم خرج زهير بن القين البجلي و هو [يرتجز] و روي أن زهيرا لما أراد الحملة،

وقف على الحسين (عليه السلام) و ضرب على كتفه و قال:

Zuhair ibn al-Qayn then set out into the battlefield, reciting [verses announcing his dedication to al-Hussain (a) and the family of the Prophet (s)]. It is narrated that when Zuhair wanted to join the battle, he stood before al-Hussain (a), put his hand on his shoulder, and recited,

اقدم حسين هاديا مهديّا * * * اليوم تلقى جدّك النبيا

و حسنا و المرتضى عليّا * * * و ذا الجناحين الفتى الكميّا

و أسد الله الشهيد الحيّا

Go forth, Hussain (a), O' guided guide

Today you will meet your grandfather the Prophet (s)

And Hassan (a) and the Chosen Ali (a)

And the winged man, [Jafar al-Tayyar]

And the Lion of God, the living martyr [Hamza]

[...] فقال الحسين (عليه السلام):

[...] Al-Hussain (a) said,

و أنا ألقاهما على أثرك.

[Go forth] and I shall meet them soon after you.

ثم قاتل قتالا شديدا، فشدّ عليه كثير بن عبد الله الشعبي و مهاجر بن أوس
التميمي، فقتلاه. فقال الحسين (عليه السلام) حين صرع زهير:

He fought valiantly until Katheer ibn Abdullah al-Shi'bi and Muhajir
ibn Aous al-Tameemi charged at him and killed him. When Zuhair was
martyred al-Hussain (a) said,

لا يبعدنّك الله يا زهير، و لعن الله قاتلك، لعن الذين مسخهم قردة
و خنازير.

*May God never distance you [from His mercy], O' Zuhair. May
God curse those who have killed you like he cursed those who he
deformed into apes and pigs.[59]*

Biographical Entry | Zuhair ibn al-Qayn

هو زهير بن القين بن قيس الأنماري البجلي. كان رجلا شريفا في قومه، نازلا فيهم بالكوفة، شجاعا له في المغازي مواقف مشهورة، و مواطن مشهودة. و كان في البداية عثمانيا ثم اهتدى إلى ولاية أهل البيت (عليهم السلام)، و لازم الحسين (عليه السلام) من الطريق، و حامى عنه كأعزّ أنصاره، حتى استشهد (رضوان الله عليه).

He is Zuhair ibn al-Qayn ibn Qays al-Anmari al-Balaji. He was a chief amongst his people and a resident of Kufa. His valor had been seen in battle through well-known stances on numerous occasions. At first, he had a leaning to Othman [the third caliph] but was then guided to the path of the Holy Household (a). He joined al-Hussain (a) on the road and defended him like his closest companions until he was martyred - may God bless his soul.

و بلغ من أهمية زهير في وقعة الطف أن وضعه الحسين (عليه السلام) على ميمنة جيشه، و جعل الصحابي حبيبا على الميسرة، و وقف هو في القلب. فكان زهير و حبيب بالنسبة للحسين (عليه السلام) مثل الجناحين بالنسبة للطائر، لا يستطيع المضي إلا بهما.

Zuhair played a critical role during the Battle of Karbala, such that al-Hussain (a) had assigned him the right flank of his army while Habib was assigned the left flank. Al-Hussain (a) remained at the heart. Thus, Zuhair and Habib were to al-Hussain (a) like the wings of a bird, without which he would not soar.

و لما صمم زهير على الشهادة، خرج برفقة الحر، و كلاهما من التائبين، فكان
إذا شدّ أحدهما و استلحم، شدّ الآخر فخلّصه، حتى قتل الحر، و لم يلبث أن
قتل زهير. و ما ذلك إلا ليبيّنا للملأ أنهما اهتديا معا، و قاتلا في سبيل الحق
معا، و استشهدا مع سيد شباب أهل الجنة معا، فزقّا إلى الجنة معا، (رضوان
الله عليهما).

When Zuhair determined to achieve martyrdom, he set out with al-
Hurr into battle. They were both repenters [who only recently joined
al-Hussain's (a) camp]. Whenever one of them charged and was
surrounded, the other would rush to the rescue. Al-Hurr was killed,
and before long Zuhair was killed as well. They did this so they can
show the world that they repented together, fought for truth together,
and were martyred in defense of the Master of the Youth of Paradise
together. They marched into paradise together, may God bless their
souls.[60]

The Martyrdom of Amr ibn Qaradha al-Ansari

و خرج عمرو بن قرظة الأنصاري، فاستأذن الحسين (عليه السلام) فأذن له.
فبرز و هو يرتجز [...]فقاتل قتال المشتاقين إلى الجزاء، و بالغ في خدمة سلطان
السماء، حتى قتل جمعا كثيرا من حزب ابن زياد، و جمع بين سداد و جهاد.

Amr ibn Qaradha al-Ansari stepped forward and asked al-Hussain (a) for permission to fight. Al-Hussain (a) granted him permission, so he joined battle reciting [verses the declared his intent to defend al-Hussain (a)]. He fought like those longing for their reward and excelled in the service of the Lord of the Heavens. He killed many of the army of Ibn Ziyad, combining both righteous deeds and excellent combat.

و جاء عمرو بن قرظة الأنصاري و وقف أمام الحسين (عليه السلام) يقيه العدو
و يتلقى السهام بصدره و جبهته، فلم يصل إلى الحسين (عليه السلام) سوء. و
لما كثر فيه الجراح التفت إلى أبي عبد الله (عليه السلام) و قال: أوفيت يابن
رسول الله؟ قال:

Amr ibn Qaradha then stood in front of al-Hussain (a) in order to protect him from the enemy and their barrage of arrows. He took the arrows with his chest and head so that no harm could reach al-Hussain (a). When his wounds grew too many, he turned to al-Hussain (a) and said, "Have I fulfilled my duty, O' son of the Messenger of God (s)?" Al-Hussain (a) replied,

نعم أنت أمامي في الجنة، فأقرئ رسول الله مني السلام و أعلمه أني
في الأثر.

Yes, and you are entering paradise before me. Give my peace and greetings to the Messenger of God (s) and tell him that I will soon follow you.

و خرّ ميّتا (رضوان الله عليه). فنادى أخوه علي بن قرظة و كان مع عمر بن سعد: يا حسين يا كذاب، غررت أخي حتى قتلته؟! فقال (عليه السلام):

Amr fell to the ground and passed away, may God bless his soul. His brother, Ali ibn Qaradha, who was in the army of Omar ibn Saad called out, "Hussain (a) you liar! You deceived my brother until you killed him!" Al-Hussain (a) replied,

إني لم أغرّ أخاك، و لكن الله هداه و أضلّك.

I did not deceive your brother, but God guided him and left you in your misguidance.

فقال: قتلني الله إن لم أقتلك. ثم حمل على الحسين (عليه السلام) ليطعنه فاعترضه نافع بن هلال الجملي، فطعنه حتى صرعه.

"May God kill me if I dont kill you," Ali ibn Qaradha said as he charged at al-Hussain (a). Nafi' ibn Hilal al-Jamali intercepted him and killed him [before he could reach al-Hussain (a)].[61]

The Martyrdom of Nafi' ibn Hilal

ثم خرج نافع بن هلال الجملي و جعل يرميهم بالسهام فلا تخطئ، و كان خاضبا

يده، و كان يرمي [ويرتجز] فلم يزل يرميهم حتى فنيت سهامه. ثم ضرب إلى

قائم سيفه فاستلّه، و حمل و هو يقول:

Nafi' ibn Hilal al-Jumali then stepped forward and began to pelt the
enemies with [poisoned] arrows and would not miss. He would
continue to shoot and recite [verses taunting his enemies] until his
arrows were depleted. He then drew his sword and charged at the
enemy, reciting,

أنا الغلام اليمنيّ الجملي * * * ديني على دين حسين و علي

إن أقتل اليوم فهذا أملي * * * و ذاك رأيي و ألاقي عملي

I am a Yemeni, Jumali man

My creed is that of Hussain (a) and Ali (a)

If I were killed today, that would be my wish

This is my belief, and I will soon see the results of my deeds

[...]فأحاطوا به يرمونه بالحجارة و النصال حتى كسروا عضديه و أخذوه أسيرا،

فأمسكه الشمر و معه أصحابه يسوقونه. فقال له ابن سعد: ما حملك على ما

صنعت بنفسك؟. قال: إن الله يعلم ما أردت. فقال له رجل و قد نظر إلى

الدماء تسيل على وجهه و لحيته: أما ترى ما بك؟!

[...] The enemies surrounded him, pelting him with rocks and arrows
until they broke his arms and took him prisoner. Al-Shimr and his
companions took him and dragged him [to Omar ibn Saad who] asked,
"What drove you to do this to yourself?" He replied, "God knows what

I wanted." A man that saw his blood pouring over his face and beard said to him, "Do you not see what has happened to you?"

فقال: و الله لقد قتلت منكم اثني عشر رجلا سوى من جرحت، و ما ألوم نفسي على الجهد، و لو بقيت لي عضد ما أسرتموني. و جرّد الشمر سيفه، فقال له نافع: و الله يا شمر لو كنت من المسلمين لعظم عليك أن تلقى الله بدمائنا، فالحمد لله الّذي جعل منايانا على يدي شرار خلقه. ثم قدّمه الشمر و ضرب عنقه.

He said, "By God, I have killed twelve of you and wounded others. I do not regret my efforts, and if I had an arm left [unbroken] you would not have captured me." Al-Shimr drew his sword, so Nafi' said to him, "By God, O' Shimr, if you were a Muslim you would have feared to meet God with our blood on your hands. Praise God who made our deaths at the hands of the most evil of his creation." Al-Shimr pushed him forward and struck him on his neck, [killing him].[62]

Biographical Entry | Nafi' ibn Hilal al-Jumali

كان نافع سيدا شريفا سريّا شجاعا. و كان قارئا كاتبا و من حملة الحديث. و كان
من أصحاب أمير المؤمنين (عليه السلام) شهد حروبه الثلاث: الجمل و صفين
و النهروان. و عندما بلغه امتناع الحسين (عليه السلام) من البيعة خرج إليه
فاستقبله في الطريق. و كان قد أوصى أن يتبع بفرسه المسمى (بالكامل)، فأتبع
مع جماعة من أصحابه. و قد قتل أسيرا (رضوان الله عليه).

Nafi' was a chief [amongst his tribe], a nobleman, of noble qualities, and a valiant warrior. He was a learned scribe and a narrator of [Prophetic] traditions. He was a companion of the Commander of the Faithful (a), fighting in all three of his wars; al-Jamal, Siffin, and al-Nahrawan. When he heard that al-Hussain (a) had refuse to pledge allegiance [to Yazid], he set out [towards Mecca] and met him on the way. He had instructed [his servant] to follow him with his horse called al-Kamil, so [the servant] did so along with a number of Nafi's companions. He was killed a captive, may God bless his soul.[63]

The Martyrdom of John the Servant of Abu Thar al-Ghafari

ثم خرج جون مولى أبي ذر الغفاري، و هو شيخ كبير السن من الموالي، و كان عبدا أسود، فجعل يحمل عليهم [وهو يرتجز] ووقف جون مولى أبي ذرّ الغفاري أمام الحسين (عليه السلام) يستأذنه، فقال (عليه السلام):

Then John, the servant of Abu Thar al-Ghafari and an elderly black man, charged at the enemy [taunting his enemies and praising al-Hussain (a) in verse]. John stood in front of al-Hussain (a) and asked permission to fight. Al-Hussain (a) said,

إنما تبعتنا طلبا للعافية، فأنت في إذن مني.

O' John, you followed us in hopes of a good outcome, so you have my permission [to leave the camp if you wish].

فوقع على قدميه يقبّلهما و يقول: أنا في الرخاء ألحس قصاعكم، و في الشدة أخذلكم!. و الله إن ريحي لنتن، و حسبي للئيم، و لوني لأسود، فتنفّس عليّ بالجنة، ليطيب ريحي، و يشرف حسبي، و يبيضّ وجهي. لا و الله لا أفارقكم حتى يختلط هذا الدم الأسود مع دمائكم. فأذن له الحسين. فقتل 25 شخصا حتى قتل (رضوان الله عليه).

John fell on al-Hussain's (a) feet and said, "In times of ease I eat from your food, but in times of hardship I would desert you! By God, my odor is rancid, my lineage is base, and my complexion is black. Breathe over me in paradise so that my odor would become pleasant, my lineage would become noble, and my face would become bright. No, by God I will not leave you until this blood mixes with your blood."

Al-Hussain (a) gave him permission to join battle. He killed twenty five enemy soldiers before being killed - may God bless his soul.

(و في رواية أبي مخنف في مقتله، ص 71) قال: «فلم يزل يقاتل حتى قتل سبعين رجلا، فوقعت في محاجر عينه ضربة، و كبا به جواده إلى الأرض، فوقع على أمّ رأسه، فأحاطوا به من كل جانب و مكان، فقتلوه». فوقف (عليه السلام) و قال:

Abu Mikhnaf narrates in his *Maqtal* (p. 71) :He continued to fight until he killed seventy men. Then a strike hit him on the eye and he fell off his horse to the ground, falling on his head. Enemy soldiers surrounded him and killed him. [Al-Hussain (a)] stood over his body and said,

اللهم بيّض وجهه و طيّب ريحه و احشره مع محمّد (ص) و عرّف بينه و بين آل محمّد (ص).

O' God, brighten his face, refine his odor, and grant him an abode with Muhammad (s) in the hereafter and alongside the family of Muhammad (s).

و روي عن الإمام الباقر (عليه السلام): أن الناس كانوا يحضرون المعركة فيدفنون القتلى، فوجدوا جونا بعد عشرة أيام تفوح منه رائحة المسك.

It is narrated that Imam al-Baqir (a) said, "Peolple used to come to the battlefield and bury their dead. They found John's body ten days after the battle with his body emitting an aroma of musk."[64]

Biographical Entry | John the Servant of Abu Thar al-Ghafari

هو جون بن حوي بن قتادة بن الأعور بن ساعدة بن عوف بن كعب بن حوي النوبي. اشتراه الإمام علي (عليه السلام) من الفضل بن العباس ابن عبد المطلب بمائة و خمسين دينارا، و وهبه لأبي ذرّ ليخدمه. فانتقل من بيئة تزخر بالثراء و الجاه إلى أخرى قد خيّم عليها جلال الزهد و التقوى، و غمرها سلطان الإيثار و القناعة و التقشف. رافق جون أباذر في حياته و عاش معه مآسيه، و كان رفيقه المخلص في (الربذة) حتى قضى (رضوان الله عليه)، فبكاه بدموع سخيّة.

He is John ibn Hawi ibn Qutada ibn al-A'war ibn Sa'eda ibn 'Aouf ibn Ka'b ibn Hawi al-Nubi. Imam Ali (a) bought him from al-Fadl ibn al-Abbas ibn Abdulmuttalib for 150 dinars, and gifted him to Abu Thar to serve him. He thus moved from an environment of wealth and luxury to one veiled by noble asceticism and piety, and deeply rooted in self-sacrifice, contentment, and austerity. John accompanied Abu Thar throughout his life and lived alongside him in his struggles. He was Abu Thar's loyal friend in al-Rabatha [where he was exiled] until he passed away - may God bless his soul. John wept for him greatly.

و حين بلغه نبأ مسير الحسين (عليه السلام) لمناهضة الباطل و تجديد الدين، تجددت في نفسه مآسيه السابقة و ذكرياته السالفة، فأسرع لنصرة الحسين (عليه السلام) و خدمة أهل البيت (ع)، حتى استشهد (رضوان الله عليه)، بعد بلاء مرير، و بعد أن أظهر لجيوش الأعداء، كيف يكون الإباء و الشمم و الإيمان بالمبدأ.

When he heard that al-Hussain (a) had set out to oppose tyranny and renew the faith, his old wounds and dreadful memories were renewed. He rushed to support al-Hussain (a) and serve the family of the Prophet (s). He was martyred - may God bless his soul - after a bitter trial, having shown the enemy army the meaning of bravery and perseverance [in his honorable stance by his principles].[65]

The Remaining Companions Race for Martyrdom

فلما رأى أصحاب الحسين (عليه السلام) [أنهم قد غلبوا] و أن الأعداء قد
كثروا، و أنهم لا يقدرون على أن يمنعوا حسينا (عليه السلام) و لا أنفسهم،
تنافسوا في أن يقتلوا بين يديه.

When al-Hussain's (a) companions saw that they had been beaten, that
the enemies remain numerous, and that they will not be able to defend
al-Hussain (a) or even themselves, they began to race toward
martyrdom before him.[66]

The Martyrdom of Handhala ibn As'ad al-Shabami

ثم جاء إليه حنظلة بن أسعد العجلي الشبامي فوقف بين يدي الحسين (عليه
السلام) يقيه السهام و الرماح و السيوف بوجهه و نحره، و أخذ ينادي:

Then Handhala ibn As'ad al-Shabami stepped forward and stood in
front of al-Hussain (a), shielding him against arrows, swords, and
spears with his own body. He cried out [the verses of the Holy Quran],

يا قَوْمِ إِنِّي أَخَافُ عَلَيْكُمْ مِثْلَ يَوْمِ الْأَحْزَابِ. مِثْلَ دَأْبِ قَوْمِ نُوحٍ وَ عَادٍ
وَ ثَمُودَ وَ الَّذِينَ مِنْ بَعْدِهِمْ وَ مَا اللَّهُ يُرِيدُ ظُلْماً لِلْعِبَادِ. وَ يَا قَوْمِ إِنِّي
أَخَافُ عَلَيْكُمْ يَوْمَ التَّنَادِ. يَوْمَ تُوَلُّونَ مُدْبِرِينَ ما لَكُمْ مِنَ اللَّهِ مِنْ عاصِمٍ
وَ مَنْ يُضْلِلِ اللَّهُ فَما لَهُ مِنْ هادٍ.

*'O' my people! Indeed I fear for you [a day] like the day of the
[heathen] factions; like the case of the people of Noah, of 'Ad and
Thamud, and those who came after them, and God does not desire
any wrong for [His] servants. O' my people! I fear for you a day
of mutual distress calls, a day when you will turn back [to flee],
not having anyone to protect you from God, and whomever God
leads astray has no guide' (The Holy Quran, 40:30-33).*

و يا قوم لا تقتلوا حسينا فيسحتكم الله بعذاب وَ قَدْ خابَ مَنِ افْتَرَى. فقال له
الحسين (عليه السلام):

"O' my people, do not kill Hussain (a) and elicit the punishment of
God, 'Whoever fabricates lies certainly fails' (The Holy Quran, 20:61)."
Al-Hussain (a) said to him,

يابن أسعد رحمك اللّه، إنّهم قد استوجبوا العذاب حين ردّوا عليك ما دعوتهم إليه من الحق، و نهضوا إليك يشتمونك و أصحابك، فكيف بهم الآن و قد قتلوا إخوانك الصالحين!

O' Ibn As'ad, may God have mercy on you! They had become deservant of punishment when they answered your call toward truth [earlier] by cursing you and your companions. What do you expect of them now after they have killed your righteous brethren!

فقال: صدقت جعلت فداك، أفلا نروح إلى ربنا فنلحق بإخواننا! فقال له الحسين (عليه السلام):

Handhala replied, "True, may I be sacrificed for you! Then shall we not head towards our Lord and join our brethren?" Al-Hussain (a) said,

رح إلى ما هو خير لك من الدنيا و ما فيها، و إلى ملك لا يبلى.

Go forth to what is better for you then the entirety of the world and what is in it. [Go forth] to a kingdom that will never perish.

فقال: السلام عليك يابن رسول اللّه، و على أهل بيتك، و جمع اللّه بيننا و بينك في الجنة. فقال الحسين (عليه السلام):

Handhala said, "Peace be upon you, O' son of the Messenger of God (s), and upon your family. May God unite us again in paradise." Al-Hussain (a) replied,

آمين آمين.

Amen, amen.

ثم تقدم فقاتل قتالا شديدا، فحملوا عليه فقتلوه.

Handhala stepped forward and fought valiantly, but the enemies charged at him and killed him.[67]

The Martyrdom of Shawthab the Servant of Bani Shakir

و أقبل عابس بن شبيب الشاكري و معه شوذب مولى بني شاكر. و كان شوذب من الرجال المخلصين، و داره مألف للشيعة يتحدثون فيها فضل أهل البيت (عليهم السلام). فقال: يا شوذب ما في نفسك أن تصنع؟. قال: أقاتل معك دون ابن بنت رسول الله (ص) حتى أقتل.

Abis ibn Shabeeb al-Shakiri approached alongside Shawthab, the servant of Bani Shakir. Shawthab was a loyal man and his house was a hub for the Shia in which they recited the virtues of the Holy Household (a). Abis said, "O' Shawthab, what would you like to do?" Shawthab replied, "I will fight by your side in defense of the son of the Messenger of God's (a) daughter until I am killed."

قال: ذلك الظن بك، فتقدم بين يدي أبي عبد الله (عليه السلام) حتى يحتسبك كما احتسب غيرك، و حتى أحتسبك أنا، فإن هذا يوم نطلب فيه الأجر بكل ما نقدر عليه، فإنه لا عمل بعد اليوم، و إنما هو الحساب. فتقدم شوذب فقال: السلام عليك يا أبا عبد الله و رحمة الله و بركاته، أستودعك الله. ثم قاتل حتى قتل.

Abis said, "Just as expected from you! Go forth before Abu Abdullah (a) so that he may grieve for you just as he grieved for the others, and so that I may grieve for you as well. This is a day in which we do all we can to attain the rewards [of God Almighty], for there are no deeds after today - only judgment awaits." Shawthab stepped forward and said, "May the peace, mercy, and blessings of God be upon you, O'

Abu Abdullah (a). I leave you in God's care!" He fought until he was killed.[68]

The Martyrdom of Abis ibn Shabeeb al-Shakiri

و جاء عابس بن شبيب الشاكري، فتقدم و سلّم على الحسين (عليه السلام)
و قال له: يا أبا عبد الله، أما و الله ما أمسى على ظهر الأرض قريب و لا
بعيد أعزّ عليّ و لا أحبّ منك. و لو قدرت على أن أدفع عنك الضيم و القتل
بشيء أعزّ عليّ من نفسي و دمي لفعلت! السلام عليك يا أبا عبد الله، أشهد
أني على هداك و هدى أبيك. ثم مشى بالسيف نحوهم.

Abis ibn Shabeeb al-Shakiri stepped forward and greeted al-Hussain
(a). He said, "O' Abu Abdullah (a), by God night has not fell on anyone
atop this earth - near of kin or not - more dear and beloved to me than
you! If I were able to repel evil and death from you with anything more
valuable than my life and blood, I surely would! Peace be upon you, O'
Abu Abdullah. I witness that I am a follower of your guidance and the
guidance of your father." He approached the enemy with his sword.

قال ربيع بن تميم: فلما رأيته مقبلا عرفته- و قد كنت شاهدته في المغازي فكان
أشجع الناس- فقلت للقوم: أيها الناس، هذا أسد الأسود، هذا ابن شبيب، لا
يخرجنّ إليه أحد منكم. فأخذ ينادي: ألا رجل؟ ألا رجل لرجل! فتحاماه الناس
لشجاعته. فقال لهم عمر بن سعد: ارضخوه بالحجارة فرموه بالحجارة من كل
جانب. فلما رأى ذلك ألقى درعه و مغفره، و شدّ على الناس فهزمهم بين يديه.

Rabi' ibn Tameem said, "When I saw him coming, I recognized him;
having seen him in battle fighting as the bravest of men. I said to the
people, 'This is the valiant lion! This is Ibn Shabeeb! Let none of you
fight him [alone].'" Abis cried out, "Are there no men amongst you
who would fight man to man?" The enemies evaded him because of

what they knew of his bravery. Omar ibn Saad said to them, "Overpower him with stones!" They pelted him with stones from every direction. Abis threw his shield and helmet and charged at them, repelling them away.

(قال الراوي): فو الله لقد رأيته يطرد أكثر من مئتين من الناس، ثم أحاطوا به من كل جانب فقتلوه، فرأيت رأسه في أيدي الرجال، كلّ يقول: أنا قتلته.

The narrator said, "By God, I saw him repelling more than two hundred men until they surrounded him from every direction and killed him. I saw his head passed about by soldiers, each crying, 'I killed him!'"[69]

Biographical Entry | Abis ibn Shabeeb al-Shakiri

بنو شاكر بطن من همدان. ذكر أرباب السير أن عابسا كان رئيسا شجاعا خطيبا
ناسكا مجتهدا. و كان من رجال الشيعة، و كذلك بنو شاكر كانوا من المخلصين
بولاء أمير المؤمنين (عليه السلام)، و فيهم قال علي (عليه السلام) يوم صفين:

Banu Shakir are a branch of Hamadan. Biographers say that Abis was a valiant leader, eloquent speaker, and dedicated worshipper. He was a notable Shia, and all the Banu Shakir were loyal to the Commander of the Faithful (a). Ali (a) said of them on the day of Siffin,

لو تمّت عدّتهم ألفا لعبد الله حقّ عبادته.

If they numbered a thousand men, God would have been worshipped like He truly deserves.

و كانوا من شجعان العرب و حماتهم، و كانوا يلقبون (فتيان الصباح). و كان
عابس رسول مسلم بن عقيل إلى الحسين (عليه السلام) و قد أرسله بكتابه
إليه، و قد صحبه (شوذب) مولاه، و استشهد معه.

They were amongst the bravest and most valiant of the Arabs, earning the nickname *Fityan al-Sabah* [i.e. the Men of Battle]. Abis was the messenger of Muslim ibn Aqeel [from Kufa] to al-Hussain (a) [in Mecca]. He was accompanied by his servant Shawthab who was martyred by his side.[70]

The Martyrdom of Saad ibn Handhala al-Tameemi

ثم خرج من بعده سعد بن حنظلة التميمي، و هو [يرتجز] ثم حمل و قاتل قتالا
شديدا، حتى قتل (رضوان الله عليه).

After [the martyrdom of Abis], Saad ibn Handhala al-Tameemi joined
the battle, reciting [verses of encouragement to inspire himself and his
companions]. He charged and fought valiantly until he was killed - may
God bless his soul.[71]

The Martyrdom of Omair ibn Abdullah al-Mithhiji

ثم خرج من بعده عمير بن عبد الله المذحجي، و هو [يرتجز] و لم يزل يقاتل

قتالا شديدا، حتى قتله مسلم الضبابي و عبد الله البجلي، اشتركا في قتله.

Then Omair ibn Abdullah al-Mithhiji stepped forward into the battlefield, [chanting verses that declare his bravery and taunt his enemies]. He continued to fight valiantly until he was killed by Muslim al-Dababi and Abdullah al-Bajali.[72]

The Martyrdom of Abdulrahman al-Yazani

ثم خرج عبد الرحمن بن عبد الله اليزني، و هو [يرتجز] ثم حمل فقاتل حتى
قتل (رضوان الله عليه).

Then Abdulrahman ibn Abdullah al-Yazani stepped forward, [reciting verses of his commitment to his cause]. He charged at the enemy and fought until he was killed - may God bless his soul.[73]

The Martyrdom of Yahya ibn Saleem al-Mazini

ثم خرج من بعده يحيى بن سليم المازني، و هو [يرتجز] ثم حمل فقاتل حتى قتل
(رضوان الله عليه).

Then Yahya ibn Saleem al-Mazini stepped forward, reciting [verses of poetry to taunt his enemies]. He charged at the enemy and fought until he was killed - may God bless his soul.[74]

The Martyrdom of Qurra ibn Abu Qurra al-Ghafari

ثم خرج من بعده قرّة بن أبي قرة الغفاري، و هو [يرتجز] ثم حمل فقاتل حتى
قتل (رضوان الله عليه).

Then Qurra ibn Abu Qurra al-Ghafari joined the battle, [announcing in verse his unwavering commitment to protect the family of the Prophet (s)]. He charged at the enemy and fought until he was killed - may God bless his soul.[75]

The Martyrdom of a Man from Banu Asad

قال العريان بن الهيثم: كان أبي يتبدّى [أي ينزل في البدو، أي يقيم في الصحراء] فينزل قريبا من الموضع الّذي كانت فيه معركة الحسين (عليه السلام)، فكنا لا نبدو إلا وجدنا رجلا من بني أسد هناك. فقال له أبي: أراك ملازما هذا المكان! قال: بلغني أن حسينا (عليه السلام) يقتل ههنا، فأنا أخرج إلى هذا المكان، لعلي أصادفه فأقتل معه. فلمّا قتل الحسين (عليه السلام)، قال أبي: انطلقوا بنا ننظر هل الأسدي فيمن قتل مع الحسين (عليه السلام)؟ فأتينا المعركة و طوّفنا، فإذا الأسدي مقتول.

Al-'Aryan ibn al-Haytham said, "My father would [spend some nights in the desert] and set his camp close to the area where al-Hussain's (a) battle took place. Whenever we did so, we would always find a man from Banu Asad there. My father said to him, 'I see that you are always in this place.' He said, 'I have been told that Hussain (a) would be killed here, so I come to this place so that perhaps I may meet him and be killed with him.' When al-Hussain (a) was killed my father said, 'Let us go and see if al-Asadi is amongst those killed with al-Hussain (a)?' We came to the battlefield and walked through. We found al-Asadi amongst the dead."

لعل هذا الشهيد هو أنس بن الحارث الكاهلي أو الأسدي، لأن الكاهلي أسدي. و هو نفسه أنس بن كاهل الأسدي الّذي ذكر في زيارة الناحية المقدسة. و ذكر في بعض المصادر: مالك بن أنس الكاهلي، و هو تصحيف.

Perhaps this martyr is the same as Anas ibn al-Harith al-Kahili or al-Asadi, as the Banu Kahil are a branch of the Banu Asad. He is the same Anas ibn Kahil al-Asadi mentioned in *Ziyarat al-Nahiyya al-Muqadasa*.

In some sources, Malik ibn Anas al-Kahili is mentioned, which is a typographical error.[76]

The Martyrdom of Anas ibn al-Harith al-Kahili

و كان أنس بن الحارث بن نبيه الكاهلي شيخاً كبيراً صحابياً، رأى النبي (ص) و
سمع حديثه، و شهد معه بدراً و حنيناً. فاستأذن الحسين (عليه السلام) و برز
شادّاً وسطه بالعمامة، رافعاً حاجبيه بالعصابة. و لما نظر إليه الحسين (عليه
السلام) بهذه الهيئة بكى، و قال:

Anas ibn al-Harith ibn Nabeeh al-Kahili was an elder companion who
had seen the Prophet (s) and carried his traditions, witnessing the
battles of Badr and Hunayn alongside the Prophet (s). He took
permission from al-Hussain (a) and joined the battle with his turban
wrapped around his abdomen [to support his back] and his eyebrows
tied back with a band. When al-Hussain (a) saw him like this, he wept
and said,

شكر الله سعيك يا شيخ.

May God reward your efforts, O' shaykh.

ثم حمل و لم يزل يقاتل حتى قتل على كبره ثمانية عشر رجلاً، و قُتِلَ أَمَامَ
الحسين (عليه السلام).

He charged at the enemy and fought until he killed eighteen men
despite his old age, before being slain before al-Hussain's (a) eyes.[77]

Biographical Entry | Anas ibn al-Harith al-Kahili

هو أنس بن الحارث بن نبيه بن كاهل الأسدي. كان صحابيا كبيرا ممن رأى النبي
(ص) و سمع حديثه. و كان فيما سمع منه و حدّث به، ما رواه جمّ غفير من
العامة و الخاصة عنه، أنه قال: سمعت رسول الله (ص) يقول و الحسين في
حجره:

Anas ibn al-Harith ibn Nabeeh ibn Kahil al-Asady. He was a companion who saw the Prophet (s) and heard his traditions. Among the traditions that he narrated is one tradition that many Shia and other scholars narrate through him. He said, "I heard the Messenger of God (s) say while al-Hussain (a) is in his lap,

إن ابني هذا يقتل بأرض من أرض العراق. ألا فمن شهده فلينصره.

This son of mine will be killed in a land in the region of Iraq. Surely, whoever witnesses him [on that day] should support him.

فلما رآه أنس في العراق و شهده، نصره و قتل معه.

When Anas witnessed al-Hussain on that day in Iraq, he supported him and was martyred alongside him. (This is mentioned by al-Jazari in *Osod al-Ghaba*, Ibn Hajar in *al-Isaba*, and numerous other authors.)[78]

The Martyrdom of Amr ibn Muta' al-Ju'fi

ثم خرج من بعده عمرو بن مطاع الجعفي، و هو [يرتجز] و لم يزل يقاتل حتى
قتل ثلاثين رجلا، ثم قتل (رضوان الله عليه).

Then Amr ibn Muta' al-Ju'fi joined the battle, chanting [verses declairing his intent to protect al-Hussain (a)]. He continued to fight until he killed thirty soldiers, then he was killed - may God bless his soul.[79]

The Martyrdom of Anees ibn Ma'qil al-Asbahi

ثم خرج من بعده أنيس بن معقل الأصبحي، فجعل [يرتجز] ثم حمل و لم يزل
يقاتل حتى قتل [على رواية ابن شهر اشوب] نيّفا و عشرين رجلا، ثم قتل
(رضوان الله عليه).

Then Anees ibn Ma'qil al-Asbahi entered the battlefield. He cried out
[verses in praise of al-Hussain (a) that announced his dedication to the
protection of the Holy Household (a)]. He charged at the enemy and
fought until he killed twenty some men [according to Ibn
Shahrashoob] before he was killed - may God bless his soul.[80]

The Martyrdom of al-Hajjaj ibn Masrouq al-Ju'fi

ثم برز من بعده الحجاج بن مسروق الجعفي، و هو مؤذّن الحسين (عليه
السلام)، و كان قد خرج من الكوفة إلى مكة فالتحق بالحسين (عليه السلام)،
و صحبه منها إلى العراق، فجعل [يرتجز] ثم حمل على القوم و قاتل قتال
المشتاقين، حتى قتل منهم ثمانية عشر رجلا، ثم قتل (رضوان الله عليه).

Then al-Hajjaj ibn Masrouq al-Ju'fi, who was al-Hussain's (a) *Muazzin*,*
set out into battle. He had left Kufa for Mecca, where he joined al-
Hussain (a) and came with him to Iraq. He [rushed into battle, chanting
verses in praise of the Holy Household (a)]. He charged and fought
like a man longing [for death]. He killed eighteen enemy men before
he was killed - may God bless his soul.[81]

---

* A *Muazzin* is an individual who recites the call to daily prayer at dawn, noon, and
dusk.

Al-Hussain's (a) companions Enter the Battle in Groups

و لما نظر من بقي من أصحاب الحسين (عليه السلام) إلى كثرة من قتل منهم،

أخذ الرجلان و الثلاثة و الأربعة يستأذنون الحسين (عليه السلام) في الذبّ

عنه و الدفع عن حرمه، و كل واحد يحمي الآخر من كيد عدوه.

When the remainder of al-Hussain's (a) companions saw the many casualties of their camp, they began to approach in groups of two, three, and four, and seek permission to fight in his defense and the defense of his family. [They would enter the battlefield in groups] and each would protect the other from the charges of their enemies.[82]

The Martyrdom of the Ghafari Brothers

لجاءه عبد الله و عبد الرحمن ابنا عروة [أو عزرة] الغفاريان، فقالا: يا أبا عبد

الله عليك السلام، قد حازنا الناس إليك، فأحببنا أن نقتل بين يديك (و ندفع

عنك). قال:

Then Abdullah and Abdulrahman, the sons of Urwa [or Uzra, as per some accounts] al-Ghafari, came to al-Hussain (a) and said, "Peace be upon you, O' Abu Abdullah. The people have grouped us with you, so we wish to be killed before you and in your defense." He said to them,

مرحبا بكما، ادنوا مني.

Welcome! Come closer.

فدنوا منه، و جعلا يقاتلان. و جعل عبد الرحمن يرتجز [...]فقاتل حتى قتل.

The drew closer to him and began to to fight, while Abdulrahman recited [verses taunting his enemies]. They fought until they were killed.[83]

131

The Martyrdom of the Jabiri Brothers

و أتاه فتيان، و هما سيف بن الحارث بن سريع، و مالك بن عبد الله بن سريع الجابريان [في مقتل الخوارزمي: بطن من همدان يقال لهم بنو جابر]، و هما ابنا عم و أخوان لأم، و هما يكيان. فقال لهما الحسين (عليه السلام):

Then two young men came to al-Hussain (a) crying. They were Saif ibn al-Harith ibn Saree' al-Jabiri and Malik ibn Abdullah ibn Saree' al-Jabiri [al-Khawarizmi says, "Banu Jabir are a branch of the Hamadan tribe"]. They were paternal cousins but brothers to the same mother [i.e. the father of one of them had married his brother's widow]. Al-Hussain (a) said to them,

يا ابني أخي، ما يبكيكما؟ فو الله إني لأرجو أن تكونا بعد (عن) ساعة قريري العين.

O' sons of my brethren, why do you cry? By God, I only wish that you soon be well.

فقالا: جعلنا الله فداك، و الله ما على أنفسنا نبكي، و لكن نبكي عليك، نراك و قد أحيط بك، و لا نقدر على أن ننفعك. فقال (عليه السلام):

They said, "May we be sacrificed for you! By God, we do not cry for ourselves, but rather for you. We see you surrounded but we cannot defend you." Al-Hussain (a) said,

جزاكما الله يا ابني أخي بوجدكما [أي حزنكما] من ذلك، و مواساتكما إياي بأنفسكما أحسن جزاء المتقين.

May God reward you, O' sons of my brethren, for your sadness at this situation and your [sacrifice of your lives] with the best of rewards given to the pious.

ثم استقدما و قالا: السلام عليك يابن رسول الله. فقال:

They stepped forward and said, "Peace be upon you, O' son of the Messenger of God (s)." He replied,

و عليكما السلام و رحمة الله و بركاته. فقاتلا حتى قتلا.

May God's peace, mercy, and blessings be with you as well.

و قد أورد الخوارزمي في مقتله ج 2 ص 23 هذا الكلام منسوبا للأخوين الغفاريين.

They fought until they were killed. Al-Khawarizmi gave this same account (v. 2 p. 23) in his *Maqtal*, but attributed it to the Ghafari brothers.[84]

The Martyrdom of Junada ibn al-Harth al-Ansari

ثم خرج من بعده جنادة بن الحرث الأنصاري، و هو [يرتجز] فحمل و لم يزل
يقاتل حتى قتل [على رواية ابن شهر اشوب] ستة عشر رجلا، ثم قتل
(رضوان الله عليه).

Then Junada ibn al-Harth al-Ansari stepped forward, reciting [verses
in praise of his lineage]. He charged at the enemy and fought until he
killed sixteen men [according to Ibn Shahrashoob] before he was killed
- may God bless his soul.[85]

The Martyrdom of Amr ibn Junada al-Ansari

ثم خرج من بعده عمرو بن جنادة و هو [يرتجز] ثم حمل فقاتل حتى قتل.

Then Amr ibn Junada joined the battle reciting verses [decrying the wretchedness of his foes]. He charged at the enemy and fought until he was killed.[86]

The Martyrdom of a Young Man

لعل السيد عبد الرزاق المقرّم (رحمه الله) في مقتله اشتبه بأن هذا الشاب هو
عمرو بن جنادة الأنصاري، مع أن أغلب المصادر تورده منفصلاً عن عمرو بن
جنادة، مما يدل على أنه شخص آخر.

Perhaps Sayyid Abdulrazzaq al-Muqarram was mistaken when he
considered this young man to be Amr ibn Junada al-Ansari, as most
historical texts mention him in a seperate account indicating that this
is an entirely different person.

و قد ذكر السيد عبد الكريم الحسيني القزويني في كتابه (الوثائق الرسمية) ص
182: أن أباه الّذي قتل في أول المعركة هو جنادة بن كعب الخزرجي. [...] أما
الخوارزمي فيقول في مقتله:

Sayyid Abdulkarim al-Qazwini mentioned in his book *al-Watha'eq al-
Rasmiyya* (p. 182) that this young man's father was Junada ibn Ka'b al-
Khazraji. [...] Al-Khawarizmi mentions the following account in his
Maqtal.

ثم خرج من بعده شاب قتل أبوه في المعركة، و كانت أمه معه. فقالت: يا بني
اخرج فقاتل بين يدي ابن رسول الله حتى تقتل. فقال: أفعل. فخرج يستأذن
الحسين (عليه السلام) فأبى، و قال:

Then a young man whose father was killed in the battle set out to fight.
His mother was with him [in al-Hussain's (a) camp]. She had said to
him, "My son, go out and fight before the son of the Messenger of
God (s) until you are killed." He said "I will" and walked out to ask
permission. Al-Hussain (a) refused to grant him leave to fight and said,

هذا شاب قتل أبوه في (الحملة الأولى) و لعل أمه تكره خروجه.

This is a young man whose father was killed in the first wave and perhaps his mother may not want him to go out into battle.

فقال الشاب: أمي أمرتني يابن رسول الله. و في (الناسخ) قال الحسين (عليه السلام):

The young man said, "My mother is the one who instructed me so, O' son of the Messenger of God (s)!" In an account mentioned in *al-Nasikh*, al-Hussain (a) says,

يا فتى قتل أبوك، و إذا قتلت فإلى من تلتجئ أمك في هذا القفر؟

Young man, your father has been killed, so who will your mother find to protect her in this land if you were killed?

فأراد أن يرجع، فجاءته أمه و قالت: يا بني تختار سلامة نفسك على نصرة ابن بنت رسول الله (ص)، فلا أرضى عنك أبدا! فبرز الشاب و قاتل قتال الأبطال، و أمه تنادي خلفه: أبشر يا بني، ستسقى من يد ساقي حوض الكوثر. فبرز و هو يقول:

The young man wanted to return, but his mother came to him and said, "My son, would you choose your personal well-being rather than support teh son of the daughter of the Messenger of God (s)? Then I would never be please with you!" The young man set out for the battlefield while his mother was calling behind him, "Glad tidings, my son! You will soon be given a drink by the hand of the one standing at the Pond of Kawthar [in paradise]!" The young man joined the battle, calling,

أميري حسين و نعم الأمير * * * سرور فؤاد البشير النذير

عليّ و فاطمة والداه * * * فهل تعلمون له من نظير

My master is Hussain (a), glory to such a master!

The joy of the heart of the Warning Messenger (s)

Ali (a) and Fatima (a) are his parents

So do you know of anyone who would equal him?

فما أسرع أن قتل و رمي برأسه إلى جهة الحسين (عليه السلام)، فأخذت أمه رأسه و مسحت الدم عنه، و قالت له: أحسنت يا بني، يا قرة عيني و سرور قلبي. [...] و عادت إلى المخيم فأخذت عمود خيمة و حملت على القوم و هي تقول:

The young man was soon killed and his head was thrown back to al-Hussain's (a) camp. His mother took his head and wiped the blood off it, saying, "Well done, my son! [Well done], O' apple of my eye and joy of my heart!" [...] She returned to the tent, took a pole, and charged at the enemy, chanting,

أنا عجوز في النساء ضعيفه * * * خاوية بالية نحيفه

أضربكم بضربة عنيفه * * * دون بني فاطمة الشريفه

I am an elder woman, weak amongst women

Barren, ailing, and sickly

But I will strike you a heavy stike

In protection of the sons of the Noble Fatima (a)

فضربت رجلين فقتلتهما، فردّها الحسين (عليه السلام) إلى الخيمة و دعا لها.

She struck and killed two men before al-Hussain (a) returned her to the tent and prayed for her.[87]

Sayyid Muhsin al-Ameen's Comment on the Martyrd Young Man

و هذا منتهى علوّ النفس و صدق الولاء، من هذه المرأة و ابنها، أن يكون
زوجها قد قتل و هي تنظر إليه، ثم تأمر ولدها الشاب بنصرة الحسين (ع)، و
هي تعلم أنه مقتول، فتسوقه إلى القتل مختارة طائعة، و يطيعها ابنها في ذلك،
فيقدم على القتل غير مبال و لا وجل.

The apex of nobility in spirit and true allegiance can be seen in this
woman and her son. Her husband was killed as she looked on, but she
still instructed her son to support al-Hussain (a). She knew he would
be killed, but she lead him to his martyrdom with her own choice and
volition. Her son obeyed her in this. He marched to his death without
any fear or sorrow.

ثم يرخّص له الحسين (عليه السلام) في ترك القتال مخافة أن تكون أمه تكره
قتاله، بعدما قتل أبوه في المعركة، فيأبى و يقول: أي أمرتني بذلك. حقا إنه لمقام
عظيم و موقف جليل، تزلّ فيه الأقدام و تذهل فيه الألباب.

Al-Hussain (a) grants him leave to sit the battle out for fear that his
mother would not want him to fight after his father had been killed in
battle. But the young man refused and said, "My mother instructed me
so!" Truely, it is a great status and a glorious stance, [in a circumstance
where] others had slipped and their minds had lapsed.[88]

The Martyrdom of Wadih al-Turki Servant of al-Harth al-Mithhiji

كان (واضح) غلاما تركيا شجاعا قارئا، و هو مولى للحارث المذحجي السلماني. و قد أبلى في كربلاء بلاء حسنا. و لما صرع واضح التركي [أي سقط و به رمق]، استغاث بالحسين (عليه السلام)؛ فأتاه أبو عبد الله (عليه السلام) و اعتنقه و هو يجود بنفسه، فقال: من مثلي و ابن رسول الله (ص) واضع خدّه على خدي!. ثم فاضت نفسه الطاهرة.

Wadih was a young turkish man, a brave warrior, and a reciter [of the Holy Quran]. He was a servant of al-Harth al-Mithhiji al-Salmani. He made a valiant stand in the land of Karbala. When Wadih al-Turki was felled, he called al-Hussain (a) for help. Abu Abdullah (a) came to him and hugged him as he was taking his last breaths. Wadih said, "Who is like me when the son of the Messenger of God (a) has put his cheek on my cheek!" His holy soul then departed this world.[89]

The Martyrdom of Abu Omar al-Nahshali

و حدّث مهران مولى بني كاهل، قال: شهدت كربلاء مع الحسين (عليه السلام)

فرأيت رجلا يقاتل قتالا شديدا؛ لا يحمل على قوم إلا كشفهم، ثم يرجع إلى

الحسين (عليه السلام) و هو يرتجز [...] فقلت: من هذا؟ فقالوا: أبو عمر

النهشلي، و قيل الخثعمي. فاعترضه عامر بن نهشل، فقتله و احتزّ رأسه. و كان

أبو عامر هذا متهجّدا كثير الصلاة.

Mahran the Servant of Banu Kahil said, "I witnessed Karbala alongside
al-Hussain (a) and saw a man fighting valiantly. Whenever he charged
at the enemy, he repelled them. Then he would return to al-Hussain
(a), reciting [verses of encouragement and praise]. I asked, 'Who is this
man?' They said, 'Abu Omar al-Nahhshali' or 'al-Khath'ami.' Then
Amir ibn Nahshal fought him, killed him, and severed his head. Abu
Omar used to spend the nights in worship and continuous prayers."[90]

The Martyrdom of Aslam al-Turki the Servant of al-Hussain (a)

ذكر العلامة الأمين في (أعيان الشيعة) أنه قرأ في أحد كتب الرجال لبعض المعاصرين: أنه كان للحسين (عليه السلام) مولى اسمه أسلم بن عمرو، و كان اشتراه بعد وفاة أخيه الحسن (عليه السلام)، و وهبه لابنه علي بن الحسين (عليه السلام). و كان أبوه (عمرو) تركيا. و كان (أسلم) هذا كاتبا عند الحسين (عليه السلام) في بعض حوائجه. لما خرج الحسين (عليه السلام) من المدينة إلى مكة كان أسلم ملازما له، حتى أتى معه كربلاء. فلما كان اليوم العاشر و شبّ القتال، استأذن في القتال.

[Al-Allama al-Ameen mentions in *A'yan al-Shia* that he read in some of the biographical books to a contemporary scholar that al-Hussain (a) had a servant names Aslam ibn Amr. He had bought him after the martyrdom of his brother al-Hassan (a) and gifted him to his son Ali ibn al-Hussain (a). His father, Amr, was turkish. Aslam was also a scribe for al-Hussain (a) in some instances. When al-Hussain (a) left Medina towards Mecca, Aslam accompanied him and was with him until they reached Karbala. On the tenth of Muharram when the battle commenced, Aslam sought permission to fight.]

و خرج غلام تركي من موالي الحسين (عليه السلام)، و كان قارئا للقرآن و عارفا بالعربية و كاتبا، فجعل يقاتل و يرتجز [...]فقتل [في رواية ابن شهر اشوب] سبعين رجلا، فتحاوشوه حتى سقط صريعا، فجاء إليه الحسين (عليه السلام) فبكى، و وضع خده على خده، ففتح عينيه فرأى الحسين (عليه السلام) فتبسم، ثم صار إلى ربه.

A turkish servant of al-Hussain (a) set out for battle, and he was a reciter of the Quran, had knowledge of the Arabic language, and was also a scribe. He fought as he recited [verses taunting his enemies]. He killed seventy men [according to Ibn Shahrashoob] before he was surrounded and felled. Al-Hussain (a) came to him, wept, and placed his cheek over Aslam's cheek. Aslam opened his eyes and saw al-Hussain (a). He smiled and his soul departed this world to the next.[91]

The Martyrdom of Malik ibn Thawdan

ثم برز مالك بن ذودان [وهو يرتجز] فقاتل حتى قتل (رضوان الله عليه).

Then Malik ibn Thawdan joined the battle, reciting [verses that declared his might and his intent to protect the family of the Prophet (s)]. He fought until he was killed, may God bless his soul.[92]

The Martyrdom of Ibrahim ibn al-Hossayn al-Asadi

و برز إبراهيم بن الحصين الأسدي و هو يرتجز [...]فقتل [على رواية ابن شهر اشوب] أربعة و ثمانين رجلا [...]و قاتل حتى قتل (رضوان الله عليه).

Ibrahim ibn al-Hossayn set out for the battlefield, [taunting his enemies with a poetic battle cry]. He killed eighty four men [according to Ibn Shahrashoob] and began to recite [verses of poetry in praise of al-Hussain (a) and his noble lineage]. He fought until he was killed - may God bless his soul.[93]

The Martyrdom of Sawwar al-Fahmi al-Hamadani

و قاتل سوّار بن أبي عمير من ولد فهم بن جابر الهمداني، قتالا شديدا حتى
ارتثّ بالجراح و أخذ أسيرا، فأراد ابن سعد قتله، و تشفّع فيه قومه، و بقي
عندهم جريحا إلى أن توفي على رأس ستة أشهر، (رحمه الله).

Sawwar ibn Abu Omair, a descendent of Fahm ibn Jabir al-Hamadani, joined the battle and fought until he was overburdened by his wounds and taken as a captive. Omar ibn Saad wanted to kill him, but his kin interceded for him. He remained with them a wounded prisoner until he died after six months - may God bless his soul.[94]

The Martyrdom of Saad ibn al-Harith and his Brother Abu al-Hutuf

و لما سمع الأنصاريان: سعد بن الحارث و أخوه أبو الحتوف، استنصار الحسين
(عليه السلام) و استغاثته، و كانا في جيش عمر بن سعد، فمالا بسيفيهما على
أعداء الحسين، و قاتلا حتى قتلا.

Saad ibn al-Harith al-Ansari and his brother Abu al-Hutuf heard the
calls of al-Hussain (a) for aid and support while they were in the army
of Omar ibn Saad. They took their swords and charged at the enemies
of al-Hussain (a), and fought until they were killed.

قال حميد بن أحمد في كتابه (الحدائق الوردية): و من المقتولين يوم الطف مع
الحسين (عليه السلام): أبو الحتوف الأنصاري و أخوه سعد بن الحرث، و كانا
من الخوارج، فخرجا مع عمر بن سعد إلى حرب الحسين (عليه السلام). فلما
كان يوم العاشر من المحرم و قتل أصحاب الحسين (عليه السلام) و لم يبق معه
غير سويد بن عمرو ابن أبي المطاع الخثعمي و بشير بن عمرو الحضرمي، جعل
الحسين (عليه السلام) ينادي:

Hameed ibn Ahmad writes in *al-Hada'eq al-Wardiyya*: And amongst
those killed with al-Hussain (a) in the Battle of Karbala were Abu al-
Hutuf al-Ansari and his brother Saad ibn al-Harth. They were
Kharijites who had joined Omar ibn Saad to fight against al-Hussain
(a). On the tenth day of Muharram when all the companions of al-
Hussain (a) had been killed and none remained with him but Sowaid
ibn Amr ibn Abu Muta' al-Khath'ami and Basheer ibn Amr al-
Hadrami, al-Hussain (a) began to call,

ألا من ناصر فينصرنا، ألا من ذابّ يذبّ عن حرم رسول الله (ص)؟

Is there no supporter who would support us? Is there no protector who would protect the sanctity [of the family and women] of the Messenger of God (s)?

فسمعن النساء و الأطفال نداء الحسين (عليه السلام) فتصارخن بالعويل و البكاء. فلما سمع سعد بن الحرث و أخوه أبو الحتوف أصوات النساء و الأطفال من آل الرسول (ص)، و كان بعد صلاة الظهر، و هما في حومة الحرب، قالا: إنا لله و لا حكم إلا لله، و لا طاعة لمن عصاه. و هذا الحسين ابن بنت نبينا محمّد (ص)، و نحن نرجو شفاعة جده يوم القيامة، فكيف نقاتله و هو بهذا الحال، نراه لا ناصر له و لا معين؟

The women and children heard al-Hussain's (a) cries and their voices rose in mourning and weeping. When Saad ibn al-Harth and his brother Abu al-Hutuf heard the voices of the women and children from the family of the Messenger (s) - it was after the noon prayers as they were in the heat of battle - they said, "We are of God [and to Him we shall return]! There is no judgment except by God! We shall not obey anyone who disobeys Him! This is al-Hussain (a), the son of the daughter of our Prophet Muhammad (s), and we hope to gain the intercession of his grandfather on the Day of Resurrection. How can we fight him while he is in this state, having no supporter or aid?"

مالا بين يدي الحسين (عليه السلام) على أعداء الله و أعدائه، فجعلا يقاتلان قريبا منه، حتى قتلا من القوم جماعة كثيرة و جرحا آخرين؛ ثم قتلا معا في مكان واحد، (رضوان الله عليهما).

They charged before al-Hussain (a) against the enemies of God and his enemies. The fought close to him, killing many enemy soldiers and wounding others. They were killed together in one spot - may God bless their souls.[95]

The Martyrdom of Sowaid ibn Amr ibn Abu Muta' al-Khath'ami

و أما سويد بن أبي المطاع فكان قد صرع، فوقع بين القتلى مثخنا بالجراحات (و ظنّ أنه قتل). فلما قتل الحسين (عليه السلام) و سمعهم يقولون: قتل الحسين (عليه السلام)، فوجد خفّة، فتحامل و أخرج سكّينة من خفّه (و كان سيفه قد أخذ)، فقاتلهم بسكينه ساعة. و كان يرتجز [...]و تعطّفوا عليه فقتلوه. قتله عروة بن بطان الثعلبي و زيد بن رقّاد الجبني. و كان سويد آخر من قتل من أصحاب الحسين (عليه السلام).

As for Sowaid ibn Abi al-Muta', he had been felled and left wounded amongst the dead. When al-Hussain (a) was killed and he heard the enemy cry out the news, he reached into his satchel and grabbed a knife [his sword had been taken]. He stood and fought the enemy for some time, reciting [verses in praise of al-Hussain (a) and his noble lineage]. The enemy charged at him and finished him off. He was killed by Urwa ibn Bitan al-Tha'labi and Zaid ibn Raqqad al-Jubni. Sowaid was the last martyr of the companions of al-Hussain (a).

و في (تاريخ الطبري) ج 6 ص 255: أنه آخر من بقي مع الحسين (عليه السلام) من أصحابه، قتله عروة بن بطار التغلبي و زيد بن رقاد الجبني.

Al-Tabari says in his *Tareekh al-Rusul wa al-Muluk* (v. 6 p. 255), "He was the last companion to remain with al-Hussain (a). He was killed by Urwa ibn Battar al-Taghlibi and Zayd ibn Ruqad al-Jubni."[96]

Every Individual Killed in the Way of God is a Martyr

و كان يأتي الحسين الرجل بعد الرجل، فيقول: السلام عليك يابن رسول الله،
فيجيبه الحسين (عليه السلام):

One by one, the companions would come to al-Hussain (a) and say,
"Peace be upon you, O' son of the Messenger of God (s)." He would
reply,

و عليك السلام، و نحن خلفك، فَمِنْهُمْ مَنْ قَضَى نَحْبَهُ وَ مِنْهُمْ مَنْ
يَنْتَظِرُ [الأحزاب: 23]

*Peace be upon you. We will soon follow you. 'There are some among
them who have fulfilled their pledge, and some of them who still
wait' (The Holy Quran 33:23).*

ثم يحمل فيقتل. حتى قتلوا عن آخرهم (رضوان الله عليهم)، و لم يبق مع الحسين
(عليه السلام) إلا أهل بيته. (يقول الخوارزمي): و هكذا يكون المؤمن، يؤثر
دينه على دنياه، و موته على حياته، في سبيل الله، ينصر الحق و إن قتل. قال
تعالى:

Each would charge at the enemy and fight until he is killed. Every
single one of the companions was killed - may God bless their souls -
and no one remained with al-Hussain (a) but his family members. Al-
Khawarizmi says: This is how a believer should be; preferring his faith
over his material gains and his death over his life, all for the sake of
God. He should support the truth, even if he is to be killed. God
Almighty says,

وَ لَا تَحْسَبَنَّ الَّذِينَ قُتِلُوا فِي سَبِيلِ اللَّهِ أَمْوَاتاً بَلْ أَحْيَاءٌ عِنْدَ رَبِّهِمْ يُرْزَقُونَ [آل عمران: 169].

Do not suppose those who were slain in the way of God to be dead; no, they are living and provided for near their Lord.

و قال النبي (صلى الله عليه و آله و سلم):

The Prophet (s) said,

كل قتيل في جنب الله شهيد.

Every individual killed in the way of God is a martyr.

و لما وقف رسول الله (صلى الله عليه و آله و سلم) على شهداء أحد و فيهم حمزة بن عبد المطلب، قال:

When the Messenger of God (s) stood over the martyrs of Uhud, and amongst them was Hamza ibn Abdulmuttalib, he said,

أنا شهيد هؤلاء القوم، زمّلوهم بدمائهم، فإنهم يحشرون يوم القيامة و كلومهم رواء، و أوداجهم تشخب دما؛ فاللون لون الدم، و الريح ريح المسك.

I am the witness over these people. Wrap them in their [bloodied garments]. They will be revived on the Day of Resurrection with their wounds pouring and their [severed] veins streaming with blood. It's color will be the color of blood, but its odor will be the aroma of musk.[97]

The Martyrdom of Ahlulbayt

The Martyrs of the Holy Household

و لما قتل أصحاب الحسين (عليه السلام)، و لم يبق إلا أهل بيته، و هم: ولد

علي (عليه السلام)، و ولد جعفر، و ولد عقيل، و ولد الحسن، و ولده (عليه

السلام)، و عددهم على الأشهر 17 شخصا، اجتمعوا و ودّع بعضهم بعضا و

عزموا على الحرب.

When the companions of Al-Hussain (a) were slain, none but his
household remained. They were the sons of Ali [ibn abi Talib] (a), the
sons of Jafar [ibn Abi Talib], the sons of 'Aqil [ibn Abi Talib], the sons
of Al-Hassan [ibn Ali ibn Abi Talib] (a), and his own [Imam Hussain's
(a)] sons. They numbered 17 individuals, as is most widely believed.
They gathered and said their farewells, preparing themselves for
battle.[98]

Ali Al-Akbar (a) Sets Out for the Battlefield

و لما لم يبق مع الحسين (عليه السلام) إلا أهل بيته، عزموا على ملاقاة الحتوف

ببأس شديد و حفاظ مرّ و نفوس أبيّة، و أقبل بعضهم يودّع بعضا. و أول من

تقدّم إلى البراز علي الأكبر (عليه السلام) و عمره سبع و عشرون سنة فإنه

ولد في 11 شعبان سنة 33 هـ. و أمه ليلى بنت أبي مرة بن عروة بن مسعود

الثقفي.

When none remained alongside Al-Hussain (a) but his household, they were determined to meet their deaths with great resolve, faithfulness despite adversity, and unwavering character. They came together to say their final farewells. The first of them to step forward was Ali Al-Akbar who was 27 years old (born on 11 Sha'ban, 33 AH). His mother was Layla bint Abi Murra ibn Orwa ibn Masood Al-Thaqafi.[99]

Layla Prays for Her Son Ali Al-Akbar

قال السيد عبد الحسين الموسوي: عندما برز علي الأكبر (عليه السلام) إلى

القتال، بادر إليه بكر بن غانم. فلما خرج إليه اللعين تغيّر وجه الحسين (عليه

السلام)، فقالت أمه ليلى: يا سيدي لعل قد أصابه شيء؟! قال (عليه

السلام):

When Ali Al-Akbar stepped forward unto the battlefield, Bakr ibn Ghanim rushed towards him. When that cursed stepped forward, Al-Hussain's (a) face changed [in fear for his son]. [Ali Al-Akbar's] mother Layla asked, "O master, has anything happened to him?" [Imam Hussain (a)] replied,

لا يا ليلى، و لكن قد خرج إليه من أخاف منه عليه؛ فادعي له، فإني

قد سمعت جدي رسول الله (صلى الله عليه و آله و سلم) يقول:

«إن دعاء الأم يستجاب في حق ولدها».

No, O' Layla, but a man has charged towards him and I fear [for my son] from him. Go pray for [Ali], for I have heard the Messenger of God (s) say, 'The prayer of the mother for her son is answered.'

كشفت رأسها و دعت له، و لعنت بكرا، إلى أن جرى بينهما ما جرى. (و في

خبر) دعت ليلى بهذا الدعاء: يا رادّ يوسف على يعقوب من بعد الفراق، و

جاعله في الدهر مسرورا، و يا رادّ إسماعيل إلى هاجر. إلهي بعطش أبي عبد

الله، إلهي بغربة أبي عبد الله، امنن عليّ بردّ ولدي.

She uncovered her head, prayed for him, and cursed Bakr until [Ali Al-Akbar was victorious and returned to the camp]. In one narration it is mentioned that she prayed with the following supplication, "O' You who returned Joseph to Jacob after their separation, and made [Jacob] ever joyous thereafter! O' You who returned Ishmael to Hagar! My Lord, by the thirst of Abu Abdillah (a)! My Lord, by the forsakenness of Abu Abdillah (a)! Grant me the return of my son!"[100]

The Martyrdom of Ali Al-Akbar

فاستأذن أباه في القتال، فأذن له. ثم نظر إليه نظرة آيس منه، و أرخى عينيه

فبكى. ثم رفع سبابتيه نحو السماء و قال:

[Ali Al-Akbar] took permission from his father to set out for battle and
he was granted permission. [Imam Hussain (a)] looked at him with
desperation and began to cry. He raised his index finger to the sky and
said,

اللّهم كن أنت الشهيد عليهم، فقد برز إليهم غلام أشبه الناس خلقا و

خلقا و منطقا برسولك محمّد (صلى الله عليه و آله و سلم) و كنا إذا

اشتقنا إلى وجه رسولك نظرنا إلى وجهه. اللّهم فامنعهم بركات

الأرض، و إن منعتهم ففرقهم تفريقا، و مزّقهم تمزيقا، و اجعلهم طرائق

قددا، و لا ترض الولاة عنهم أبدا. فإنهم دعونا لينصرونا، ثم عدوا

علينا يقاتلونا و يقتلونا.

*My God, be witness to [their deeds], for a young man has come
forward to them who is most like Your Messenger Muhammad (s)
in his countenance, morals, and demeanor. Whenever we missed
the countenance of Your Messenger (s), we would look towards
[Ali Al-Akbar]. My God, deprive them of the blessings of the
earth, and after you have deprived them so divide them into factions,
tear them apart, make them into various sects, and do not ever let
their governors be pleased with them! They invited us with the
promise that they would aid us, but they have turned against us,
fighting and killing us!*

ثم صاح الحسين (عليه السلام) بعمر بن سعد:

Al-Hussain (a) then cried out to Omar ibn Saad,

مالك قطع اللّه رحمك و لا بارك لك في أمرك، و سلّط عليك من يذبحك على فراشك، كما قطعت رحمي و لم تحفظ قرابتي من رسول اللّه (صلى اللّه عليه و آله و سلم.

What is wrong with you? May God sever your lineage and never bless you in any matter! [May God] empower over you one who would slay you on you bed! This is just as you have severed my lineage and did not respect my kinship to the Messenger of God (s).

ثم رفع صوته و قرأ:

He then raised his voice in recitation,

إِنَّ اللَّهَ اصْطَفَى آدَمَ وَ نُوحاً وَ آلَ إِبْرَاهِيمَ وَ آلَ عِمْرَانَ عَلَى الْعَالَمِينَ، ذُرِّيَّةً بَعْضُها مِنْ بَعْضٍ وَ اللَّهُ سَمِيعٌ عَلِيمٌ. [آل عمران: 33- 34]

Indeed God chose Adam and Noah, and the progeny of Abraham and the progeny of Imran above all the nations; some of them are descendants of the others, and God is all-hearing, all-knowing. (The Holy Quran, 3:33-34)

ثم حمل علي بن الحسين (عليه السلام) و هو يقول:

Ali Al-Akbar then charged while reciting in verse,

أنا علي بن الحسين بن علي * * * نحن و بيت اللّه أولى بالنبي

و اللّه لا يحكم فينا ابن الدّعي * * * أطعنكم بالرمح حتى ينثني

أضربكم بالسيف حتى يلتوي * * * ضرب غلام هاشميّ علوي

I am Ali ibn Al-Hussain ibn Ali (a)

We are, by the House of God, more worthy of the Prophet [and his example]

By God, the son of the imposter will not rule over us

I will stab you with the spear until it breaks

I will strike you with the sword until it bends

The strikes of a young Hashemite, Alid man.

و كان علي الأكبر (عليه السلام) مرآة الجمال النبوي، و مثال خلقه السامي، و أنموذجا من منطقه البليغ [...] وفي (الدمعة الساكبة): لما توجّه علي الأكبر إلى الحرب، اجتمعت النساء حوله كالحلقة، و قلن له: ارحم غربتنا، و لا تستعجل إلى القتال، فإنه ليس لنا طاقة في فراقك. قال: فلم يزل يجهد و يبالغ في طلب الإذن من أبيه، حتى أذن له. ثم ودّع أباه و الحرم، و توجّه نحو الميدان.

Ali Al-Akbar was a reflection of prophetic beauty, an example of [the Prophet's (s) teachings in] high morals, and a likeness of the [Prophet's (s)] eloquent speech. [...] In *Al-Dam'a Al-Sakiba* [by Al-Waheed Al-Behbahani] it says: When Ali Al-Akbar head towards battle, the women gathered around him in a circle and said, "Have mercy on our forsakenness and do not rush to battle, for we do not have the power to overcome your loss." He continued to ask for permission from his father until he was granted permission. He bade farewell to his father and the women and headed towards the battlefield.

فلم يزل يقاتل حتى ضجّ أهل الكوفة لكثرة من قتل منهم، حتى أنه روي أنه على عطشه قتل 120 رجلا. ثم رجع إلى أبيه الحسين (عليه السلام) و قد أصابته جراحات كثيرة. فقال: يا أبت العطش قد قتلني، و ثقل الحديد قد أجهدني،

فهل إلى شربة من ماء سبيل، أتقوى بها على الأعداء؟. فبكى الحسين (عليه السلام) و قال:

He continued to fight until the Kufans became distraught by the amount of them he had killed. It is even narrated that he had killed, despite his thirst, 120 men. He then returned to his father, having been severely injured, and said, "O' father, thirst is killing me and the weight of iron has tired me. Is there means by which I can get a sip of water to strengthen me against my enemies?" Al-Hussain (a) wept and said,

يا بنيّ عزّ على محمّد و على علي و على أبيك، أن تدعوهم فلا يجيبوك، و تستغيث بهم فلا يغيثوك.

My son, it saddens Muhammad (s), Ali (a), and your father that you call them but they do not answer you and that you plead for their aid but they do not aid you. [...]

و دفع إليه خاتمه و قال له

[Imam Hussain (a)] then gave him his ring and said,

خذ هذا الخاتم في فيك، و ارجع إلى قتال عدوك، فإني أرجو أن لا تمسي حتى يسقيك جدك بكأسه الأوفى شربة لا تظمأ بعدها أبدا.

Put this ring in your mouth and return to battle against your enemy. Surely, I hope that night does not fall before your grandfather gives you out of his overflowing cup a drink after which you will never thirst.

و أورد المقرم في مقتله: و من جهة أن ليلى أم علي الأكبر هي بنت ميمونة ابنة أبي سفيان صاح رجل من القوم: يا علي إن لك رحما بأمير المؤمنين [يزيد] و

نريد أن نرعى الرحم، فإن شئت آمنّاك!. فقال (عليه السلام): إن قرابة رسول
الله أحقّ أن ترعى.

Al-Muqarram also wrote in his *Maqtal*: Because Layla, Ali Al-Akbar's
mother, was the daughter of Maymouna bint Abi Sufyan, a man called
out, "O' Ali, you have a blood relation to the Prince of the Believers
[Yazid], and we wish to respect that blood relation. If you wish, we will
grant you sanctuary!" He replied, "Surely, the blood relation to the
Messenger of God (s) is more worthy of being respected."

فرجع علي بن الحسين إلى القتال [...]و جعل يقاتل حتى قتل تمام المئتين (و
في رواية: فقال مرّة بن منقذ العبدي: عليّ آثام العرب إن لم أثكل أباه به، فطعنه
بالرمح في ظهره). ثم ضربه (مرّة) على مفرق رأسه ضربة صرعه فيها، و ضربه
الناس بأسيافهم، فاعتنق الفرس فحمله الفرس إلى عسكر عدوه، فقطّعوه
بأسيافهم إربا إربا.

He then returned to battle. [...] He continued to fight until he killed
an even 200. [One narration states that Murra ibn Munqith Al-Abdi
said, 'May I bear all the sins of the Arabs if I do not bereave his father
by killing him.' He then struck [Ali Al-Akbar] with a spear in his back.]
Then Murra struck him on the top of his head, felling him. Men
continued to strike him with their swords, so he held on to [the neck
of] the horse which carried him into the enemy camp. They tore him
to pieces with their swords.

فلما بلغت روحه التراقي نادى بأعلى صوته: يا أبتاه! هذا جدي رسول الله قد
سقاني بكأسه الأوفى شربة لا أظمأ بعدها أبداً، و هو يقول لك: العجل، فإن
لك كأساً مذخورة. فصاح الحسين (عليه السلام):

When his soul was about to leave his body he called at the top of his voice, "O' father, here is my grandfather, the Messenger of God (s), giving me a drink out of his overflowing cup, after which I shall never thirst. He says to you, 'Make haste, for there is a cup waiting for you.'" Al-Hussain (a) called out,

قتل الله قوما قتلوك يا بني، ما أجرأهم على الله و على انتهاك حرمة رسول الله، على الدنيا بعدك العفا.

May God kill a people which have killed you, my son. What audacity do they have against God in desecrating the sanctity of the Messenger of God (s)! The world may just as well end after you!

و روي أن الحسين (عليه السلام) بكى عليه بكاء شديدا. و في (ناسخ التواريخ) أن الحسين (عليه السلام) لما جاء إلى ولده، رآه و به رمق، و فتح علي (عليه السلام) عينيه في وجه أبيه، و قال: يا أبتاه أرى أبواب السماء قد انفتحت، و الحور العين بيدها كؤوس الماء قد نزلن من السماء، و هن يدعونني إلى الجنة؛ فأوصيك بهذه النسوة، بأن لا يُخمشن عليّ وجها. ثم سكن و انقطع أنينه.

It is narrated that Al-Hussain (a) wept heavily for his loss. In *Nasikh Al-Tawareekh* it is relayed that Al-Hussain (a) reached his son while he still had a breath in him. Ali [Al-Akbar] opened his eyes and said, "Father, I see the doors of the heavens open and the servants of heaven are descending with cups of water, calling me to paradise. I ask you to instruct the women not to scratch their faces in mourning me." He then became still and his voice became quiet.

و في (الفاجعة العظمى) ص 137، قال أبو مخنف: و وضع الحسين (عليه السلام) رأس ولده علي في حجره، و جعل يمسح الدم عن ثناياه، و جعل يلثمه و يقول:

166

In *Al-Faji'a Al-'Othma* Abu Mikhnaf writes: Al-Hussain (a) put his son's
head on his lap and wiped the blood off his mouth. He would kiss him
and say,

يا بني، لعن الله قوما قتلوك، ما أجرأهم على الله و رسوله (صلى الله
عليه و آله و سلم).

My son, may God curse a people who would kill you. What
audacity do they have against God and His Messenger (s)!

و هملت عيناه بالدموع و قال:

His eyes drowned in tears as he said,

أما أنت يا بني، فقد استرحت من كرب الدنيا و محنها، و صرت إلى
روح و ريحان، و بقي أبوك، و ما أسرع لحوقه بك.

My son, you have gained comfort from the troubles and tribulations
of the world, and have reached a place of ease and abundance. Your
father remains, but will surely follow you soon.

قال: و جعل الحسين (عليه السلام) يتنفس الصعداء. و في (المنتخب): و
صاح الحسين (عليه السلام) بأعلى صوته، فتصارخن النساء. و قال لهن الحسين
(عليه السلام):

Al-Hussain (a) would take deep, heavy breaths. In *Al-Muntakhab*: Al-
Hussain (a) cried at the top of his voice and the women began to weep.
He said to them,

اسكتن، فإن البكاء أمامكنّ.

Settle down, there will be much weeping ahead.[101]

Lady Zaynab Mourns Ali Al-Akbar

و روي أن زينب (عليها السلام) خرجت مسرعة تنادي بالويل و الثبور، و
تقول: يا حبيباه. قال حميد بن مسلم: لكأني أنظر إلى امرأة خرجت مسرعة كأنها
شمس طالعة، تنادي بالويل و الثبور. تصيح: وا حبيباه! وا ثمرة فؤاداه! وا نور
عيناه! فسألت عنها، فقيل: هي زينب بنت علي (عليها السلام). ثم جاءت حتى
انكبّت عليه. فجاء إليها الحسين (عليه السلام) حتى أخذ بيدها و ردّها إلى
الفسطاط .. ثم أقبل مع فتيانه إلى ابنه، فقال:

It is narrated that Zaynab came out in a rush, warning of ill-fate and
destruction and calling "O' my beloved [nephew]." Hameed ibn
Muslim said, "I saw a woman rushing out. She appeared like the rising
sun and was warning of ill-fate and destruction while calling, 'O' my
beloved [nephew]! O' apple of my heart! O' light of my eye!' I asked
about her and was told, 'She is Zaynab bint Ali (a).' She continued until
she collapsed beside him. Al-Hussain (a) then came to her, took her by
the hand, and returned her to the tent. He came back to his son along
with the young men from his camp and said,

احملوا أخاكم.

Carry your brother.

فحملوه من مصرعه حتى وضعوه عند الفسطاط الّذي يقاتلون أمامه. و ذكر
المياني في (العيون العبرى) ص 153: و في الزيارة المروية عن الصادق (عليه
السلام):

They carried him back and placed him before the tent [...]." Al-Mayaniji
wrote in *al-Oyoon al-'Abra*: And in the visitation narrated from Al-Sadiq
(a),

بأبي أنت و أمي من مذبوح مقتول من غير جرم، و بأبي أنت و أمي
دمك المرتقى به إلى حبيب الله [أي النبي (صلى الله عليه و آله و
سلم)]، و بأبي أنت و أمي من مقدّم بين يدي أبيك يحتسبك و يبكي
عليك، محترقا عليك قلبه، يرفع دمك بكفّه إلى أعنان السماء، لا ترجع
منه قطرة، و لا تسكن من أبيك زفرة.

May my father and mother be sacrificed for you, O' you who were slaughtered without a crime. May my father and mother be sacrificed for you, O' you whose blood was raised to God's Beloved [Prophet (s)]. May my father and mother be sacrificed for you, O' you who laid at his father's hands, grieving and weeping over you while his heart burns for you. He would raise your blood in his hands to the highest of the heavens and not a drop of it would return, while his heavy breaths never calm.[102]

كان يكنّى أبا الحسن، و يلقّب (بالأكبر) لأنه أكبر أولاد الحسين (عليه السلام) على ما رواه صاحب (الحدائق الوردية). و روى ابن إدريس في (السرائر)، و المفيد في (الإرشاد): أنه ولد بعد وفاة جده أمير المؤمنين علي (عليه السلام) بسنتين (و قيل: ولد في أوائل خلافة عثمان). أمه ليلى بنت أبي مرّة بن عروة بن مسعود الثقفي، و هي (ليلى) بنت ميمونة ابنة أبي سفيان. و كان علي الأكبر (عليه السلام) أول المستشهدين يوم الطف من أهل البيت (عليه السلام)، و قيل كان عمره 27 و قيل 25 و قيل 19 و قيل 18 و الأول هو الأصح. و كان علي الأكبر أشبه الناس خلقا و خلقا برسول الله (صلى الله عليه و آله و سلم)، لا بل إنه شابه الخمسة أصحاب الكساء، و هم: محمّد و فاطمة و علي و الحسنان (عليهم السلام). فأما شباهته بجده رسول الله (صلى الله عليه و آله و سلم) ففي كلامه و مقاله، و في خلقه و أخلاقه. و أما شباهته بجده الإمام علي (عليه السلام) ففي كنيته و شجاعته و تعصبه للحق. و أما شباهته بجدته فاطمة الزهراء (عليها السلام) ففي مدة حياته، إذ توفيت الزهراء و عمرها ثماني عشرة سنة. و أما شباهته بعمه الحسن (عليه السلام) فقد شابهه بالبهاء و الهيبة، فكان وجهه يتلألأ نورا. و أما شباهته بأبيه الحسين (عليه السلام) فقد شابهه بالإباء و الكرم، و يكفيه إباء و كرما أنه أول من برز من أهل البيت الطاهر يوم كربلاء، و ما زال يضرب في القوم [ضرب غلام هاشميّ علوي] حتى استشهد (رضوان الله عليه).

Ali ibn al-Hussain ibn Ali ibn Abi Talib, given the kunya of Abu al-Hassan, was nicknamed *al-Akbar* because he was the eldest of Imam Hussain's (a) sons. There is much discrepancy in regards to his age, but the most accurate accounts say that he was 27 years old during the Battle of Karbala. His mother is Layla bint Abi Murra ibn Orwa ibn Masood al-Thaqafi, and her mother was Maymouni bint Abi Sufyan. Ali al-Akbar was the first of the Hashemite martyrs in the Battle of Karbala. His traits were said to be very similar to the Holy Prophet Muhammad (s). Rather, it is said that he bore the traits of the five Immaculate *Ahl al-Kisa'*. He resembled the great-grandfather the Holy Prophet (s) in his speech and demeanor. He resembled his grandfather Imam Ali (a) in his kunya, as well as in his courage and pride. He was like his grandmother Lady Fatima (a) in his death at a young age - Lady Fatima (a) had passed away at the age of 18. He resembled his uncle Imam Hassan (a) in his splendor and stature. He bore the honor and determination of his father Imam Hussain (a), and the height of that honor and determination came on the day of Ashura when he was the first of the Hashemites to be martyred in the battle.[103]

How old was Ali Al-Akbar?

قال المياني في (العيون العبرى) ص 154: ولد (عليه السلام) في 11 من شعبان، كما في (أنيس الشيعة) في أوائل خلافة عثمان. أمه ليلى بنت أبي مرة بن عروة ابن مسعود الثقفي. قال صاحب (نفس المهموم): اختلفوا في سنّه الشريف اختلافا عظيما، فقال محمّد بن شهر اشوب و محمد بن أبي طالب الموسوي: إنه ابن 18 سنة. و قال الشيخ المفيد: إن له 19 سنة. فعلى هذا يكون هو أصغر من أخيه زين العابدين (عليه السلام).

Al-Mayaniji writes in *Al-Oyoon Al-Abra* (p. 154), "He was born on the 11th of Sha'ban, and it is said in *Anees Al-Shia* that it was in the beginnings of the caliphate of Othman. His mother is Layla bint Abi Murra ibn Orwa ibn Masood Al-Thaqafi." The author of *Nafs Al-Mahmoom* wrote, "There is great discrepancy with respect to his honorable age. Muhammad ibn Shahrashoob and Muhammad ibn Abi Talib Al-Musawi said that he was 18 years of age. Al-Shaykh Al-Mufeed said that he was 19 years of age. This would mean that he was younger than his brother Zayn Al-Abidin (a).

و قيل إنه ابن 25 سنة، فيكون هو الأكبر، و هذا هو الأصح و الأشهر. و قال السيد عبد الرزاق المقرّم في كتابه (علي الأكبر): ولد علي الأكبر و يكنّى بأبي الحسن في حدود سنة 33 هـ، فله يوم الطف ما يقارب 27 سنة. و يلقّب بالأكبر، لأنه أكبر من الإمام السجّاد (عليه السلام) الّذي له يوم الطف 23 سنة.

It is also said that he was 25 years of age, which would make him the eldest. That opinion is the more accurate and wide-spread." Sayyid

Abdulrazzaq Al-Muqarram wrote in his book *Ali Al-Akbar*, "Ali Al-Akbar, known as Abu Al-Hassan, was born around the year 33 AH. He was about 27 years of age on the day of [Ashura]. He is given the title 'Al-Akbar' because he was older than Imam Sajjad (a) who was 23 years of age on the day of [Ashura]."

و لعل هذا القول (أي أنه هو الأكبر) هو الأوجه، و يؤيده ما ورد في (تاريخ اليعقوبي)، و معارف ابن قتيبة، و تاريخ ابن خلّكان: بأنه ليس للحسين (عليه السلام) عقب إلا من علي بن الحسين الأصغر، و هو زين العابدين (عليه السلام).

And this opinion (that he was the eldest) is perhaps the most accurate, and is supported by what is relayed in *Tareekh Al-Yaqoubi*, *Ma'arif ibn Qutayba*, and *Tareekh ibn Khalkan* - that Al-Hussain (a) did not have any living descendants except through the younger Ali ibn Al-Hussain, who is known as Zayn Al-Abidin (a).[104]

The Martyrdom of Abdullah ibn Muslim ibn Aqeel

و برز عبد الله بن مسلم بن عقيل بن أبي طالب (عليه السلام)، و أمه رقية بنت علي (عليها السلام) [...] فقتل ثلاثة رجال فرماه عمرو بن صبيح الصيداوي [و في رواية: الصدائي] بسهم، فوضع عبد الله بن مسلم يده على جبهته يتّقيه، فأصاب السهم كفّه و نفذ إلى جبهته فسمّرها فلم يستطع أن يحرّكها. ثم طعنه أسيد بن مالك بالرمح في قلبه فقتله.

Abdullah ibn Muslim ibn Aqeel, whose mother was Ruqaya bint Ali (a), set out for the battlefield [...]. He killed three men but then was struck by the arrow of Amr ibn Subayh al-Saydawi. Abdullah lifted his hand to his forehead to guard against the arrow, but it pierced through his palm and reached his forehead. His hand was pinned to his forehead and he could not move it. Osaid ibn Malik then struck him with a spear in his chest, killing him.

(و قيل) إن قاتل عبد الله بن مسلم هو يزيد بن الرّقّاد الجهني، و كان يقول: رميته بسهم و كفّه على جبهته يتقي النبل، فأثبتّ كفّه في جبهته، فما استطاع أن يزيل كفه عن جبهته. و قال حين رميته: اللّهم إنهم استقلّونا و استذلّونا، فاقتلهم كما قتلونا. ثم رماه بسهم آخر، و كان يقول: جئته و هو ميّت، فنزعت سهمي من جوفه، و لم أزل أنضض الآخر عن جبهته حتى أخذته و بقي النصل.

It is also said that the killer of Abdullah ibn Muslim was Yazid ibn al-Raqqad al-Juhani. [Yazid] would say, "I shot him with an arrow while his hand was in front of his forehead guarding against the arrows. I pinned his hand to his forehead so that he could not move it. He said when I shot him so, 'O' God, they have isolated and subdued us, so kill them just as they killed us!'" [Yazid] then struck him with another arrow and would say afterwards, "I came to him after he had died and removed my arrow from his body. I continued to tug at the other arrow to remove it from his forehead until it separated and the arrowhead remained."[105]

Biographical Entry | Ruqaya bint Ali ibn Abi Talib (a)

من زوجات الإمام علي (عليه السلام): الصهباء (أم حبيب) التغلبية بنت عباد
بن ربيعة بن يحيى، من سبي اليمامة أو عين التمر. اشتراها أمير المؤمنين (عليه
السلام) فأولدها عمر الأطرف و رقية، و هما توأمان. تزوّج رقية هذه مسلم بن
عقيل (عليه السلام) فولدت له: عبد الله و عليا. و قد قتل ولدها عبد الله بن
مسلم (عليه السلام) يوم كربلاء، و كانت هي مع نساء الحسين في كربلاء بعد
أن قتل زوجها مسلم في الكوفة.

One of the wives of Imam Ali (a) was Al-Sahba' Al-Taghlibiyya, also
known as Umm Habib. She gave birth to twins - Omar and Ruqaya.
Ruqaya was wed to Muslim ibn Aqeel and bore him two sons by the
names Abdullah and Ali. Her son Abdullah was martyred in the Battle
of Karbala and she was amongst the women taken captive by the
Umayyad army.[106]

The Martyrdom of Muhammad ibn Muslim ibn Aqeel

و خرج محمّد بن مسلم بن عقيل بن أبي طالب (عليه السلام)، فقاتل حتى
قتل. قتله أبو جرهم الأزدي و لقيط بن ياسر الجهني.

Then Muhammad ibn Muslim ibn Aqeel set out for the battlefield and fought until he was felled. His killers were Abu Jarham al-Azdi and Laqeet ibn Yasir al-Juhani.[107]

The Martyrdom of the Remainder of the Hashemites

يقول السيد المقرم في مقتله، ص 328: و لما قتل عبد الله بن مسلم، حمل آل
أبي طالب حملة واحدة. فصاح بهم الحسين (عليه السلام):

Sayyid Abdulrazzaq al-Muqarram says in his *Maqtal*: And when Abdullah ibn Muslim ibn Aqeel was killed, the family of Abu Talib set out onto the battle field in a single push. Al-Hussain (a) called out to them,

صبرا على الموت يا بني عمومتي، و الله لا رأيتم هوانا بعد هذا اليوم
أبدا.

Be patient in the face of death, O' cousins. By God, you will never experience meekness after this day.[108]

The Martyrdom of Some of the Sons of Aqeel

فخرج جعفر بن عقيل بن أبي طالب (عليه السلام)، فحمل [...] فقتل خمسة عشر فارسا [على رواية محمّد بن أبي طالب]، و راجلين [على رواية ابن شهر اشوب]. فقتله عبد الله بن عروة الخثعمي، و قيل بشر بن سوط الهمداني.

Then Jafar ibn Aqeel ibn Abi Talib stepped forward unto the battlefield [...] killing 15 cavalrymen [according to the historical account of Muhammad ibn Abi Talib] and 2 infantrymen [according to ibn Shahrashoob]. He was killed by Abdullah ibn Orwa al-Khath'ami, or [as in other historical accounts] Bishr ibn Sawt al-Hamadani.

ثم خرج من بعده أخوه عبد الرحمن بن عقيل، فحمل [...] فقتل [على رواية محمّد بن أبي طالب و ابن شهر اشوب] سبعة عشر فارسا. فحمل عليه عثمان بن خالد الجهني و بشر بن سوط الهمداني فقتلاه.

He was followed by his brother Abdulrahman ibn Aqeel [...] who killed seventeen cavalrymen [according to both Muhammad ibn Abi Talib and Ibn Shahrashoob]. He was attacked and killed by Othman ibn Khalid al-Juhani and Bishr ibn Sawt al-Hamadani.

و خرج عبد الله الأكبر بن عقيل بن أبي طالب (عليه السلام) فما زال يضرب فيهم حتى أثخن بالجراح و سقط إلى الأرض. فجاء عثمان بن خالد التميمي و بشر بن سوط فقتلاه.

Then Abdullah the Elder ibn Aqeel ibn Abi Talib set out for the battlefield. He continued to fight until he was severly wounded and fell to the ground. Othman ibn Khalid al-Tamimi and Bishr ibn Sawt came to him and finished him off.

و أصابت الحسن المثنّى ابن الإمام الحسن (عليه السلام) ثماني عشرة جراحة و قطعت يده اليمنى، و لم يستشهد. ثم برز من بعده موسى بن عقيل (عليه السلام) [...] ثم حمل على القوم و لم يزل يقاتل حتى قتل سبعين فارسا، ثم قتل (رحمه الله).

[Amongst the sons of Aqeel was] al-Hassan II, the son of Imam Hassan (a), who was wounded and his right hand was severed, but he was not martyred.
Musa ibn Aqeel then set out to the battle field [...] and was charged by the enemies. He continued to fight until he killed 70 cavalrymen, but was eventually killed.[109]

The Martyrdom of Ibrahim ibn Al-Hussain (a)

و برز من بعده إبراهيم بن الحسين، و هو [يرتجز] ثم حمل على القوم فقتل
خمسين فارسا، و قتل (رحمه الله).

Then Ibrahim ibn Al-Hussain (a) stepped forward unto the battlefield
[reciting verses of poetry written in honor of his father.] He charged
the enemies, killing fifty cavalrymen before being killed - may God
have mercy on his soul.[110]

The Martyrdom of Ahmad ibn Muhammad al-Hashemi

و برز من بعده أحمد بن محمد الهاشمي، و هو يرتجز [...] ثم حمل على القوم، و

لم يزل يقاتل حتى قتل ثمانين فارسا، ثم قتل (رضوان الله عليه).

Then Ahmad ibn Muhammad al-Hashemi stepped forward, [declaring in verse his intent to defend Imam Hussain (a).] He charged the enemy and fought valiantly until he killed eighty cavalrymen before being killed - may God be pleased with him.[111]

Martyrdom of Muhammad and Aoun, the Sons of Abdullah ibn Jafar

و حمل الناس على الحسين (عليه السلام) و أهل بيته من كل جانب. فخرج محمّد بن عبد الله بن جعفر بن أبي طالب (عليه السلام)، و أمه زينب الكبرى بنت أمير المؤمنين (عليه السلام)، و قيل الخوصاء من بني تيم اللات، و هو [يرتجز] ثم قاتل حتى قتل عشرة أنفس، فحمل عليه عامر بن نهشل التميمي فقتله.

The enemies attacked al-Hussain (a) and his household from every direction. Muhammad ibn Abdullah ibn Jafar ibn Abi Talib stepped forward. His mother was [Lady] Zaynab, the daughter of the Commander of the Faithful (a), or according to some sources al-Khawsa', a woman from the tribe of Taim al-Laat. [He declared in verse his contempt for an enemy that had abandoned the teachings of the Holy Quran.] He fought and killed ten enemies, but was attacked and killed by 'Amir ibn Nahshal al-Tamimi.

و خرج أخوه عون بن عبد الله بن جعفر (عليه السلام) و أمه زينب الكبرى (عليها السلام) و هو [يرتجز] ثم قاتل حتى قتل [على رواية ابن شهر اشوب] ثلاثة فوارس و ثمانية عشر راجلا. فحمل عليه عبد الله بن قطبة الطائي فقتله.

His brother Aoun ibn Abdullah ibn Jafar then set out, and his mother was [Lady] Zaynab. He [stepped onto the battlefielding declaring his lineage and praising his father in verse.] He fought and killed [according to the account of Ibn Shahrashoob] three cavalrymen and eighteen infintrymen. He was attacked by Abdullah ibn Qutba al-Taei and killed.

قال صاحب (نفس المهموم) ص 155: اعلم أنه كان لعبد الله بن جعفر ابنان مسميان بعون: (الأكبر) و أمه زينب العقيلة (عليها السلام)، (و الأصغر) و أمه جماعة بنت المسيّب بن نجبة. و الظاهر أن المقتول بالطف هو الأول.

The author of *Nafas al-Mahmoom* said, "Know that Abdullah ibn Jafar had two sons named Aoun, the elder's mother was [Lady] Zaynab and the younger's mother was Juma'a bint al-Musayyab ibn Najaba. It seems that the one killed in [Karbala] was the former of the two."[112]

The Martyrdom of Abdullah al-Akbar ibn al-Hassan (a)

و خرج أبو بكر بن الحسن (عليه السلام) و هو عبد الله الأكبر، و أمه أم ولد يقال لها رملة، و هي أم القاسم (عليه السلام)، برز [وهو يرتجز] فقاتل حتى قتل. و كان عبد الله بن الحسن (عليه السلام) قد تزوج من ابنة عمه سكينة بنت الحسين (عليه السلام) قبيل المعركة [....].

[Abdullah al-Akbar] ibn al-Hassan (a), [whose mother was Ramla] the mother of al-Qasim, set out unto the battlefield [reciting battle verses adapted from the poetry of his grandfather the Commander of the Faithful (a).] He fought until he was slain. He had been recently married to his cousin Sukayna bint al-Hussain (a) [at the time of the Battle of Karbala].

قال السيد إبراهيم الميانجي في (العيون العبرى) ص 158: يظهر أنه كان للإمام الحسن (ع) ابنان مسمّيان بعبد الله: أحدهما إليه الأصغر)، و الآخر (الأكبر) و هو المكنى بأبي بكر، و كان أخا للقاسم لأبويه، و قد زوّجه عمه الحسين (عليه السلام) ابنته سكينة.

Sayyid Ibrahim al-Mayaniji said in *al-Oyoon al-Abra* (p. 158), "It seems that Imam Hassan (a) had two sons by the name of Abdullah, one of whom was called al-Asghar ["the Younger"] while the other was called al-Akbar ["the Elder"] and "Abu Bakr." [Abdullah al-Akbar] was the full brother of al-Qasim and was married by his uncle al-Hussain (a) to [his cousin] Sukayna."[113]

The Martyrdom of al-Qasim ibn al-Hassan (a)

و خرج من بعده أخوه لأمه و أبيه القاسم بن الحسن (عليه السلام)، و أمه أم
ولد، و هو غلام لم يبلغ الحلم. فلما نظر الحسين (عليه السلام) إليه قد برز،
اعتنقه و جعلا يبكيان حتى غشي عليها. ثم استأذن عمه في المبارزة فأبى أن
يأذن له، فلم يزل الغلام يقبّل يديه و رجليه، حتى أذن له. فخرج و دموعه
تسيل على خديه و هو يقول:

[After the martyrdom of Abdullah al-Akbar ibn al-Hassan (a)], his full
brother al-Qasim ibn al-Hassan (a) came forward... and he had not yet
reached the age of adolescence. When al-Hussain saw him come
forward he embraced him and they wept until they fainted. [Al-Qasim]
asked his uncle for permission to enter the battlefield but his request
was denied. He continued to [beg his uncle for permission] kissing his
hands and feet, until he was granted permission. [Al-Qasim] stepped
forward unto the battlefield with tears running down his cheeks as he
said [in verse],

إن تنكروني فأنا ابن الحسن * * * سبط النبي المصطفى و المؤتمن

هذا حسين كالأسير المرتهن * * * بين أناس لا سقوا صوب المزن

If you do not know me, I am the son of al-Hassan (a)

The grandson of the Chosen and Trusted Prophet (s)

And this is Hussain (a) like a ransomed captive

*Amongst a [cursed] people; may the sky never rain its mercy upon
them!*

فقاتل قتالا شديدا، حتى قتل على صغر سّنه [على بعض الروايات] خمسة و
ثلاثين رجلا. و في (المنتخب) للطريحي، ص 374 ط 2: ثم إن القاسم تقدم
إلى عمر بن سعد، و قال له: يا عمر أما تخاف الله، أما تراقب الله يا أعمى
القلب، أما تراعي رسول الله (صلى الله عليه و آله و سلم)؟! فقال عمر: أما
كفاكم التجبر، أما تطيعون يزيد؟ فقال القاسم (عليه السلام): لا جزاك الله خيرا،
تدّعي الإسلام، و آل رسول الله (صلى الله عليه و آله و سلم) عطاشى ظماء،
قد اسودّت الدنيا بأعينهم.

He fought valiantly until he killed [according to some accounts] thirty
five men. Al-Turaihi wrote in *al-Muntakhab* (p. 374), "Al-Qasim
approached Omar ibn Saad and said, 'O' Omar, do you not fear God?
Has your heart been so blinded that you do not heed [God's wrath]?
Do you not take account of [the rights of] the Messenger of God (s)?"
Omar replied, "Enough with your pride! Why do you not obey Yazid?"
Al-Qasim said, "May God not reward you for any deed! You claim
Islam while the household of the Messenger of God (s) are thirsty and
the world grows dark in their eyes!"

و في (اللواعج) قال حميد بن مسلم: كنت في عسكر ابن سعد، حين خرج علينا
غلام كأن وجهه شقة قمر، و في يده سيف، و عليه قميص و إزار و نعلان، قد
انقطع شسع إحداهما، ما أنسى أنها كانت اليسرى [و أنف ابن النبي (صلى الله
عليه و آله و سلم) أن يحتفي في الميدان، فوقف يشدّ شسع نعله] [...].

In *al-Lawa'ij*, Hamid ibn Muslim says: I was in the camp of [Omar] ibn
Saad when a young man came forward whose face was like the shining
moon. He carried a sword... and the strap of one shoe was torn - I will
never forget that it was the left. [Al-Qasim refused to walk bearfoot in

battle, as that was seen to be disgraceful. He stopped in the middle of the battlefield and knelt down to fix his shoe.] [...]

فقال لي عمرو بن سعد بن نفيل الأزدي: و الله لأشدّنّ عليه. فقلت: سبحان الله و ما تريد بذلك! و الله لو ضربني ما بسطت إليه يدي، دعه يكفيكه هؤلاء الذين تراهم قد احتوشوه. فقال: و الله لأفعلنّ. فشدّ عليه، فما ولّى حتى ضرب رأسه بالسيف ففلقه، و وقع الغلام إلى الأرض لوجهه، و نادى: يا عماه!

Amr ibn Saad ibn Nufayl al-Azdi said to me, 'By God, I shall assault him!' I said, 'Glory be to God! What do you hope to achieve by this! By God, if he were to strike me I would not extend my hand [to strike him back]. Leave him, for those who have gathered around him will be enough. He replied, 'By God, I will do [as I have said].' He charged toward [al-Qasim] and did not stop until he struck him on his head with the sword, cutting it in half. The young man fell on his face and called, 'O' uncle.'

فانقضّ عليه الحسين (عليه السلام) كالصقر، و تخلل الصفوف، و شدّ شدة ليث أغضب، فضرب عمرو بن سعد بن نفيل بالسيف، فاتقاها بالساعد فقطعها من لدن المرفق، فصاح صيحة سمعها أهل العسكر. ثم تنحّى عنه الحسين (عليه السلام) فحملت خيل أهل الكوفة ليستنقذوه، فاستقبلته بصدورها و وطئته بحوافرها، فمات.

Al-Hussain (a) charged toward him like a falcon, tearing through [enemy] lines like a angered lion. He struck Amr ibn Saad ibn Nufayl with the sword. [Amr] guarded against the blow with his forearm, leaving his arm severed at the elbow. He cried out so that the entire camp could hear him. Al-Hussain (a) moved back away from him while the Kufan cavalry approached, trying to save [Amr]. But as the cavalry charged, the horses hit him with their chests and trampled him under their feet, killing him.

و انجلت الغبرة فإذا بالحسين (عليه السلام) قائم على رأس الغلام و هو يفحص برجليه، و الحسين (عليه السلام) يقول:

When the dust settled, al-Hussain (a) was standing over the boy's head while he was digging with his feet [out of pain]. Al-Hussain (a) would say,

بُعداً لقوم قتلوك و من خصمهم يوم القيامة فيك جدك و أبوك. ثم قال (عليه السلام): عزّ و الله على عمك أن تدعوه فلا يُجيبك أو يُجيبك فلا ينفعك [أو يعينك فلا يغني عنك]. صوت و الله كثر واتره، و قلّ ناصره!

Away with the people who have killed you! Who is their adversary on the Day of Judgement other than your grandfather and your father? By God, it saddens your uncle that you should call him while he cannot answer you, or that he answers but cannot help you, [or that he helps but cannot suffice you]. By God, our voice is one opposed by many and supported by few!

ثم حمله و وضع صدره على صدره. و كأني أنظر إلى رجلي الغلام يخطان الأرض. فجاء به حتى ألقاه مع ابنه علي و القتلى من أهل بيته. ثم رفع طرفه إلى السماء و قال (عليه السلام):

[Al-Hussain (a)] carried [Al-Qasim], putting the boy's chest to his. It is as if I could see the boy's feet dragging on the floor. He carried him until he placed him with his son Ali [al-Akbar] and the rest of the fallen from his household. He raised his eyes to the heavens and said,

اللّهم أحصهم عددا و اقتلهم بددا و لا تغادر منهم أحدا [و لا تغفر لهم أبدا].

My God, mark their numbers, kill them off bit by bit, do not leave any of them [out of Your punishment, and do not ever forgive them].

و صاح الحسين (عليه السلام) في تلك الحال:

In that condition, al-Hussain (a) called out,

صبرا يا بني عمومتي، صبرا يا أهل بيتي، فو الله لا رأيتم هوانا بعد هذا اليوم أبدا.

Be patient, my cousins! Be patient, O' members of my family! By God, you will never experience meekness after this day.[114]

Al-Qasim's Wedding

ذكر فخر الدين الطريحي في كتابه (المنتخب في المراثي و الخطب) ص 373، و كذلك المياني في (العيون العبرى) ص 158، قصة زواج القاسم (عليه السلام). و ملخصها أن الإمام الحسن (عليه السلام) كان قد أوصى بتزويج ابنه القاسم (عليه السلام) من ابنة أخيه الحسين (عليه السلام) المسماة زبيدة. ذلك أن الحسين (عليه السلام) بعد وفاة زوجته شهربانو أم زين العابدين (عليه السلام) تزوج بأختها شاهزنان، فولدت له زبيدة هذه، و قبر زبيدة خاتون في الري جنوبي طهران على مسافة ثلاثة ضرائح من قبر الشاه عبد العظيم الحسني (راجع أسرار الشهادة، ص 310).

The story of al-Qasim's wedding was recounted in al-Turaihi's *al-Muntakhab fi al-Marathi wa al-Khutb* (p. 373) and al-Mayaniji's *al-Oyoon al-Abra* (p. 158). In summary, they state that Imam Hassan (a) instructed in his will that his son al-Qasim be married to Imam Hussain's (a) daughter Zubayda. Imam Hussain (a) had been married to Shahrbanu, the mother of Imam Sajjad (a), but after she passed away he married her sister Shahzanan, who gave birth to their daughter Zubayda. Lady Zubayda's tomb can be found in modern day Iran, south of the capital Tehran.

لذلك قام الحسين (عليه السلام) في كربلاء بإجراء عقد الزواج بين القاسم و زبيدة في خيمة، بعد أن ألبسه ثيابا جديدة. لكن القاسم رغم ذلك فضّل الشهادة على الزواج، و قال لخطيبته: لقد أخّرنا عرسنا إلى الآخرة. فبكت الهاشميات. يقول المحقق السيد عبد الرزاق المقرّم في كتابه (القاسم بن الحسن) ص 320:

كل ما يذكر في عرس القاسم غير صحيح، لعدم بلوغ القاسم سن الزواج، و لم
يرد به نص صحيح من المؤرخين.

Thus, Imam Hussain (a) wed the couple to one another in one of the tents. Despite this, al-Qasim favored martyrdom over marriage and said, "We have delayed our wedding to the hereafter." The Hashemite women wept when they heard this.

Sayyid Abdulrazzaq al-Muqarram writes in his book *al-Qasim ibn al-Hassan (a)*, "Everything that is mentioned about the al-Qasim's wedding is untrue. He had not reached the age of marriage yet and there is not an accurate historical account of the event."[115]

Biographical Entry | Al-Qasim ibn al-Hassan (a)

في بعض الكتب: توفي الإمام الحسن (عليه السلام) و للقاسم سنتان، فربّاه عمه الحسين (عليه السلام) في حجره، و كفله مع سائر إخوته. و كان يوم عاشوراء غلاما لم يبلغ الحلم (عمره 13 سنة). و كان وجهه من جماله كفلقة القمر. أمه و أم عبد اللّه: رملة. [و في طبقات ابن سعد]: نفيلة.

Imam Hassan (a) passed away when al-Qasim was two years old. Al-Qasim was raised by his uncle al-Hussain (a), who took him into his household and became his and his siblings' guardian. On the day of Ashura, he was still a boy who had not reached the age of adolescence. His face shined like the bright moon. His full brother was Abdullah and his mother was Ramla [or according to *Tabaqat ibn Saeed*, her name was Nufayla].[116]

The Martyrdom of Some of Imam Hussain's (a) Brothers

و تقدمت إخوة الحسين (عليه السلام) عازمين على أن يموتوا دونه. فأول من خرج منهم أبو بكر بن علي (عليه السلام) و اسمه عبد الله، و أمه ليلى بنت مسعود من بني نهشل، فتقدم و هو يرتجز [...] فلم يزل يقاتل حتى قتله زجر بن بدر النخعي. ثم خرج من بعده أخوه عمر بن علي (عليه السلام)، أمه أم حبيب الصهباء بنت ربيعة التغلبية، فحمل على زجر قاتل أخيه فقتله، و استقبل القوم و جعل يضرب بسيفه ضربا منكرا، و هو [...] فلم يزل يقاتل حتى قتل.

Al-Hussain's (a) brothers stepped forward, intent on dying in his service and protection.

The first to rush into the battlefield was [Abdullah] ibn Ali (a), whose [nickname was Abu Bakr]. His mother was Layla bint Masood of the Nahshal clan. He rushed into the battlefield [declaring in verse his lineage and his intent to die in protection of his brother]. He continued to fight until he was killed by Zajr ibn Badr al-Nakha'ei.

Then his brother Omar ibn Ali (a) stepped forward. His mother was al-Sahba' bint Rabe'a al-Taghlibiyya [known as Umm Habib]. He charged toward Zajr, his brother's killer, and killed him. He rushed toward the enemies, swinging his sword with might and valor while [taunting his enemies with prideful verses]. He continued to fihgt until he was killed.

و خرج محمّد الأصغر بن علي (عليه السلام) و أمه أم ولد، فرماه رجل من تميم من بني أبان بن دارم، فقتله و جاء برأسه. و خرج عبد الله بن علي (عليه السلام) و أمه ليلى بنت مسعود النهشلية، فقاتل حتى قتل. و هو أخو أبي

194

بكر بن علي (ع) لأمه و أبيه، و هو غير عبد الله الأصغر بن علي (عليه
السلام) شقيق العباس (عليه السلام)، كما صرح بذلك الشيخ المفيد في
(الإرشاد).

Then Muhammad al-Asghar ibn Ali (a) [...] set out unto the battlefield.
A man from the tribe of Tameem, from the descendants of Aban ibn
Darim, struck him with an arrow and returned with his head.

Abdullah ibn Ali (a) stepped forward and fought until he was killed.
His mother was Layla bint Masood al-Nahshaliyya and he was Abu
Bakr ibn Ali's (a) full brother. He is not Abdullah al-Asghar ibn Ali (a),
the full brother of al-Abbas, as was expressly stated by al-Shaykh al-
Mufeed in *al-Irshaad*.[117]

The Martyrdom of al-Abbas's Full Brothers

و لما رأى العباس بن علي (ع) كثرة القتلى من أهله قال لإخوته من أمه و أبيه،
و هم عبد الله و جعفر و عثمان (عليه السلام)، و أمهم أم البنين فاطمة بنت
حزام بن خالد الكلابية: يا بني أمي تقدموا حتى أراكم قد نصحتم لله و لرسوله،
فإنه لا ولد لكم [...]. فبرز عبد الله الأصغر بن علي (عليه السلام) و عمره
خمس و عشرون سنة و هو [يرتجز] فاختلف هو و هاني بن ثبيت الحضرمي
ضربتين، فقتله هاني.

When al-Abbas saw the great number of family members who had
been martyred, he turned to his full brothers - Abdullah, Jafar, and
Othman. Their mother was Fatima bint Hizam ibn Khalid al-Kilabiyya,
known as Umm al-Baneen. He said to them, "O' sons of my mother,
step forward so that I can see you be faithful to God and His
Messenger (s); for you have no children [to worry about in case of your
martyrdom]." [...]

Abdullah al-Asghar, a man of 25 years, stepped forward [while taunting
the enemy with verses in praise of his father]. He fought Hani ibn
Thubayt al-Hadrami, who slayed him.

ثم برز بعده أخوه جعفر بن علي (عليه السلام) و كان عمره تسع عشرة سنة
و هو [يرتجز] فحمل عليه هاني بن ثبيت الحضرمي أيضا فقتله، و جاء برأسه.

ثم برز بعده أخوه عثمان بن علي (عليه السلام) فقام مقام إخوته، و كان عمره
إحدى و عشرين سنة و هو [يرتجز] فرماه خولي بن يزيد الأصبحي على جبينه
فسقط عن فرسه، و حمل عليه رجل من بني أبان بن دارم فقتله، و جاء برأسه.

Then his brother Jafar ibn Ali (a), who was 19 years of age, stepped forward [reciting verses in praise of his family and declaring his intent to die protecting Imam Hussain (a)]. Hani ibn Thubayt al-Hadrami charged at him and killed him, returning with his head.

Their brother Othman ibn Ali (a), a man of 21, then stepped forward like his brothers [reciting verses in praise of his father, the Prophet (s), and Imam Hussain (a)]. Khawli ibn Yazid al-Asbahi shot him with an arrow to the forehead, knocking him off his horse. A man from the clan of Aban ibn Darim charged at him and killed him, returning with his head.[118]

Al-Abbas Martyred While Seeking Water for the Camp

قال العباس (عليه السلام): قد ضاق صدري من هؤلاء المنافقين و أريد أن
آخذ ثأري منهم. فأمره الحسين (عليه السلام) أن يطلب الماء للأطفال، فذهب
العباس (عليه السلام) إلى القوم و وعظهم و حذّرهم غضب الجبار فلم ينفع،
فنادى بصوت عال: يا عمر بن سعد هذا الحسين ابن بنت رسول الله، قد قتلتم
أصحابه و أهل بيته، و هؤلاء عياله و أولاده عطاشى فاسقوهم من الماء، فقد
أحرق الظمأ قلوبهم، و هو مع ذلك يقول:

Al-Abbas said, "I grow impatient with these hypocrites and I wish to seek redress against them." Al-Hussain (a) instructed him to fetch water for the children first. Al-Abbas went towards the enemy and advised them, warning them of the Almighty's wrath; but this was to no avail. He then called out, "O' Omar ibn Saad, this is al-Hussain (a), the son of the daughter of Messenger of God (s). You have killed his companions and family. His wards and children are thirsty, so give them some water to quench their burning hearts. All the while, [al-Hussain (a)] has been saying,

دعوني أذهب إلى الروم أو الهند و أخلّي لكم الحجاز و العراق.

Let me go to Rome or India and leave Hijaz and Iraq to you."

فأثّر كلام العباس (عليه السلام) في نفوس القوم حتى بكى بعضهم. و لكن
الشمر صاح بأعلى صوته: يابن أبي تراب لو كان وجه الأرض كله ماء و هو
تحت أيدينا لما سقيناكم منه قطرة، إلا أن تدخلوا في بيعة يزيد. ثم إنه ركب جواده
و أخذ القربة، فأحاط به أربعة آلاف و رموه بالنبال.

Al-Abbas's words effected the hearts of the enemy such that some of them began to cry. Shimr, however, called out, "O' son of Abu Turab [Imam Ali (a)], if the face of the earth was all water and under our control, we would not give you a single drop unless you pledge allegiance to Yazid." [Al-Abbas] rode his horse and took the waterskin. He was surrounded by four thousand enemies who pelted him with arrows.

فلم ترعه كثرتهم و أخذ يطرد أولئك الجماهير وحده، و لواء الحمد يرفرف على رأسه، فلم تثبت له الرجال، و نزل إلى الفرات مطمئنا غير مبال بذلك الجمع. و لما اغترف من الماء ليشرب تذكّر عطش أخيه الحسين (عليه السلام) و من معه، فرمى الماء و قال:

Their numbers did not discourage him and he began to repel them by himself while the banner of glorification [to God Almighty] waved above his head. Men could not stand in his way and he was able to reach the Euphrates despite the great number amassed against him. But when he took a handful of water to drink, he remembered the thirst of his brother al-Hussain (a) and those with him. He threw the water back [into the river] and said,

يا نفس من بعد الحسين هوني * * * و بعده لا كنت أن تكوني

هذا الحسين وارد المنون * * * و تشربين بارد المعين

تالله ما هذا فعال ديني * * * و لا فعال صادق اليقين

O' self, [be second] to al-Hussain (a)

As after him, it matters not whether you be or not

This is Hussain (a) approaching death

And you [dare] drink sweet, cold water?

By God, this is not an act of my faith

Nor an act of a man of true certainty

ثم ملأ القربة و ركب جواده و توجّه نحو المخيم فقطع عليه الطريق، و جعل يضرب حتى أكثر القتل فيهم و كشفهم عن الطريق و هو يقول:

He filled the waterskin and rode his horse back towards the camp. Enemies blocked the way and he fended them off again, killing much of them. He would recite,

لا أرهب الموت إذا الموت رقى   *   *   *   حتى أواري في المصاليت لقى

نفسي لسبط المصطفى الطهر وقى   *   *   *   إني أنا العباس أغدو بالسّقا

و لا أخاف الشرّ يوم الملتقى

I do not fear death if it approached

Leaving brave men felled beside me

I will give my soul in protection of the Prophet's (s) pure grandson

I am al-Abbas, and I will return with the water

I do not fear harm on the day of battle

فكمن له زيد بن الرقّاد الجهني من وراء نخلة و عاونه حكيم بن الطفيل السنبسي، فضربه على يمينه فبراها، فقال (عليه السلام):

Zaid ibn al-Raqqad al-Juhani and Hakeem ibn al-Tufail al-Sunbusi ambushed him from behind a palm tree. The struck him on his right arm, severing it. [But al-Abbas pushed on], saying,

و الله إن قطعتم يميني   *   *   *   إني أحامي أبدا عن ديني

و عن إمام صادق اليقين   *   *   *   سبط النبي الطاهر الأمين

200

By God, if you have severed my right arm

I will continue to defend my faith

And [protecting] an Imam of true certainty

The grandson of the pure and trusted Prophet (s)

فلم يعبأ بيمينه بعد أن كان همه إيصال الماء إلى أطفال الحسين (عليه السلام) و

عياله، و لكن الحكيم بن الطفيل كمن له من وراء نخلة، فلما مرّ به ضربه على

شماله فقطعها فقال (عليه السلام):

He did not give any attention to his severed right arm, as his sole concern was delivering the water to al-Hussain's (s) wards and children. But Hakeem ibn al-Tufail ambushed him once again from behind a palm tree, striking him on his left arm and severing it. [Yet al-Abbas continued to push on], saying,

يا نفس لا تخشي من الكفّار * * * و أبشري برحمة الجبّار

مع النبي السيد المختار * * * مع جملة السادات و الأطهار

قد قطّعوا ببغيهم يساري * * * فأصلهم يا ربّ حرّ النار

O' self, do not fear this band of disbelievers

And rejoice for the mercy of the Almighty

Alongside our master, the Chosen Prophet (s)

Along with the other noble and pure souls

They have severed my left arm by their wretchedness

O' Lord, deliver them to a blazing Hell!

و تكاثروا عليه و أتته السهام كالمطر، فأصاب القربة سهم و أريق ماؤها، و

سهم أصاب صدره و ضربه رجل بالعمود على رأسه ففلق هامته، و سقط على

الأرض ينادي: عليك مني السلام أبا عبد الله. فأتاه الحسين (عليه السلام) و

قد استشهد، فقال:

The enemies surrounded him as arrows rained down; one struck the waterskin and spilling its water, while another struck him in his chest. A man hit him on his head with a pole, cracking his skull. He fell to the ground calling, "Farewell, O' Abu Abdullah (a)." Al-Hussain (a) rushed to him and found that he had been martyred. He said,

الآن انكسر ظهري و قلّت حيلتي.

Now my back has been broken and I have been left powerless.[119]

Imam Hussain (a) Bids Farewell to al-Abbas

أخذ الحسين (عليه السلام) رأسه و وضعه في حجره، و جعل يمسح الدم عن

عينيه، فرآه و هو يبكي. فقال الحسين (عليه السلام):

Al-Hussain (a) took al-Abbas's head and placed it in his lap. He began to wipe the blood off his eyes and saw that he was crying. Al-Hussain (a) asked,

ما يبكيك يا أبا الفضل؟

What has made you cry, O' Abu al-Fadl?

قال: يا نور عيني، و كيف لا أبكي و مثلك الآن جئتني و أخذت رأسي، فبعد

ساعة من يرفع رأسك عن التراب، و من يمسح التراب عن وجهك! و كان

الحسين (عليه السلام) جالسا، إذ شهق العباس شهقة، و فارقت روحه الطيبة.

فصاح الحسين (عليه السلام):

[Al-Abbas] replied, "O' light of my eys! How can I not cry when you have come to me and taken my head [in your lap]? But in an hour who will lift you head from the ground and wipe the sand off your face?"Al-Hussain (a) was sitting there when al-Abbas took his last breath and his blessed soul departed his body. He cried out,

وا أخاه، وا عباساه، وا ضيعتاه!

O' my brother! O' Abbas! O' what a loss![120]

Historians Neglect the Account of al-Abbas's Martyrdom

أورد الخوارزمي في مقتله مصرع العباس باختصار كبير، ج 2 ص 29 قال: ثم
خرج من بعده العباس بن علي (عليه السلام) و أمه أم البنين، و هو السّقّاء،
فحمل و هو [يرتجز] فلم يزل يقاتل حتى قتل جماعة من القوم ثم قتل. فقال
الحسين (عليه السلام): الآن انكسر ظهري و قلّت حيلتي.

Al-Khawarizmi excerpted the account of al-Abbas's martyrdom in his
Maqtal (v. 2 p. 29). He wrote "Then al-Abbas stepped forward, and his
mother was Umm al-Baneen. He was in charge of maintaining the
water supply. He charged, [declaring his intent to die protecting his
brother in verse]. He continued to fight and killed a group of enemies
but was killed. Al-Hussain (a) then said, 'Now my back has been
broken and I have been left powerless.'"

و أما الطبري فمن العجب العجاب أنه لم يذكر شيئا أبدا عن مصرع العباس. و
اعتبر السيد ابن طاووس في (اللهوف) مقتل العباس (عليه السلام) آخر أهل
البيت (عليهم السلام) و ذلك باختصار.

It is astonishing that al-Tabari did not mention anything at all about
the martyrdom of al-Abbas. As for al-Sayyid ibn Tawoos, he wrote in
al-Luhoof that the martyrdom of al-Abbas was the last amongst the
Household [of the Prophet (s)], recounting the story with brevity.[121]

Biographical Entry | Al-Abbas ibn Ali (a)

أبو الفضل العباس (عليه السلام) هو ابن أمير المؤمنين علي بن أبي طالب. أمه فاطمة بنت حزام الكلابية، اختارها له أخوه عقيل لتلد له غلاما فارسا، و قد اشتهرت عشيرتها بالشجاعة و البأس، و كان آباؤها و أخوالها فرسان العرب في الجاهلية. و قد ولدت للإمام (عليه السلام) أربعة أولاد، فسميت لذلك (أم البنين) و هم: العباس و جعفر و عثمان و عبد الله، و قد استشهدوا جميعا في كربلاء. و كانت أم البنين من أفضل النساء، عارفة بحق أهل البيت (عليهم السلام) و مخلصة في ولائهم. كان أكبر أولادها العباس (عليه السلام)، ولد في 4 شعبان سنة 26 ه.

Abu al-Fadl al-Abbas is the son of the Commander of the Faithful Ali ibn Abi Talib (a). His mother is Fatima bint Hizam al-Kilabiyya, who was chosen for [Imam Ali (a)] by his brother Aqeel so that she can bear a courageous son. Her family was famed for their bravery and resolve. Her forefathers were foremost amongst the knights of Arabia during the Age of Ignorance. She gave birth to four sons - earning the honorific title "Umm al-Baneen" [i.e. the mother of male children] - by the names of al-Abbas, Jafar, Othman, and Abdullah, all of whom were martyred in Karbala. Umm al-Baneen was the best of women. She knew well the rights of the Holy Household and was loyal and devoted to them. Her eldest child was al-Abbas, who was born on the 4th of Shaaban, 26 AH.

و قد اجتمعت في العباس كل صفات العظمة، من بأس و شجاعة و إباء و نجدة من جهة، و جمال و بهجة و وضاءة و طلاقة من جهة أخرى، و لما تطابق فيه الجمالان الخَلقي و الخُلقي، قيل فيه (قمر بني هاشم). و قد عاش (عليه السلام)

مع أبيه أمير المؤمنين (عليه السلام) أربع عشرة سنة، و حضر معه حروبه، و لكنه لم يأذن له أبوه بالنزال بها. و قتل مع أخيه الحسين (عليه السلام) بكربلاء و عمره 34 سنة، و كان صاحب رايته.

Al-Abbas manifested all the qualities of greatness; from resolve, bravery, pride, and courage as well as charm, cheerfulness, good-nature, and eloquence. And because he combined the best of moral and physical qualities, he was given the nickname "Moon of the Hashemites." He lived for fourteen years with his father the Commander of the Faithful [before the Imam's (a) martyrdom]. He participated in the battles fought by his father but was not granted permission to duel [in one-on-one combat]. He was martyred alongside his brother al-Hussain (a) at the age of 34 and was the standard bearer [during the Battle of Karbala].

من ألقاب العباس (عليه السلام): (السّقّاء) لأنه استسقى الماء لأهل البيت (عليهم السلام) يوم الطف. و (أبو الفضل) لأنه كان له ولد اسمه الفضل. و (باب الحوائج) لكثرة ما صدر عنه من الكرامات يوم كربلاء و بعده. و منها (قمر بني هاشم) لما ذكرنا من جمال هيئته و وسامته. و كان يركب الفرس المطهّم و رجلاه تخطّان في الأرض.

Al-Abbas's nicknames include *al-Saqqa'* (the water-bearer) because he fetched the water for the Holy Household during the Battle of Karbala, and *Abu al-Fadl* because he has a son named al-Fadl.

He is called *Bab al-Hawa'ej* (the Gate of Answered Needs) because of his many *Karamat** on the day of Karbala and thereafter. He is also

---

* A *Karama* (plural: *Karamat*) is a gift given by God to an individual honored by Him. This often includes the individual's intercession to answer prayers and cure the ill.

called *Qamar Bani Hashem* (the Moon of the Hashemites) because of his charm and good looks. He used to ride the most magnificent of steeds while his feet would still touch the ground.

و لقد شهدت الأمة بطولة العباس (عليه السلام) و مواقفه مع أخيه الحسين (عليه السلام) يوم الطف، و استماتته في الدفاع من أجله، حتى أن الحسين (عليه السلام) خاطبه قائلا: بنفسي أنت، فأقامه مقام نفسه الزكية، و هذا شرف لم يبلغه أحد من الناس.

The world witnessed the bravery of al-Abbas and his stance alongside his brother al-Hussain (a) during the Battle of Karbala; sacrificing himself in defense of his brother. Al-Hussain (a) would even say to al-Abbas, "May I be sacrificed for you," placing al-Abbas at the level of his pure soul - an honor not reached by any other individual.

و عن منزلة العباس (عليه السلام) ذكر السيد عبد الحسين الموسوي في (الفاجعة العظمى) ص 147: [...] قال الإمام الصادق (عليه السلام):

In regards to al-Abbas's stature, Sayyid Abdulhussain al-Mousawi said in *al-Faji'a al-'Othma* (p. 147): [...] Imam Sadiq (a) said,

كان عمّنا العباس ابن علي (عليه السلام) نافذ البصيرة صلب الإيمان، جاهد مع أبي عبد الله (عليه السلام) و أبلى بلاء حسنا، و مضى شهيدا.

Our uncle al-Abbas ibn Ali (a) was of astute insight and firm faith. He strived alongside [Imam Hussain (a)], distinguished himself, and passed as a martyr.

و عن (الأمالي) بإسناده عن أبي حمزة الثمالي عن الإمام زين العابدين (عليه السلام) قال:

In *al-Amali*, it is relayed by the way of Abu Hamza al-Thamali that Imam Zayn al-Abideen (a) said,

رحم الله عمي العباس، فلقد آثر و أبلى و فدى أخاه بنفسه حتى قطعت يداه، فأبدله الله عزّ و جلّ جناحين يطير بهما مع الملائكة في الجنة، كما جعل لجعفر بن أبي طالب (عليه السلام). و إن للعباس عند الله تبارك و تعالى منزلة يغبطه بها جميع الشهداء يوم القيامة.

May God bless my uncle al-Abbas. He was forebearant, distinguished himself, and sacrificed himself for his brother so that his hands were severed [and he was martyred]. God has given him wings by which he will fly with the angels in paradise, just as God gave to Jafar ibn Abi Talib. Al-Abbas has a stature in the eyes of God for which he is envied by all other martyrs on the Day of Judgment.

و يقع مرقد العباس (عليه السلام) في كربلاء المقدسة على مسافة بسيطة من قبر الحسين (عليه السلام)، و يلاحظ أن مرقده الشريف منفرد عن مرقد الحسين و الشهداء (عليهم السلام)، و يبعد عن مرقد الحسين (عليه السلام) نحو 350 مترا، و قد أقيمت فوقه قبة من الذهب شبيهة بقبة الحسين (عليه السلام).

The tomb of al-Abbas is in Karbala, short distance from the tomb of al-Hussain (a). It is separate from the shrine of al-Hussain (a) and the martyrs, about 350 meters away. Above his tomb is a golden dome similar to the dome of the shrine al-Hussain (a).[122]

The Rewards of Providing Water for the Thirsty

بما أن أبا الفضل العباس (عليه السلام) كان ساقي عطاشى كربلاء، نذكر هذين الحديثين: قال الإمام زين العابدين (عليه السلام):

Because Abu al-Fadl al-Abbas was the water bearer of Karbala, let us mention the following two Hadiths. Imam Zayn al-Abideen (a) said,

من سقى مؤمناً من ظمأ، سقاه اللّه من الرحيق المختوم.

Whoever provides drink to a thirsty believer, God will serve him from the Sealed Pure Wine [of Paradise].

و عن الإمام الصادق (عليه السلام) قال:

It is also narrated that Imam Sadiq (a) said,

من سقى الماء في موضع يوجد فيه الماء، كان كمن أعتق رقبة. و من سقى الماء في موضع لا يوجد فيه الماء، كان كمن أحيا نفساً، و من أحيا نفساً فكأنما أحيا الناس جميعاً.

Whoever provides water in a place where water is readily available, he is like one who has emancipated a slave. Whoever provides water in a place where water is not readily available, he is like one who has saved a life, and whoever saved a life is as though he saved all mankind.[123]

The Martyrdom of the sons of al-Abbas ibn Ali (a)

ذكر السيد عبد الرزاق المقرم في كتابه (العباس قمر بني هاشم) ص 195: أنه كان للعباس (عليه السلام) خمسة أولاد: الفضل و عبيد الله و الحسن و القاسم و بنت واحدة. وعدّ ابن شهر اشوب في مناقبه من الشهداء يوم الطف من ولد العباس (عليه السلام): محمّد بن العباس (عليه السلام) أمه لبابة بنت عبيد الله بن العباس بن عبد المطلب. و ليس للعباس (عليه السلام) نسل إلا من ولده عبيد الله.

Sayyid Abdulrazzaq al-Muqarram mentioned in his book *al-Abbas Qamar Bani Hashem* (p. 195), "Al-Abbas had five children; al-Fadl, Obaydillah, al-Hassan, al-Qasim, and a daughter."

Ibn Shahrashoob counted Muhammad ibn al-Abbas amongst the martyrs of Karbala in his book *al-Manaqib*. [Muhammad's mother was said to be] Lubaba bint Obaydillah ibn al-Abbas ibn Abdulmuttalib. Al-Abbas did not have any surviving lineage except through his son Obaydillah.[124]

Al-Hussain's (a) Cry for Help

و لما قتل العباس (عليه السلام) التفت الحسين (عليه السلام) فلم ير أحدا

ينصره. و نظر إلى أهله و صحبه مجزّرين كالأضاحي، و هو إذ ذاك يسمع عويل

الأيامى و صراخ الأطفال، صاح بأعلى صوته:

After the martyrdom of al-Abbas, al-Hussain (a) looked around and
did not see anyone who would aid him. He saw his companions and
family members slaughtered like sacrificial lambs, while the wails of the
widows and the cries of the orphans rung in his ears. He cried in the
loudest of voices,

هل من ذابّ يذبّ عن حرم رسول الله (صلى الله عليه و آله و

سلم)؟ هل من موحّد يخاف الله فينا؟ هل من مغيث يرجو الله في

إغاثتنا؟ هل من معين يرجو ما عند الله في إعانتنا؟

Is there a defender who will defend the sanctity of the family of the
Messenger of God (s)? Is there a monotheist who fears God [and
will stand with us]? Is there a helper who will seek God by helping
us? Is there an aid who will seek the rewards of God by aiding
us?[125]

Al-Hussain (a) Bids the Hashemite Women Farewell

في (المنتخب): فدعا (عليه السلام) ببردة رسول الله (صلى الله عليه و آله و سلم) و التحف بها، و أفرغ عليه درعه الفاضل، و تقلّد سيفه، و استوى على متن جواده و هو غائص في الحديد. فأقبل على أم كلثوم (عليها السلام) و قال لها:

Al-Hussain (a) called for the mantle of the Messenger of God (s) and cloaked himself with it. He wore his blessed armor, carried his sword, and rode his horse, fully dressed in iron armor. He approached Umm Kulthum and said,

أوصيك يا أخيّة بنفسك خيرا، و إني بارز إلى هؤلاء القوم.

Take care of yourself, sister. I am stepping forward to battle this group.

فأقبلت سكينة و هي صارخة و كان يحبها حبا شديدا، فضمّها إلى صدره و مسح دموعها بكمه، و قال:

[His daughter] Sukayna ran to him wailing, and he used to love her immensly. He hugged her, wiped her tears with his sleave, and said [in verse],

سيطول بعدي يا سكينة فاعلمي * * * منك البكاء إذا الحمام دهاني

لا تحرقي قلبي بدمعك حسرة * * * ما دام مني الروح في جثماني

فإذا قتلت فأنت أولى بالذي * * * تأتينه يا خيرة النسوان

Know, O' Sukayna, that after me you will

212

Cry much, when death will over come me

Do not burn my heart with your agonizing tears

So long as my soul remains in my body

If I were slain, you will more justly

Continue your cries, O' best of women[126]

Al-Hussain (a) Elegizes Himself

قال أبو مخنف: ثم نادى (عليه السلام):

Al-Hussain (a) then cried out,

يا أم كلثوم و يا زينب و يا سكينة و يا رقية و يا عاتكة و يا صفية،
عليكنّ مني السلام، فهذا آخر الاجتماع، و قد قرب منكن الافتجاع.

*O' Umm Kulthum. O' Zaynab. O' Sukayna. O' Ruqaya. O'
'Atika. O' Safiyya. I bid you farewell, for this is our last meeting.
You will soon be grieving.*

فصاحت أم كلثوم: يا أخي كأنك استسلمت للموت! فقال لها الحسين (عليه
السلام):

Umm Kulthum cried out, "Brother! It is as if you have submitted to
death!" Al-Hussain (a) said to her,

يا أختاه فكيف لا يستسلم من لا ناصر له و لا معين!

*How can one who does not have a helper nor an aid not submit to
death?*

فقالت: يا أخي ردّنا إلى حرم جدنا. فقال لها:

She said, "Then return us to the [city] of our grandfather." He replied,

يا أختاه هيهات هيهات، لو ترك القطا ليلا لنام.

*O' Sister! Woe! Woe! [If there was any possible way for me to
fulfill your wish, I surely would have].*

رفعت سكينة صوتها بالبكاء و النحيب، فضمّها الحسين (عليه السلام) إلى
صدره الشريف و قبّلها و مسح دموعها بكمّه.

Sukayna began to cry and wail. Al-Hussain (a) hugged her, kissed her,
and wiped her tears with his sleeve.[127]

Another Farewell

(و في رواية) فنادى في تلك الحالة:

[In another narration] Al-Hussain (a) then called,

يا زينب يا أم كلثوم و يا سكينة يا رقية يا فاطمة، عليكنّ مني السلام.

O' Zaynab. O' Umm Kulthum. O' Sukayna. O' Ruqaya. O'
Fatima. I bid you farewell.

فأقبلت زينب (عليها السلام) فقالت: يا أخي، أيقنت بالقتل؟ فقال (عليه
السلام):

[Lady] Zaynab came to him and said, "O' brother, have you become
certain of your death [here]?" He replied,

كيف لا أيقن و ليس لي معين و لا نصير؟

How can I not be certain when I have no aid or supporter?

فقالت: يا أخي ردّنا إلى حرم جدنا. فقال (عليه السلام):

She said, "Brother, return us to the [city] of our grandfather." He
replied,

هيهات، لو تركت ما ألقيت نفسي في المهلكة، و كأنكم غير بعيد
كالعبيد، يسوقونكم أمام الركاب، و يسومونكم سوء العذاب.

Woe! If I were left to be I would not be [mourning myself]. You
will be soon like slaves, driven before the caravan and made to taste
the worst of torture.

فلما سمعته زينب (عليها السلام) بكت، و جرى الدموع من عينيه، و نادت: وا وحدتاه، وا قلة ناصراه، وا سوء منقلباه، وا شؤم صباحاه. فشقّت ثوبها و نشرت شعرها و لطمت على وجهها. فقال الحسين (عليه السلام):

When [Lady] Zaynab heard him, she cried. Tears flowed in his eyes. She cried out, "O' solitude! O' lack of support! O' dreadful end! O' cursed morn!" She tore her dress, disheveled her hair, and struck her face.* Al-Hussain (a) said to her,

مهلا لها، يا بنت المرتضى، إن البكاء طويل.

Have patience, O' daughter of al-Murtada. There is much time for weeping.

فأراد أن يخرج من الخيمة، فلصقت به زينب (عليها السلام) فقالت: مهلا يا أخي، توقّف حتى أزوّد من نظري، و أودّعك وداع مفارق لا تلاق بعده... فمهلا يا أخي قبل الممات هنيئة، لتبرد مني لوعة و غليل. فجعلت تقبّل يديه و رجليه. و أحطن به سائر النسوان...

He wanted to walk out of the tent, but she rushed to him and said, "Wait, brother! Stay so my sight can take its fill of you and so I can bid you the proper farewell after which we will never meet again... Wait here brother before rushing to death so that I can cool my anguish and thirst." She began to kiss his hands and feet as he was surrounded by the rest of the women.[128]

---

* Lady Zaynab was still in her tent when this took place.

Al-Hussain (a) Wears a Worn Cloth under his Clothes

ثم قال (عليه السلام) لأخته:

Al-Hussain (a) then said to his sister,

اتيني بثوب عتيق لا يرغب فيه أحد من القوم، أجعله تحت ثيابي لئلا أجرّد منه بعد قتلي.

Bring me an old piece of cloth that no one would want and that I can wear under my clothes so that I would not be robbed of it after my death.

فارتفعت أصوات النساء بالبكاء و النحيب. يقول السيد المقرّم في مقتله، ص 341: فأتوه بتبّان، فلم يرغب فيه لأنه من لباس الذلة. و أخذ ثوبا خلقا [أي باليا] و خرّقه و جعله تحت ثيابه، و دعا بسراويل حبرة ففزرها و لبسها لئلا يسلب منها.

The voices of the women rose in cries and wails. Al-Sayyid al-Muqarram says in his *Maqtal* (p. 341): They brought him a short trouser, but he refused it as it was a mark of humiliation. He took a piece of worn out clothing, ripped it, and wore it under his clothes. He called for knitted trousers and tore them before wearing them so that he would not be robbed of them.

و يقول السيد عبد الكريم الحسيني القزويني في (الوثائق الرسمية) ص 223: ثم إنه (عليه السلام) دعا بسروال يماني محكم النسج، يلمع فيه البصر، فخرّقه و

فزره، حتى لا يطمع فيه أحد، لأنه (عليه السلام) يعلم أنه يسلب بعد مقتله.

فقيل له: لو لبست تحته تبّانا- و هو سروال صغير- فقال (عليه السلام):

Sayyid Abdulkarim al-Hussaini al-Qazwini says in *al-Watha'eq al-Rasmiyya* (p. 223): He called for a Yemeni trouser of strurdy knitting [...]. He ripped and tore it so that no one would desire it, as he knew that he would be plundered after his martyrdom. He was asked, "Why do you not wear a short trouser under it?" He said,

ذلك ثوب مذلة، لا ينبغي لي أن ألبسه.

That is a mark of humiliation, it is not becoming of me to wear it.[129]

The Martyrdom of Another of al-Hussain's (a) Sons

و بينما الحسين (عليه السلام) جالس، عليه جبّة خز دكناء، و النبل يقع حوله،

فوقعت نبلة في ولد له ابن ثلاث سنين. فلبس لامته [أي درعه]. (أقول): لا

يبعد أن يكون هذا هو علي الأصغر (عليه السلام).

As al-Hussain (a) was sitting wearing a dark woolen cloak and arrows were raining around him, an arrow hit a son of his who was three years of age. He wore his armor [and set out to battle]. [This may be a reference to Ali al-Asghar].[130]

Zayn al-Abideen (a) Attempts to Enter Battle Despite Illness

ثم التفت الحسين (عليه السلام) عن يمينه و شماله فلم ير أحدا من الرجال. فخرج علي ابن الحسين (عليها السلام) و هو زين العابدين- و هو أصغر من أخيه علي القتيل- و كان مريضا بالذّرب. و نهض السجّاد (عليه السلام) يتوكأً على عصا و يجرّ سيفه، لأنه لا يقدر على حمله لمرضه، و أم كلثوم تنادي خلفه: يا بني ارجع. فقال:

Al-Hussain (a) looked left and right, but could not see a single man by his side. Ali ibn al-Hussain (a) - known as Zayn al-Abideen (a) and the younger brother of Ali al-Akbar - who was stricken by a stomach illness came out of his tent. He was leaning on a walking stick and dragging his sword, as he could not carry it due to his illness. Umm Kulthm was running behind him calling, "Come back, my son!" He replied,

يا عمتاه! ذريني أقاتل بين يدي ابن بنت رسول الله (صلى الله عليه و آله و سلم).

O' aunt. Leave me fight before the son of the daughter of the Messenger of God (s).

فصاح الحسين (عليه السلام) بأم كلثوم:

Al-Hussain (a) called to Umm Kulthum,

احبسيه لئلا تخلو الأرض من نسل آل محمّد (صلى الله عليه و آله و سلم).

Restrain him so that the earth is not deprived of the lineage of the family of Muhammad (s).

فأرجعته إلى فراشه.

Umm Kulthum took him back to his bed.[131]

Why did God Strike Zayn al-Abideen with illness?

حاول الإمام زين العابدين (عليه السلام) أن يخرج للجهاد رغم مرضه، فمنعه سيد الشهداء (عليه السلام). و الواقع أن الله تعالى قد أمرض سيد الساجدين، فطال زمان كونه عليلا ليسقط عنه الجهاد، حفظا للعالم عن أن ينهدم و يبيد. و قد أثر عن الحسين (عليه السلام) قوله:

Imam Zayn al-Abideen (a) attempted to go out for battle despite his illness, but [Imam Hussain] (a) prevented him from doing so. In reality, God Almighty has struck the Master of Worshippers (a) with an illness so that he would be relieved of the obligation of battle. This was so that the world does not crumble and dissipate [due to the eradication of the entire lineage of the Holy Prophet (s)]. It is narrated that al-Hussain (a) said,

و حاشا الله عزّ و جلّ شأنه الكبير المتعال، أن يبقي الأرض بلا حجة من نسلي.

Far be it from God - the Almighty, Most High, and Supremely Exalted - to leave the earth without a proof from my progeny.[132]

Al-Hussain (a) Asserts Multiple Times that Zayn al-Abideen (a) is Successor to Role of Imam

اعلم أن وصية سيد الشهداء (عليه السلام) على ولده سيد الساجدين (عليه السلام) و تنصيصاته بإمامته، كما أنها قد وقعت مرات عديدة قبل خروجه (عليه السلام) من المدينة، فكذا إنها قد وقعت مرات في كربلاء. و ما استفيد من الأخبار أنها وقعت في كربلاء أربع مرات: مرة في ليلة عاشوراء، و مرة في طلب زين العابدين (عليه السلام) الجهاد، و مرة قبيل شروع الإمام الحسين (عليه السلام) في الجهاد، و مرة بعد صدور مجاهدات كثيرة و قتل آلاف من الناس في جملة من الحملات منه (عليه السلام).

Know that the Master of Martyrs (a) bequested [his status as Imam] to his son, the Master of Worshippers (a), and asserted mutliple times that his son [Zayn al-Abideen (s)] is the successor to the role of Imam. This occured mutliple times in Medina and also multiple times in Karbala. What can be deduced from the narrations is that this occured four times in Karbala: Once on the eve of Ashura, once when Zayn al-Abideen (a) requested permission to enter battle, once before Imam Hussain (a) entered battle, and once after a number of skirmishes when [Imam Hussain (a)] had killed thousands of men in one of his assults.[133]

Imam Hussain's (a) Bequest to Zayn al-Abideen

عن (إثبات الوصية) قال: ثم أحضر علي بن الحسين (عليه السلام) و كان عليلا، فأوصى إليه بالاسم الأعظم و مواريث الأنبياء. و عرّفه أنه قد دفع العلوم و الصحف و المصاحف و السلاح إلى أم سلمة (رضي الله عنها) و أمرها أن تدفع جميع ذلك إليه.

In *Ithbat al-Wasiyya* it is said, "Then [Imam Hussain (a)] broguht forth Ali ibn al-Hussain (a), who was ill at the time, and bequested to him the Great Name of God along with the remainder of the inheritance of the prophets. He told him that he gave the books, scrolls, scriptures, and arms to Umm Salama and asked her to give them all to him [upon his return to Medina]."

و عنه أيضا: أن الحسين (عليه السلام) أوصى إلى أخته زينب بنت علي (عليها السلام) في الظاهر، فكان ما يخرج من علي بن الحسين (عليها السلام) في زمانه من علم ينسب إلى زينب (عليها السلام) عمته، سترا على علي بن الحسين (عليها السلام) و تقيّة و اتقاء عليه. و عن العلامة الكليني عن أبي جعفر الباقر (عليه السلام) أنه قال:

He also narrates, "Al-Hussain (a) outwardly bequested to his sister [Lady] Zaynab bint Ali (a), so that everything that came from Ali ibn al-Hussain (a) in that time was attributed to his aunt [Lady] Zaynab as a way of sheltering Ali ibn al-Hussain (a) and protecting him from harm." Allama al-Kulayni also narrates that Abu Jafar al-Baqir (a) said,

إن الحسين (عليه السلام) لما حضره الّذي حضر، دعا ابنته الكبرى فاطمة بنت الحسين (عليها السلام) فدفع إليها كتابا ملفوفا و وصية ظاهرة. و كان علي بن الحسين (عليه السلام) مبطونا معهم، لا يرون إلا أنه لما به. فدفعت فاطمة (عليها السلام) الكتاب إلى علي بن الحسين (عليها السلام). فيه و الله ما يحتاج إليه ولد آدم، منذ خلق الله آدم إلى أن تفنى الدنيا. و الله إن فيه الحدود، حتى أن فيه أرش الخدش.

When al-Hussain (a) met what he had met, he called to his eldest daughter Fatima bint al-Hussain (a) and gave her an apparent bequest along with a sealed scroll. Ali ibn al-Hussain (a) was amongst those present and those present did not see in him anything but his illness. Fatima then gave the scroll to Ali ibn al-Hussain (a) [away from the sights of those present]. By God, it contains everything that the sons of Adam may need, from the time of Adam's creation until the end of the world. By God, it contains all punishments, even the monetary damages for a scratch.[134]

The Martyrdom of Ali al-Asghar

اختلف الرواة في عدد أولاد الحسين (عليه السلام) الذين حضروا كربلاء، كما اختلفوا في أسمائهم. و قد حققنا سابقا أن عددهم أربعة هم: علي الأكبر (عليه السلام)- علي الأوسط و هو زين العابدين (عليه السلام)- علي الأصغر - عبد الله الرضيع. فمن الرواة ما اعتبر زين العابدين (عليه السلام) هو الأصغر، و لم يذكر علي الأصغر. و منهم من سمّى عبد الله الرضيع عليا الأصغر، و اعتبر عددهم ثلاثة.

Historians disagree about the number of al-Hussain's (a) children at the Battle of Karbala, as well as what their names were. We previously showed that they were in fact four; Ali al-Akbar, Ali al-Awsat who was known as Zayn al-Abideen (a), Ali al-Asghar, and the infant Abdullah.

Some historians considered Zayn al-Abideen as Ali al-Asghar and did not mention any other Ali al-Asghar. Others gave the name Ali al-Asghar to the infant Abdullah. Either way, these historians considered [the number of Imam Hussain's (a) children] at Karbala to be three.

و قد ذكر القرماني في (أخبار الدول و آثار الأول) شهادة علي الأصغر قبل شهادة علي الأكبر (عليه السلام)، و قال: و طلب الحسين (عليه السلام) ماء لولده الصغير علي الأصغر، فذهب علي الأكبر بركوة و ملأها من الشريعة و رجع. و أجلس الحسين (عليه السلام) ابنه على فخذه و همّ بسقيه، فأتاه سهم... يقول الفاضل الدربندي في (أسرار الشهادة) ص 404: و هذه الرواية كما ترى غير مستقيمة، و هي تنافي ما في الزيارة المروية من الناحية القائمية المقدسة.

Al-Qirmani recounted the martyrdom of Ali al-Asghar before Ali al-Akbar in his *Akhbar al-Duwal wa Aathar al-Uwal.* He wrote, "Al-Hussain (a) asked for water for his young son Ali al-Asghar. Ali al-Akbar took a pouch, filled it with water from the river, and returned. Al-Hussain (a) sat his son [Ali al-Asghar] on his lap and proceeded to give him the water. However, an arrow struck [Ali al-Asghar and killed him]."

Al-Fadil al-Darabandi says in *Asrar al-Shahada* (p. 404), "And this narration, as you can see, is not accurate. It contradicts what was mentioned in *Ziyarat al-Nahiya.*"

ثم يقول القرماني في (أخبار الدول) ص 108: و أصاب سهم ابنا للحسين (عليه السلام) و هو في حجره، فجعل يمسح الدم عنه و يقول:

Al-Qirmani continues in *Akhbar al-Duwal* (p. 108): And an arrow struck one of the sons of al-Hussain (a) while he was in his lap. [Al-Hussain (a)] wiped the blood off him and said,

اللّهم احكم بيننا و بين قوم دعونا لينصرونا فقتلونا.

O' God, be the judge between us and a people who called us in order to support us but are instead killing us.

و أتي بصبي صغير من أولاده (عليه السلام) اسمه عبد الله [الظاهر أنه الرضيع]، فحمله و قبّله، فرماه رجل من بني أسد [لعله حرملة بن كاهل الأسدي] فذبح ذلك الغلام. فتلقى الحسين (عليه السلام) دمه في يده و ألقاه نحو السماء، و قال:

Another of al-Hussain's (a) children, Abdullah [the infant], was brought to him. He carried the boy and kissed him. A man from the tribe of Asad shot an arrow and killed the boy. Al-Hussain (a) took the blood in his hands and threw it towards the sky, saying,

يا رب إن تكن حبست عنا النصر من السماء، فاجعله لنا خيرا، و
انتقم من الظالمين.

*O' Lord, if you have kept victory away from us, make [death] a
blessing for us and exact vengeance from the oppressors.*

ابن أعثم في (كتاب الفتوح) ج 5 ص 209 يقول: فبقي الحسين (عليه السلام)
فريدا وحيدا، ليس معه ثان إلا ابنه علي (عليه السلام) و هو يومئذ ابن سبع
سنين [أقول: هذا خطأ من الناسخ، و لعل عمره سبع عشرة سنة، و هو زين
العابدين (عليه السلام)]. و له ابن آخر يقال له علي في الرضاع. فتقدم إلى باب
الخيمة، فقال:

As for Ibn al-A'tham, he writes in *al-Futuh* (v. 5 p. 209): Al-Hussain (a)
remained alone with no supporters. No one remained with him but his
son Ali (a) who was then [seventeen] years old. He had another son
named Ali who was an still an infant. Al-Hussain (a) came o the tent
and said,

ناولوني ذلك الطفل حتى أودّعه.

Hand me the child so that I can bid him farewell.'

و إذا بسهم قد أقبل حتى وقع في لبّة الصبي، فقتله.

Suddenly, an arrow struck boy at the base of the neck, killing him.[135]

The Martyrdom of the Infant Abdullah

ثم تقدم (عليه السلام) إلى باب الخيمة و قال:

Al-Hussain (a) then went to the tent and said,

ناولوني ولدي الرضيع لأودعه.

Hand me my infant son so that I can bid him farewell.

فأتته زينب (عليها السلام) بابنه عبد الله [و قد سماه ابن شهر اشوب: علي
الأصغر] و أمه الرباب بنت امرئ القيس، فأجلسه في حجره و جعل يقبّله و
يقول:

[Lady] Zaynab came to him with his son Abdullah [who was called by
Ibn Shahrashoob 'Ali al-Asghar'], whose mother was al-Rabab bint
Imra' al-Qays. He took him in his arms and kissed him, saying,

بعدا لهؤلاء القوم، إذا كان خصمهم جدك المصطفى.

*May God distance these people [from His mercy], as their
adversary [on the Day of Judgment will be] your great-grandfather
al-Mustafa (s).*

ثم أتى (عليه السلام) بالرضيع نحو القوم يطلب له الماء، و قال لهم:

He took the infant and approach the enemy, asking them to give him
some water. He said to them,

لقد جفّت محالب أمه، فهل إلى شربة من ماء سبيل؟ [...] يا قوم،
إذا كنت أقاتلكم و تقاتلوني، فما ذنب هذا الطفل حتى تمنعوا عنه
الماء؟!

*His mother's milk has dried up, so is there a way for him to have
a sip of water? [...] O' people, if I fight you and you fight me,
what is the crime of this child that you deny him water?*

(و في رواية) أنه قال:

Another narrations states that he said,

إذا لم ترحموني فارحموا هذا الطفل.

If you will not have mercy on me, then have mercy on this child.

فمنهم من رقّ قلبه للطفل، و قال: اسقوه شربة من ماء، و منهم من قال: لا
تسقوه و لا ترحموه! فخاف عمر بن سعد أن يدبّ النزاع في صفوف جيشه،
فقال لحرملة بن كاهل الأسدي و كان راميا: اقطع نزاع القوم.

Some amongst them felt sympathetic and said, "Give him a sip of
water." Other said, "Do not give him water or show him ant mercy!"
Omar ibn Saad feared that there would be discord in the ranks of his
army. He turned to Harmala ibn Kahil al-Asadi, a well-known archer,
and said, "End these people's dispute!"

فسدد حرملة سهمه نحو عنق الصبي، فرماه بسهم فذبحه من الوريد إلى الوريد،
و هو لائذ بحجر أبيه. فأخذ الطفل يفحص من ألم الجروح، و يرفرف كما يرفرف
الطير المذبوح، و دمه يشخب من أوداجه، و الحسين (عليه السلام) يتلقّى
دمه من نحره حتى امتلأت كفه، ثم رمى به نحو السماء. قال الإمام الباقر (عليه
السلام):

Harmala aimed his arrow at the boy's neck. The arrow stuck the infant
and severed his jugular as he was in his father's arms. The infant began
to squirm with pain, fluttering like a wounded bird. Blood flowed from

his veins and al-Hussain (a) took it in his hands. He threw a handful of blood to the sky. Imam al-Baqir (a) said,

فما وقع منه قطرة إلى الأرض، و لو وقعت منه إلى الأرض قطرة لنزل العذاب.

Not a drop of [that blood] fell to earth. If a single drop had touched the earth, [God's] punishment would have befell [the enemy army].

ثم قال (عليه السلام):

[Al-Hussain (a)] then said,

هوّن ما نزل بي أنه بعين الله تعالى. اللّهم لا يكن أهون عليك من فصيل ناقة صالح. إلهي إن كنت حبست عنا النصر [من السماء]، فاجعله لما هو خير منه، و انتقم لنا من [هؤلاء القوم] الظالمين و اجعل ما حلّ بنا في العاجل ذخيرة لنا في الآجل. اللّهم أنت الشاهد على قوم قتلوا أشبه الناس برسولك محمّد (صلى الله عليه و آله و سلم).

What has befallen me is only eased because it is all in the eyes of God. O' God, [let this infant] not be of less significance to you than the calf of Saleh's she-camel. O' God, if you have kept victory away from us, then let it be for something greater. Exact our vengeance from the oppressors. Let what has befallen us in the present be our provision for the Hereafter. O' God, be witness to a people who have killed the one most similar to Your Messenger Muhammad (s).

فسمع (عليه السلام) مناديا من السماء:

He heard a caller from the heavens say,

دعه يا حسين فإن له مرضعا في الجنة.

Leave him, O' Hussain (a), for he has a wet-nurse [awaiting him]
in paradise!

ثم نزل (عليه السلام) عن فرسه، و حفر له بجفن سيفه، و دفنه مرمّلا بدمه،
و صلّى عليه. و يقال: وضعه مع قتلى أهل بيته.

[Al-Hussain (a)] came down from his horse, dug a grave with the
sheath of his sword, buried the child covered in dust and blood, and
prayed over him. It is also said that he put him with the rest of the
martyrs of his family.[136]

What Happened After the Martyrdom of the Infant?

و هكذا بدأ شلال الدم ينحدر على أرض كربلاء، و سحب المأساة تتجمع في آفاقها الكئيبة، و صيحات العطش و الرعب تتعالى من حول الحسين (عليه السلام) و تنبعث من حناجر النساء و الأطفال.

Thus, the deluge of blood soaked the sands of Karbala as the clouds of tragedy amassed over its mournful horizon. The cries of thirst and terror coming from the women and children grew louder around al-Hussain (a).[137]

Al-Hussain (a) Mourns his Martyred Companions

ثم توجّه (عليه السلام) نحو القوم و قال:

[Al-Hussain (a)] then turned to the enemy and said,

يا ويلكم علام تقاتلوني؛ على حقّ تركته، أم على سنّة غيّرتها، أم على
شريعة بدّلتها؟!

*Woe to you! Why do you fight me? For a truth that I have
abondened? Or for a tradition that I have replaced? Or for a divine
ruling that I have changed?*

فقالوا: بل نقاتلك بغضا منا لأبيك و ما فعل بأشياخنا يوم بدر و حنين. فلما
سمع كلامهم بكى و جعل ينظر يمينا و شمالا فلم ير أحدا من أنصاره إلا من صافح
التراب جبينه، و من قطع الحمام أنينه. فنادى:

They replied, "We fight you out of hatred for your father and for what
he did to our elders on the days of Badr and Hunayn." When he heard
their words, he began to cry and looked left and right. He did not find
any of his companions that had not embraced the dust and had death
end his sighs. He cried out,

يا مسلم بن عقيل و يا هانئ بن عروة و يا حبيب بن مظاهر و يا
زهير بن القين [...]يا أبطال الصفا، و يا فرسان الهيجا، مالي أناديكم
فلا تجيبون، و أدعوكم فلا تسمعون! أنتم نيام، أرجوكم تنتبهون، أم
حالت مودتكم عن إمامكم فلا تنصروه! هذه نساء الرسول (صلى الله
عليه و آله و سلم) لفقدكم قد علاهن النحول.

235

O' Muslim ibn Aqeel! O' Hani ibn Urwa! O' Habib ibn Mudhahir! O' Zuhair ibn al-Qayn! [...] O' heroes in times of peace! O' knights in times of war! Why is it that I call you and you do not answer? Why do I cry out to you and you do not listen? If you are asleep, please awaken! Has your love for your Imam been shaken so that you are not aiding him? These are the women of the [family of the] Messenger of God (s), weakened by your absence.

فقوموا عن نومتكم أيها الكرام، و ادفعوا عن حرم الرسول الطغاة اللئام. و لكن صرعكم و الله ريب المنون، و غدر بكم الدهر الخؤون، و إلا لما كنتم عن نصرتي تقصّرون، و لا عن دعوتي تحتجبون. فها نحن عليكم مفتجعون، و بكم لاحقون. فإنا لله و إنا إليه راجعون.

Wake up from your slumber, O' most honorable of men! Repel these evil tyrants away from the family of the Messenger of God (s)! Alas! By God, the calamities of the time have beaten you! This treacherous age has betrayed you! Otherwise, you would not fall short in aiding me! You would not ignore my calls! We are bereaved [at your loss] and will soon follow you. Indeed, we are of God and to Him we shall return.[138]

Al-Dahhak ibn Abdullah al-Mashriqi Leaves the Battle

عن الضحاك بن عبد الله المشرقي، قال: لما رأيت أصحاب الحسين (عليه السلام) قد أصيبوا، و قد خلص إليه و إلى أهل بيته، و لم يبق معه غير سويد بن عمرو بن أبي المطاع الخثعمي و بشير بن عمرو الحضرمي، قلت له: يابن رسول الله، قد علمت ما كان بيني و بينك؛ قلت لك: أقاتل عنك ما رأيت مقاتلا، فإذا لم أر مقاتلا فأنا في حلّ من الانصراف! فقلت لي: نعم! فقال (عليه السلام):

Al-Dahhak ibn Abdullah al-Mashriqi said: When I saw that the companions of al-Hussain (a) were felled and none remained except him and his household along with only Suwaid ibn Amr ibn Abi al-Muta' al-Khath'ami and Basheer ibn Amd al-Hadrami, I said to him, 'O' son of the Messenger of God (s), you remember what occured between you and I. I told you, "I will fight protecting you so long as I see other fighting so. When I see that no fighter remaining, I will be free to have my leave." You said to me, "Yes [I accept your condition].'" [Al-Hussain] (a) said,

صدقت، و كيف لك بالنجاة؟ إن قدرت على ذلك فأنت في حل!

Yes, it is true. But how will you escape? If you are able to do so, then you are free [of any obligation to me].

فأقبلت إلى فرسي، و قد كنت - حيث رأيت خيل أصحابنا تعقر- أقبلت بها حتى أدخلتها فسطاطا لأصحابنا من البيوت، و أقبلت أقاتل معهم راجلا، فقتلت يومئذ بين يدي الحسين (عليه السلام) رجلين، و قطعت يد آخر [...]. فلما

أذن لي استخرجت الفرس من الفسطاط [...] و اتّبعني منهم خمسة عشر رجلا، حتى انتهيت إلى (شفية) قرية قريبة من شاطئ الفرات.

So I went to my horse - which I had hid in a tent when I saw our horses being slain and began to fight on foot, killing two in protection of al-Hussain (a) and severing the arm of another. [...] When he gave me permission I pulled the horse out of the tent [and rode off with it]. Fifteen enemy soldiers followed me until I reached Shafya, a town close to the banks of the Euphrates.

فلما لحقوني عطفت عليهم، فعرفني كثير بن عبد الله الشعبي و أيوب بن مشرح الخيواني و قيس بن عبد الله الصائدي، فقالوا: هذا الضحاك بن عبد الله المشرقي، هذا ابن عمنا، ننشدكم الله لما كففتم عنه. فقال ثلاثة نفر من بني تميم كانوا معهم: بلى و الله لنجيبنّ إخواننا و أهل دعوتنا إلى ما أحبوا من الكف عن صاحبهم. قال: فلما تابع التميميون أصحابي كفّ الآخرون. قال: فنجّاني الله.

When they caught up to me, I turned and faced them. I was recognized by Katheer ibn Abdullah al-Sha'bi, Ayyoub ibn Mashrah al-Khaywani, and Qays ibn Abdullah al-Sa'edi, who said, 'This is al-Dahhak ibn Abdullah al-Mashriqi. He is our cousin. By God, we beseach you to let him be.' Three individuals of Bani Tameem said, 'Yes. By God, we will answer the call of our brothers and supporters to what they like by leaving their companion be.' When the men of Tameem followed my companions, the rest stopped. Thus, God saved me [from death].[139]

The Martyrdom of al-Hussain

Verses of Poetry from al-Hussain (a)

ثم وثب (عليه السلام) قائمًا، و [إمتدح جده رسول الله (ص) وأباه أمير المؤمنين (ع) وأمه فاطمة الزهراء]. ثم حمل (عليه السلام) على الميمنة، و هو يقول:

Al-Hussain (a) then stood and [recited verses of poetry in praise of his grandfather the Prophet (s), his father the Commander of the Faihtful (a), and his mother Lady Fatima (a)]. He then charged at the enemy's right flank, saying,

الموت أولى من ركوب العار * * * و العار أولى من دخول النار

و الله من هذا و هذا جاري

Death is better than living in humiliation

And humiliation is better than entering hellfire

But God is my refuge from both these ills!

و حمل على الميسرة، و هو يقول:

He charged at the enemy's left flank, saying,

أنا الحسين بن علي * * * آليت ألا أنثني

أحمي عيالات أبي * * * أمضي على دين النبي

I am al-Hussain ibn Ali (a)!

I have sworn not to bend [to my enemies]!

I will protect the family of my father!

I will continue on the religion of the Prophet (s)![140]

An Arrow Strikes al-Hussain's (a) Jaw (1)

و اشتدّ العطش بالحسين فمنعوه. فحصل له شربة ماء، فلمّا أهوى ليشرب رماه

حصين بن نمير بسهم في حنكه، فصار الماء دما. ثمّ رفع يده إلى السماء و هو

يقول:

Thirst overpowered al-Hussain (a), but the enemies blocked him [from reaching the river]. He was finally able to acquire a bit of water, but when he attempted to drink it Hossayn ibn Numair struck him with an arrow in his jaw. Blood flowed into the water [and he was no longer able to drink it]. Al-Hussain (a) then raised his hands to the heavens and said,

اللّهم أحصهم عددا، و اقتلهم بددا، و لا تذر على الأرض منهم أحدا.

O' God, tally their number, kill them in small groups, and do not leave a single one of them on this earth![141]

An Arrow Strikes al-Hussain's (a) Jaw (2)

و اشتد العطش بالحسين (عليه السلام) فركب المسناة يريد الفرات، فاعترضته

خيل ابن سعد، فرمى رجل من بني دارم الحسين (عليه السلام) بسهم، فأثبته

في حنكه الشريف، فانتزع السهم و بسط يديه تحت حنكه حتى امتلأت راحتاه

من الدم، ثم رمى به و قال:

Thirst overpowered al-Hussain (a) so he rode towards the river bank. The cavalry of Ibn Saad cut off his route and a man from Banu Darim shot him with an arrow that struck his noble jaw. He pulled out the arrow and placed his hands under his jaw until his palms were filled with blood. He then threw it toward the heavens and said,

اللّهم إني أشكو إليك ما يفعل بابن بنت نبيك.

O' God, I complain to you of what is being done to the son of You Prophet's (s) daughter![142]

Al-Hussain (a) was Killed Thirsty

و منعوا الحسين (عليه السلام) من الماء في يوم شديد الحر، و صاروا يتراءون إليه بكيزان من البلور مملوءة ماء باردا، فيقول:

[The enemy army] cut off water from al-Hussain (a) on a day of severe heat. They began to parade crystalline cups filled with cold water as he would say,

أقسم عليكم بجدّي إلا سقيتموني شربة أبرّد بها كبدي.

I swear to you by my grandfather that you should give me a sip to cool my body!

فلم يجيبوه.

They would not answer his call.[143]

Thirst Takes its Toll on al-Hussain (a)

و لقد أثر العطش في الحسين (عليه السلام) في أربعة مواضع من أعضائه الشريفة: الكبد و الشقّة و اللسان و العين. الشفة ذابلة من الأوام، و الكبد مفتّت من حرّ الظمأ، و اللسان مجروح من كثرة اللوك في الفم، و العين من شدة العطش مظلمة.

Thirst affected al-Hussain (a) in four areas of his noble body; his livers, lips, tongue, and eyes. His lips were withered and his liver was severly damaged due to thirst. His tongue was gashed [due to the failure of his salvitory glands]. His eyesight was blurred [due to dehydration].[144]

Al-Hussain (a) is Cut Off from his Camp

ثم إنه (عليه السلام) دعا الناس إلى البراز، فلم يزل يقتل كلّ من دنا إليه من
عيون الرجال، حتى قتل منهم مقتلة عظيمة، فحالوا بينه و بين رحله، فصاح بهم:

Al-Hussain (a) then called the enemy to duel. He continued to fell any
warrior who would approach him until he killed a great many of them.
The enemy then cut him off from his camp. Al-Hussain (a) called out,

و يحكم يا شيعة آل أبي سفيان، إن لم يكن لكم دين، و كنتم لا تخافون
المعاد، فكونوا أحرارا في دنياكم هذه، و ارجعوا إلى أحسابكم إن كنتم
عربا كما تزعمون!

*Woe to you, followers of Abu Sufyan's family! If you have no
religion and you do not fear the Resurrection, then [at least] be free
in this world of yours! Return to your roots if you are Arabs as
you claim!*

فناداه شمر: ما تقول يا حسين؟ فقال (عليه السلام):

Al-Shimr asked, "What are you saying, O' Hussain (a)?" He replied,

أقول أنا الّذي أقاتلكم و تقاتلوني، و النساء ليس عليهن جناح، فامنعوا
عتاتكم و طغاتكم و جهّالكم عن التعرّض لحرمي ما دمت حيّا.

*I say that I am the one fighting you and you are fighting me. The
women have committed no crime. Forbid your defiant, savage, and
ignorant [soldiers] from attacking my family so long as I live!*

قال له شمر: لك ذلك يا بن فاطمة. ثم صاح شمر بأصحابه: إليكم عن حرم الرجل
و اقصدوه بنفسه، فلعمري لهو كفو كريم.

Al-Shimr said, "You shall have that, O' son of Fatima (a)." Then he looked at his soldiers and cried out, "Leave the man's family and attack him! By my life, he is a noble opponent!"[145]

The Enemies Deceive al-Hussain (a)

فقصده القوم، و هو مع ذلك يطلب شربة من الماء. و كلما حمل بفرسه على الفرات حملوا عليه بأجمعهم فخلّوؤه عنه. ثم حمل على الأعور السلمي و عمرو بن الحجاج و كانا في أربعة آلاف رجل، على الشريعة ففرّقهم، و أقحم الفرس في الفرات. فلما ولغ الفرس برأسه ليشرب، قال (عليه السلام):

The enemies charged at him while he continued to seek a drink of water. Whenever he approached the Euphrates on his horse, the enemy would charge at him and repel him [from the river].

Al-Hussain (a) then charged at al-A'war al-Salami and Amr ibn al-Hajjaj, who were commanding four thousand men. He scrambled their troops and rode his horse into the Euphrates. When the horse lowered its head to drink, al-Hussain (a) said,

أنت عطشان و أنا عطشان، و الله لا ذقت حتى تشرب!

You are thirsty and I am thirsty. By God, I will not drink until you do!

فرفع الفرس رأسه كأنه فهم الكلام. فقال الحسين (عليه السلام):

The horse raised its head as if it had understood his words. Al-Hussain (a) then said,

اشرب.

Drink!

و لما مدّ الحسين (عليه السلام) يده فغرف من الماء غرفة ليشرب، ناداه رجل من القوم: يا أبا عبد الله، أتتلذّ بشرب الماء و قد هتك حرمك؟! فنفض الماء من يده، و حمل على القوم فكشفهم، فإذا الخيمة سالمة، فعلم أنها حيلة.

And when al-Hussain (a) took a handful of water to drink, an enemy soldier called out, "O' Abu Abdullah (a)! Do you saver a drink of water while your family is being attacked?" He threw the water in his hand and charged at the enemy, repelling them [from his way]. [When he got to the camp] he saw that the tents were safe and knew that the enemy had deceived him.[146]

A Second Farewell

ثم إنه (عليه السلام) ودّع عياله ثانيا، و أمرهم بالصبر و لبس الأزر، و قال:

Al-Hussain (a) then bade farewell to his family again, instructing them to remain patient and perseverant. He said,

استعدوا للبلاء، و اعلموا أن الله تعالى حاميكم و حافظكم و سينجيكم
من شرّ الأعداء، و يجعل عاقبة أمركم إلى خير، و يعذّب عدوكم بأنواع
العذاب، و يعوّضكم عن هذه البلية بأنواع النعم و الكرامة، فلا
تشكوا، و لا تقولوا بألسنتكم ما ينقص من قدركم.

Be ready for tribulation. Know that God Almighty will guard and protect you, saving you from the evils of the enemy. He will deliver you to a great end. He will punish your enemy with all kinds of punishments. He will reward you for this trial with all kinds of blessings and honors. So do not complain and do not say with your own tongues what would reduce of your status.

فقال ابن سعد: و يحكم اهجموا عليه مادام مشغولا بنفسه و حرمه، و الله إن
فرغ لكم لا تمتاز ميمنتكم عن ميسرتكم. فحملوا عليه يرمونه بالسهام، حتى تخالفت
السهام بين أطناب الخيم. و شكّ سهم بعض أزر [جمع إزار] النساء، فدهشن
و أرعبن و صحن، و دخلن الخيمة ينظرن إلى الحسين (عليه السلام) كيف يصنع.

Omar ibn Saad then said [to his soldiers], "Woe to you! Attack him while he is preoccupied with himself and his family. By God, if he were to turn to you, [he would scatter you so that] your right flank will be indistinguishable from your left!"

They attacked him, pelting him with arrows that ripped through the tents. Some tents ripped through the veils of the women. They began to cry, startled and terrified. They rushed to al-Hussain's (a) tent to see what he will do.[147]

An Arrow Strikes al-Hussain's (a) Forehead

فقصده القوم بالحرب من كل جانب، فجعل يحمل عليهم و يحملون عليه، و هو في ذلك يطلب الماء ليشرب منه شربة، فكلما حمل بفرسه على الفرات حملوا عليه حتى أجلوه عنه. ثم رماه رجل يقال له أبو الحتوف الجعفي بسهم فوقع السهم في جبهته (و في مقتل أبي مخنف: أن الّذي رماه هو خولي، و قيل إنه قدامة العامري). فنزع الحسين (عليه السلام) السهم و رمى به، فسال الدم على وجهه و لحيته. فقال:

The enemies attacked al-Hussain (a) from every direction. He charged at them as they charged at him. He would try to charge toward the river to get a drink, but whenever his horse approached the Euphrates, the enemies would charge at him and repel him from the river.

Then a man name Abu al-Hutuf al-Ju'fi shot him with an arrow that hit him in the forehead [Abu Makhnaf says the archer was Khawli, while others say it was Qudama al-Amiri]. Al-Hussain (a) pulled the arrow out and threw it to the ground, while blood gushed on his face and beard. He said,

اللّهم قد ترى ما أنا فيه من عبادك هؤلاء العصاة العتاة، اللّهم فأحصهم عددا، و اقتلهم بددا، و لا تذر على وجه الأرض منهم أحدا، و لا تغفر لهم أبدا.

O' God, You see what I suffer at the hands of your disobedient and defiant servants! O' God, tally their number, kill them in small groups, do not leave a single one of them on this earth, and do not ever forgive their misdeeds!

ثم حمل عليهم كالليث المغضب، فجعل لا يلحق أحدا إلا بعجه بسيفه و ألحقه بالحضيض، و السهام تأخذه من كل ناحية، و هو يتلقاها بنحره و صدره و يقول:

He charged at the enemy like an angered lion. He would strike each man once with his sword and fell him. All the while, arrows rained down on him from every direction, striking him in his chest and neck. He would say,

يا أمة السوء، بئسما خلّفتم محمدا في عترته. أما إنكم لن تقتلوا بعدي عبدا من عباد الله الصالحين فتهابوا قتله، بل يهون عليكم عند قتلكم إياي. و ايم الله إني لأرجو أن يكرمني ربي بهوانكم، ثم ينتقم منكم من حيث لا تشعرون.

O' nation of misfortune! How wrongly you have treated Muhammad's (s) family after his passing! Surely, you will never kill any of God's righteous servants after me and fear the consequence. Rather, it will pale in comparison after you kill me. By God, I hope that my Lord will honor me through your demise, and that He should avenge me while you are unaware [of His reprisal]!

فصاح به الحصين بن مالك السكوني: يابن فاطمة، بماذا ينتقم لك منا؟ فقال (عليه السلام):

Al-Hossayn ibn Malik al-Sakuni asked him, "O' son of Fatima (a)! How will He avenge you?" He said,

يلقي بأسكم بينكم، و يسفك دماءكم، ثم يصبّ عليكم العذاب الأليم.

He will turn your enmity toward one another, [so that you] shed [each other's] blood. He will then heap upon you a most painful punishment.

(و في مقتل المقرم، ص 350) قال: و رجع إلى مركزه يكثر من قول:

Al-Muqarram says in his *Maqtal* (p. 350): Then he returned to his base, continuously saying,

لا حول و لا قوة إلا بالله العلي العظيم.

There is no power or authority save from God, the Most High and Glorious.

و طلب في هذا الحال ماء، فقال الشمر: لا تذوقه حتى ترد النار. و ناداه رجل: يا حسين ألا ترى الفرات كأنه بطون الحيات؟ فلا تشرب منه حتى تموت عطشا! فقال الحسين (عليه السلام):

In this state, he asked [the enemy] for water, but al-Shimr said, "You will not taste it until you reach hellfire!" Another man called out, "O' Hussain, do you not see the Euphrates [flowing] like the belly of a snake? You will not drink of it until you die of thirst!" Al-Hussain (a) said,

اللهم أمته عطشا.

O' God, kill him of thirst.

فكان ذلك الرجل يطلب الماء، فيؤتى به فيشرب حتى يخرج من فيه، و ما زال كذلك إلى أن مات عطشا.

[Afterwards], that man would continue to ask for water and drink until it would spew out of his mouth. He was like this until he died thirsty.[148]

The Enemies Split into Three Divisions

إن الشمر أقبل إلى ابن سعد و قال له: أيها الأمير إن هذا الرجل يفنينا عن

آخرنا مبارزة. قال: كيف نصنع به؟. قال: نتفرّق عليه ثلاث فرق: فرقة بالنبال

و السهام، و فرقة بالسيوف و الرماح، و فرقة بالنار و الحجارة، نعجل عليه.

فجعلوا يرشقونه بالسهام، و يطعنونه بالرماح، و يضربونه بالسيوف، حتى أثخنوه

بالجراح.

Al-Shimr approached Ibn Saad and said, "Commander, this man will kill us all [if we continue to] duel him [one by one]." Ibn Saad asked, "So what should we do?" Al-Shimr replied, "We should split against him into three divisions; one [to pelt him] with arrows and bolts, one [to strike him] with swords and spears, and one [to attack him] with fire and stones. Thus, we will soon fell him." They began to pelt him with their arrows, stab him with their spears, and strike him with their swords until he was overcome with wounds.[149]

A Man Almost Killed al-Hussain (a)

روى الطبري عن أبي مخنف عن الحجاج بن عبد الله بن عمار بن عبد يغوث
البارقي، أنه عتب على عبد الله بن عمار مشهده قتل الحسين (عليه السلام).
فقال عبد الله بن عمار: إن لي عند بني هاشم ليدا [أي معروفا]. قلنا له: و ما
يدك عندهم؟ قال: حملت على حسين بالرمح، فانتهيت إليه، فو الله لو شئت
لطعنته. ثم انصرفت عنه غير بعيد، و قلت: ما أصنع بأن أتولى قتله، يقتله
غيري!

Al-Tabari relays from Abu Makhnaf from al-Hajjaj ibn Abdullah ibn
Ammar al-Bariqi that Abdullah ibn Ammar was once chastised for
witnessing the killing of al-Hussain (a) [and being in the army of Omar
ibn Saad]. Abdullah ibn Ammar replied, "Surely, I have gained favor
with the Banu Hashem!" He was asked, "And what favor have you
gained?" He said, "I charged at al-Hussain (a) with a spear. I reached
him and - by God - I could have stabbed him had I wanted to. But I
turned and walked away, saying, 'Why would I bear the responsibility
of killing him? Let another man kill him!'"[150]

Al-Hussain's (a) Bravery and Resolve

فشدّ عليه رجّالة ممن عن يمينه و شماله، فحمل على من عن يمينه حتى ابذعرّوا،
و على من عن شماله حتى ابذعرّوا، و عليه قميص له من خز، و هو معتمّ.

Infantrymen charged at him from left and right. He charged at his
enemies at the right and fought them until he repelled them. He
charged at his enemies at the left and fought them until he repelled
them. He was wearing a woolen robe and a turban.[151]

Al-Hussain (a) on the Battlefield

قال عبد الله بن عمار بن يغوث: [فو الله] ما رأيت مكثورا قط، قد قتل ولده و أهل بيته و صحبه، أربط جأشا منه، و لا أمضى جنانا، و لا أجرأ مقدما. و لقد كانت الرجال تنكشف بين يديه إذا شدّ فيها، و لم يثبت له أحد.

Abdullah ibn Ammar ibn Yaghuth said, "By God, I have not seen a man outnumbered so, with his sons, kin, and companions all murdered, with stronger resolve, nor a more firm heart, nor more valor in his actions! Men would scatter before him if he charge at them so that no man stood before him!"

(و في رواية اللّهوف، ص 67): و إن كانت الرجال لتشدّ عليه فيشدّ عليها بسيفه، فتنكشف عنه انكشاف المعزى إذا شدّ فيها الذئب. و لقد كان يحمل فيهم و قد تكمّلوا ثلاثين ألفا، فينهزمون بين يديه كأنهم الجراد المنتشر، ثم يرجع إلى مركزه و هو يقول:

[Ibn Tawwus] says in *al-Luhuf* (p. 67): Men would charge at him and he would charge at them, scattering them like sheep attacked by a wolf. He would charge at an army of thirty thousand men and scatter them like a swarm of locust. He would then return to his base, saying,

لا حول و لا قوة إلا بالله.

There is no power or authority save in God, the Most High and Glorious!

(و في مثير الأحزان للجواهري، ص 85): و لم يزل يقاتل حتى قتل ألف رجل و تسعمائة و خمسين رجلا، سوى المجروحين. فقال عمر بن سعد لقومه: الويل

258

لكم، أتدرون لمن تقاتلون؟ هذا ابن الأنزع البطين، هذا ابن قتّال العرب، احملوا

عليه (حملة رجل واحد) من كل جانب. فأتته أربعة آلاف نبلة.

Al-Jawahiri says in *Mutheer al-Ahzan* (p. 85): He continued to fight until he killed one thousand, nine hundred, and fifty men and wounded others.

Omar ibn Saad then said, "Woe to you, do you know who you are fighting? This is the son of [Ali ibn Abu Talib (a)]! This is the son of the killer of Arabs! Charge at him at once from every direction." [Omar Ibn Saad's army shot at al-Hussain (a)] with four thousand arrows.[152]

A Poisoned Arrow Strikes al-Hussain (a)

ثم جعل (عليه السلام) يقاتل حتى أصابته اثنتان و سبعون جراحة، فوقف يستريح و قد ضعف عن القتال. فبينا هو واقف إذ أتاه حجر فوقع على جبهته، فسالت الدماء من جبهته. فأخذ الثوب ليمسح [الدم] عن جبهته، فأتاه سهم محدّد مسموم له ثلاث شعب، فوقع في قلبه [و قيل في صدره]. فقال الحسين (عليه السلام):

Al-Hussain (a) continued to fight until he had been wounded seventy two times. He became too weak to fight and stopped to rest. As he was resting, a stone struck him on the forehead and blood began to rush out of the wound. As he took a piece of his clothes to wipe his forehead, a sharp, poisoned, three pronged arrow struck him in the chest. Al-Hussain (a) said,

بسم الله و بالله و على ملّة رسول الله.

In the name of God! [I rely] on God and follow the religion of the Messenger of God (s)!

و رفع رأسه إلى السماء، و قال:

He then raised his head to the heavens and said,

إلهي إنك تعلم أنهم يقتلون رجلا ليس على وجه الأرض ابن نبي غيره.

O' God, You surely know that they are killing a man while knowing that there is no son of a prophet on the face of the earth but him!

ثم أخذ السهم و أخرجه من وراء ظهره، فانبعث الدم كالميزاب، فوضع يده على الجرح، فلما امتلأت دما رمى به إلى السماء، فما رجع من ذلك قطرة. و ما عرفت

الحمرة في السماء حتى رمى الحسين (عليه السلام) بدمه إلى السماء. ثم وضع يده

على الجرح ثانيا، فلما امتلأت لطّخ بها رأسه و لحيته، و قال:

He took the arrow and drew it out from his back while his blood
flowed like a fountain. He put his hand on the wound until it was filled
with blood, then threw the blood toward the heavens. Not a drop of
it fell back to the earth. Redness was not seen in the sky before al-
Hussain (a) threw his blood toward it. He then placed his hand on the
wound again. When his hand was filled with blood, he took it and
stained his head and beard with it, saying,

هكذا و الله أكون حتى ألقى جدي محمدا و أنا مخضوب بدمي، و

أقول: يا رسول الله قتلني فلان و فلان.

*By God, this is how I will meet my grandfather Muhammad (s),
stained in my own blood! I will say, 'O' Messenger of God (s), I
was killed by so and so.'[153]*

Al-Hussain (a) is Struck on the Head

ثم ضعف (عليه السلام) عن القتال فوقف مكانه، فكلما أتاه رجل من الناس و انتهى إليه، انصرف عنه و كره أن يلقى الله بدمه. حتى جاءه رجل من كندة يقال له (مالك بن نسر) فضربه بالسيف على رأسه، و كان عليه برنس [أي قلنسوة طويلة] فقطع البرنس و امتلأ دما، فقال له الحسين (عليه السلام):

Al-Hussain (a) became too weak to fight, so he stopped to rest. Enemy soldiers would come to him [to kill him], but they would soon retreat hating to meet God with his blood [on their hands]. Soon a man from Kinda named Malik ibn Nisr came to al-Hussain (a) and struck him on his head, tearing his headpiece in two and filling it with blood. Al-Hussain (a) said to him,

لا أكلت بيمينك و لا شربت بها، و حشرك الله مع الظالمين.

May you never eat or drink with your right hand! May God group you along with the oppressors [on Judgment Day]!

ثم ألقى البرنس و لبس قلنسوة و اعتمّ عليها، و قد أعيى و تبلّد... (و في بعض الأخبار): أنه ألقى البرنس من رأسه، ثم جاء إلى الخيمة و طلب خرقة. فلما أتوه بها شدّها على جراحته، و لبس فوقها قلنسوة أخرى و اعتمّ عليها. و رجع عنه شمر بن ذي الجوشن و من كان معه إلى مواضعهم، فمكث هنيئة ثم عاد و عادوا إليه و أحاطوا به.

He threw his headpiece and wore a skullcap, wearing a turban over it. At this point, he had become weary and overburdened [by his wounds].

In some accounts: He threw down his headpiece, returned to the camp, and asked for a piece of cloth. When they brought one to him, he wrapped his wound with it, then wore a skullcap and wrapped a turban over it. Shimr ibn Thiljawshan and his men halted their advance and return to their positions. He rested for a while, then he returned to the battlefield and the enemy continued their advance, surrounding him.[154]

Shimr Incites the Army to Fight

ثم نادى شمر: ما تنتظرون بالرجل فقد أثخنته السهام؟ فأحدقت به الرماح و
السيوف. فضربه رجل يقال له (زرعة بن شريك التميمي) ضربة منكرة، و رماه
(سنان بن أنس) بسهم في نحره، و طعنه (صالح بن وهب المرّي) على خاصرته
طعنة منكرة، فسقط الحسين (عليه السلام) عن فرسه إلى الأرض، على خده
الأيمن. ثم استوى جالسا، و نزع السهم من نحره.

Shimr then called, "What are you waiting for? He's been overcome by
the arrows!" The swords and spears [of the enemy] surrounded him. A
man named Zur'a ibn Shurayk al-Tameemi struck him a deadly blow.
Sinan ibn Anas shot him with an arrow in his neck. Salih ibn Wahab
al-Murri gave him a fatal stab in his waist. Al-Hussain (a) fell off his
horse to the ground, falling on his right cheek. He sat up and drew the
arrow out of his neck.[155]

Al-Hussain (a) Falls off his Horse

في (مثير الأحزان): جعلوه شلوا [أي جعلوا أعضاءه مقطّعة] من كثرة الطعن و الضرب. و في (القمقام): لقد أصابته السهام حتى كأنه الطائر و عليه الريش [...].و في (البحار): كانت السهام في درعه كالشوك في جلد القنفذ، و كانت كلها في مقدّمه.

In *Mutheer al-Ahzaan* it is said, "They tore him to pieces with the strikes [of their swords] and stabs [of their spears]." And in *al-Qimqaam*, "Arrows struck him until he was like a bird with the arrows as his feathers. [...]" [Al-Majlisi records] in *al-Bihar*, "The arrows in his armor were like the spines on the skin of a hedgehog, except they were [lodged in and around his chest, rather than his back]."

أما أبو مخنف فقال في مقتله (كما في أسرار الشهادة للدربندي، ص 424): و اعترضه خولي بن يزيد الأصبحي بسهم فوقع في لبّته، فأرداه عن ظهر جواده إلى الأرض صريعا يخور بدم (و روي: أن السهم رماه أبو قدامة العامري)، فجعل (عليه السلام) ينزع السهم بيده، و يتلقّى الدم بكفيه و يخضب به لحيته و رأسه الشريف، و يقول:

Abu Mikhnaf wrote in his *Maqtal*, as did al-Darbandi in *Asrar al-Shahada* (p. 424): Khawli ibn Yazid al-Asbahi shot him with an arrow in his breastbone, felling him off his horse [...]. [Al-Hussain (a)] drew the arrow out and began to take the flowing blood in his hands and using it to stain his noble head and beard. He would say,

هكذا ألقى ربي الله، و ألقى جدي رسول الله (صلى الله عليه و آله و سلم)، و أشكو إليه ما نزل بي.

This is how I will meet my Lord, God! This is how I will meet my grandfather, the Messenger of God (s), and complain to him of what befell me!

و خرّ صريعا مغشيا عليه. فلما أفاق من غشيته وثب ليقوم للقتال فلم يقدر.
فبكى بكاء عاليا، و نادى:

He then fell unconscious. When he woke, he attempted to stand and fight, but could not. He cried out loudly and said,

وا جدّاه، وا محمداه، وا أبا القاسماه، وا أبتاه، وا علياه، وا حسناه،
وا جعفراه، وا حمزتاه، وا عقيلاه، وا عباساه، وا عطشاه، وا غوثاه،
وا قلة ناصراه. أقتل مظلوما و جدي محمّد المصطفى، و أذبح عطشانا
و أبي علي المرتضى، و أترك مهتوكا و أمي فاطمة الزهراء (عليها
السلام)!

O' grandfather! O' Muhammad (s)! O' Abu al-Qasim (s)! O' father! O' Ali (a)! O' Hassan (a)! O' Ja'far! O' Hamza! O' Aqeel! O' Abbas! O' [how strong is] my thirst! O' [who will come to my] aid! O' how few are my supporters! Will I be oppressed and killed while my grandfather is Muhammad al-Mustafa (s)? Will I be slaughtered thirsty while my father is Ali al-Murtada (a)? Will I be left massacred while my mother is Fatima al-Zahraa (a)?[156]

Al-Hussain (a) Fights on his Feet

قال أبو مخنف: حدثني الصّقعب بن زهير عن حميد بن مسلم، قال: كانت عليه جبّة من خزّ، و كان معتمّا، و كان مخضوبا بالوسمة. قال: سمعته يقول قبل أن يقتل، و هو يقاتل على رجليه قتال الفارس الشجاع:

Abu Mikhnaf said, "Al-Sa'qab ibn Zuhair relayed to me that Hameed ibn Muslim said, 'He [al-Hussain (a)] was wearing a woolen coat and a turban, and [was marked by the blood of the wounds that covered his body]. I heard him say before he was killed, as he was fighting on his feet like a valiant warrior.'" [Al-Hussain (a) then said,]

أعلى قتلي تحاثّون؟! أما و الله لا تقتلون بعدي عبدا من عباد الله، الله أسخط عليكم لقتله مني. و ايم الله إني لأرجو أن يكرمني الله بهوانكم، ثم ينتقم لي منكم من حيث لا تشعرون. أما و الله إن قتلتموني لقد ألقى الله بأسكم بينكم و سفك دماءكم، ثم لا يرضى لكم حتى يضاعف لكم العذاب الأليم.

You encourage each other to kill me?! By God, you will never kill another of God's servant for which His anger will be greater than for your killing me! By God, I hope that God will honor me by your demise and then take reribution for [my murder] from whence you are not aware! Indeed, by God, if you kill me, God will turn your enmity toward one another, [so that you] shed [each other's] blood. He will not be content until He multiplies the most painful punishment [that you have now earned].[157]

The Martyrdom of Muhammad ibn Abu Saeed ibn Aqeel

قال هاني بن ثبيت الحضرمي: إني لواقف عاشر عشرة لما صرع الحسين (عليه السلام)، إذ نظرت إلى غلام من آل الحسين (عليه السلام)، عليه إزار و قميص، و في أذنيه درّتان، و بيده عمود من تلك الأبنية، و هو مذعور يتلقّت يمينا و شمالا. فأقبل رجل يركض، حتى إذا دنا منه مال عن فرسه، و علاه بالسيف و قطعه. فلمّا عيب عليه كنّى عن نفسه. و ذلك الغلام هو محمّد بن أبي سعيد بن عقيل بن أبي طالب (عليه السلام) و كانت أمه تنظر إليه و هي مدهوشة.

Hani ibn Thubait al-Hadrami said, "I was standing [among the Umayyad soldiers] on the tenth [of Muharram] when al-Hussain (a) was felled. Suddenly, I saw a boy from the family of al-Hussain (a) wearing [...] two pearls in his ears and carrying a pillar from one of the tents. He was terrified, turning left and right. A man rushed towards him. When he got near the boy, he leaned off his horse and struck him with his sword, killing him. When he was chided for his actions, he refused to give his name [so that he would not be known]."

That boy was Muhammad ibn Abu Saeed ibn Aqeel ibn Abu Talib. His mother was watching him in shock [as he was killed].[158]

The Martyrdom of Abdullah al-Asghar ibn al-Hassan (a)

ثم إنهم لبثوا هنيئة و عادوا إلى الحسين (عليه السلام) و أحاطوا به، و هو جالس على الأرض لا يستطيع النهوض. فخرج الغلام عبد الله بن الحسن السبط (عليه السلام) و له إحدى عشرة سنة، و نظر إلى عمه و قد أحدق به القوم، فأقبل من عند النساء يشتدّ نحو عمه الحسين (عليه السلام)، فلحقته زينب (عليها السلام) لتحبسه، فقال لها الحسين (عليه السلام):

After a while, they returned to al-Hussain (a) and surrounded him as he was sitting on the ground unable to stand. A young boy, Abdullah ibn al-Hassan al-Sibt (a), ran out and he was eleven years of age. He saw his uncle surrounded by soldiers. He ran from amongst the women, rushing toward his uncle al-Hussain (a). [Lady] Zainab (a) ran after him to hold him. Al-Hussain (a) said to her,

احبسيه يا أختي.

Hold him back, sister!

فأبى و امتنع عليها امتناعا شديدا، و قال: و الله لا أفارق عمي. و أهوى أبجر ابن كعب إلى الحسين (عليه السلام) بالسيف، فقال له الغلام: ويلك يابن الخبيثة، أتقتل عمي؟ فضربه أبجر بالسيف، فاتّقاها الغلام بيده، فأطنّها إلى الجلد، فإذا هي معلّقة. فصاح الغلام: يا عمّاه. فأخذه الحسين (عليه السلام) فضمّه إليه، و قال:

The boy refused and tried as best he can to escape her.

[When the boy saw that] Abjar ibn Ka'b came close to al-Hussain (a) with his sword, he called out, "Woe to you, son of a vile woman! Would you kill my uncle?" Abjar struck [Abdullah] with his sword. When the boy tried to block the blow with his hand, it severed his arm so that it hung only by the skin. The boy cried out, "Uncle!" Al-Hussain (a) took him close and said,

يا بن أخي اصبر على ما نزل بك، و احتسب في ذلك الخير، فإن الله يلحقك بآبائك الصالحين.

O' nephew, be patient with what has befallen you and await the best of rewards for it! Surely, God will allow you to join your righteous forefathers.

و رفع الحسين (عليه السلام) يديه قائلا:

Al-Hussain (a) then raised his hand and said,

اللّهم إن متّعتهم إلى حين، ففرّقهم تفريقا، و اجعلهم طرائق قددا [أي مذاهب متفرقة]، و لا ترض الولاة عنهم أبدا، فإنهم دعونا لينصرونا، ثم عدوا علينا يقاتلوننا.

O' God, if You will provide for them for a while, then seperate them into factions, make them into various sects, and do not let the governors be pleased with them. Surely, they called us to support us, but they turned against us and fought us!

و رمى حرملة بن كاهل الغلام بسهم فذبحه و هو في حجر عمّه. و حملت الرجّالة يمينا و شمالا على من كان بقي مع الحسين (عليه السلام) فقتلوهم، حتى لم يبق معه إلا ثلاثة نفر أو أربعة.

Harmala ibn Kahil launched an arrow at the boy, killing him in his uncle's arms. The [enemy] infantry charged left and right and killed anyone who remained with al-Hussain (a). None remained at that point but three or four men [alongside al-Hussain (a)].[159]

Lady Zaynab Speaks to Omar ibn Saad

و خرجت أخته زينب (عليها السلام) إلى باب الفسطاط، فنادت عمر بن سعد

بن أبي وقاص: ويلك يا عمر، أيقتل أبو عبد الله و أنت تنظر إليه! فلم يجبها

عمر بشيء. فنادت: و يحكم أما فيكم مسلم ؟! فلم يجبها أحد بشيء.

[Lady] Zaynab walked to the tent's entrance and called out to Omar
ibn Saad, "Woe to you, Omar! Will Abu Abdullah (a) be killed while
you look on?!" He did not answer her, so she called out to the army,
"Woe to you! Is there no Muslim amongst you?!" Again, no one
answered.[160]

Al-Hussain (a) Sees his Grandfather in a Vision

فخفق الحسين (عليه السلام) برأسه خفقة، ثم انتبه و هو يقول:

Al-Hussain (a) then lowered his head for a bit [as if he had slept for a short while]. He then awoke and said,

رأيت الساعة جدي رسول الله (صلى الله عليه و آله و سلم) و هو يقول: يا بني اصبر، الساعة تأتي إلينا.

I just saw my grandfather, the Messneger of God (s), and he said, 'My son, have patience. Soon, you will be with us.'[161]

The Men Who Killed al-Hussain (a) When he was Weakened

و نادى شمر بن ذي الجوشن الفرسان و الرجالة، فقال: و يحكم ما تنتظرون
بالرجل (اقتلوه) ثكلتكم أمهاتكم؟. فحملوا عليه من كل جانب. فضربه زرعة بن
شريك على كتفه اليسرى، و ضرب الحسين (عليه السلام) زرعة فصرعه. و
ضربه آخر على عاتقه المقدس بالسيف ضربة كبا بها لوجهه، و كان قد أعيى، و
جعل ينوء و يكبّ.

Shimr ibn Thiljawshan called out to his cavalry and infantry, "Woe to
you, what are you waiting for? [Kill] the man! May your mothers grieve
for you!" They attacked al-Hussain (a) from every direction. Zar'a ibn
Shuraik struck al-Hussain (a) on his left shoulder. Al-Hussain (a) struck
back and killed Zar'a. Another man struck him on his noble shoulder
[again], so he fell [off his horse] to the ground. He had been
overpowered, burdened [by his wounds] and felled.

فطعنه سنان بن أنس بن عمرو النخعي في ترقوته. ثم انتزع الرمح، فطعنه في
بواني صدره. ثم رماه سنان أيضا بسهم فوقع السهم في نحره، فسقط (عليه
السلام) و جلس قاعدا. فنزع السهم من نحره، و قرن كفيه جميعا، فكلما امتلأتا
من دمائه خضّب بها رأسه و لحيته، و هو يقول:

Sinan ibn Anas ibn Amr al-Nakha'i stabbed him in his shoulder blade.
He took the spear and stabbed him again in his ribs. He took an arrow
and shot him with an arrow, striking him in his neck. Al-Hussain (a)
fell and sat on the ground. He drew the arrow from his neck and
clasped his hands together [gathering the blood that flowed from his

wounds]. Whenever his hands would fill with blood, he would take it to stain his head and beard, saying,

كذا ألقى الله مخضّبًا بدمي، مغصوبًا عليّ حقّي.

This is how I will meet God, stained with my own blood and usurped of my rights![162]

Shimr's Second Cry Inticing his Men to Kill al-Hussain (a)

و بقي الحسين (عليه السلام) مطروحا مليّا، و لو شاؤوا أن يقتلوه لفعلوا، إلا
أن كل قبيلة تتّكل على غيرها و تكره الإقدام... فصاح الشمر: ما وقوفكم و ما
تنتظرون بالرجل، و قد أثخنته السهام و الرماح، احملوا عليه. و ضربه زرعة بن
شريك على كتفه الأيسر، و رماه الحصين في حلقه و ضربه آخر على عاتقه، و
طعنه سنان بن أنس في ترقوته، ثم في بواني صدره، ثم رماه بسهم في نحره و
طعنه صالح بن وهب في جنبه.

Al-Hussain (a) remained lying on the ground for a while. If the enemy had wished to kill him, they could have. But each tribe would rely on the other and refuse to step forward. Al-Shimr called out, "Why do you [just] stand there? What are you waiting for? [Why don't you kill] the man, when he has been overburdened by wounds and arrows? Charge at him!"

Zar'a ibn Shuraik struck him on his left shoulder, al-Hossayn shot him with an arrow in his jaw, and another man struck him on his shoulder [again]. Sinan ibn Anas stabbed him in his shoulder blade and his ribs, then shot him with an arrow in his neck. Salih ibn Wahab stabbed him in his side.[163]

Hilal ibn Nafi' Describes al-Hussain (a) as he Takes his Final Breaths

قال هلال بن نافع: إني لواقف في عسكر عمر بن سعد، إذ صرخ صارخ: أبشر أيها الأمير، فهذا (شمر) قد قتل الحسين. قال: فخرجت بين الصفين فوقفت عليه، و إنه ليجود بنفسه. فو الله ما رأيت قتيلا مضمّخا بدمه أحسن منه و لا أنور وجها، و لقد شغلني نور وجهه و جمال هيئته عن الفكرة في قتله.

Hilal ibn Nafi' said, "I was standing in the camp of Omar ibn Saad when someone called out, 'Glad tidings, commander! Shimr has killed al-Hussain (a)! I rushed from between the lines and stood over him as he was taking his last breaths. By God, I have not seen a felled man covered in blood that was more handsome than him or of a brighter face. The brightness of his face and his handsome appearance distracted me from thinking about killing him."[164]

Al-Hussain (a) Asks for Water in his Last Breaths

فاستسقى (عليه السلام) في تلك الحال ماء، فأبوا أن يسقوه. و قال له رجل: لا تذوق الماء حتى ترد الحامية فتشرب من حميمها. فقال (عليه السلام):

In that condition, al-Hussain (a) asked for water. The enemies refused to give him. A man called out, "You will not taste water until you reach the scorching fire [of Hell] and drink its boiling waters!" Al-Hussain (a) replied,

أنا أرد الحامية فأشرب من حميمها! بل أرد على جدي رسول الله (ص)، و أسكن معه في داره، في مقعد صدق عند مليك مقتدر، و أشرب من ماء غير آسن ، و أشكو إليه ما ارتكبتم مني و فعلتم بي.

Is it me who will reach the scorching fire [of Hell] and drink its boiling waters? No! I will reach my grandfather the Messenger of God (s) and live with him in his home [in Paradise], in the abode of truthfulness with an omnipotent King, and drink it's unstaling water! I will complain to him of how you transgressed against me and done to me!

فغضبوا بأجمعهم، حتى كأن الله لم يجعل في قلب أحدهم من الرحمة شيئا. فاحتزّوا رأسه و إنه ليكلمهم. فتعجبت من قلة رحمهم، و قلت: و الله لا أجامعكم على أمر أبدا.

They were all angered [by what he said], as if God had not put a shred of mercy in any of their hearts. They severed his head as he was speaking to them. I was surprised by their lack of mercy and said, "By God, I will not go along with you in any matter again!"

و في (الأنوار النعمانية) للسيد نعمة الله الجزائري، ج 2 ص 244: قال: فأقبل عدوّ الله سنان بن أنس و شمر بن ذي الجوشن العامري في رجال من أهل الشام، حتى وقفوا على رأس الحسين (عليه السلام)، فقال بعضهم لبعض: أريحوا الرجل. فنزل سنان بن أنس و أخذ بلحية الحسين (عليه السلام) و جعل يضرب السيف في حلقه، و هو يقول: و الله إني لأجترّ رأسك، و أنا أعلم أنك ابن رسول الله (صلى الله عليه و آله و سلم) خير الناس أما و أبا.

Sayyid al-Jaza'eri says in *al-Anwar al-Nu'maniya* (v. 2 p. 244), "Then the enemy of God Sinan ibn Anas and Shimr ibn Thiljawshan approached with soldiers from the levant. They stood at al-Hussain's (a) head and said to each other, 'Finish the man off!' Sinan ibn Anas went down, grabbed al-Hussain's (a) beard, and began to strike him on his neck, saying, 'By God, I am severing your head and I know that you are the son of the Messenger of God (s) and that your mother and father are the best of parents!'"

و في (مقدمة مرآة العقول) ج 2 ص 284: قال: و جعل سنان بن أنس لا يدنو أحد من الحسين (عليه السلام) إلا شدّ عليه مخافة أن يغلب على رأسه، حتى أخذ رأس الحسين (عليه السلام) فدفعه إلى خوليّ.

Al-Askari writes in *Muqaddimat Miraat al-Oqool* (v. 2 p. 284), "Sinan ibn Anas would charge against any man who would approach al-Hussain (a), fearing that someone would beat him to al-Hussain's (a) head. He severd al-Hussain's (a) head and gave it to Khawli."[165]

Al-Hussain's (a) Prayer Before his Martyrdom

و لما اشتدّ به الحال (عليه السلام) رفع طرفه إلى السماء و قال:

When [al-Hussain's (a) condition became dire and he was taking his last breaths], he looked towads the heavens and said,

اللّهم متعال المكان، عظيم الجبروت، شديد المحال، غني عن الخلائق، عريض الكبرياء، قادر على ما يشاء. قريب الرحمة، صادق الوعد، سابغ النعمة، حسن البلاء. قريب إذا دعيت، محيط بما خلقت. قابل التوبة لمن تاب إليك. قادر على ما أردت، تدرك ما طلبت. شكور إذا شكرت، ذكور إذا ذكرت. أدعوك محتاجا، و أرغب إليك فقيرا، و أفزع إليك خائفا. و أبكي مكروبا، و أستعين بك ضعيفا، و أتوكل عليك كافيا.

O' God, you are the Most High Place, Greatest Power, and Most Terrible Punishment. You are independent of all creation, sublime in Your glory, able to act as You wish, close [to Your creations] in Your mercy, truthful in Your promise, bounteous in Your blessings, and generous in Your goodness. Your are close if You are called upon and wil accept the repentance of whoever repents to You. You are able in what You will and will have what You demand. You are appreciative of those who thank You and will remember those who remember You. I call on You while I'm in need, long for You in my dependence [on You], seek refuge in You from my fears, cry [to You] in my distress, rely on You in my weakness, and trust in You to suffice me.

اللّهم احكم بيننا و بين قومنا، فإنهم غرّونا و خذلونا و غدروا بنا و قتلونا، و نحن عترة نبيك و ولد حبيبك محمّد (صلى الله عليه و آله و سلم) الّذي اصطفيته بالرسالة، و ائتمنته على الوحي، فاجعل لنا من أمرنا فرجا و مخرجا، يا أرحم الراحمين. صبرا على قضائك يا رب، لا إله سواك، يا غياث المستغيثين. مالي ربّ سواك، و لا معبود غيرك. صبرا على حكمك. يا غياث من لا غياث له، يا دائما لا نفاد له. يا محيي الموتى، يا قائما على كل نفس بما كسبت، احكم بيني و بينهم و أنت خير الحاكمين.

O' God, judge between us and our people, for they have called decieved, deserted, betrayed, and murdered us. We are the progeny of your Prophet and the children of your Beloved Muhammad (s), whom You had chosen for the message and trusted with revelation. So grant us in our matter relief and rescue, O' most merciful of the merciful. [Grant us] patience with Your judgment. There is no God but You, O' aid of those who call [upon You] for aid. I have no Lord but You and I do not worship anyone beside You, [so grant me] patience with Your judgment. O' aid of whomever has no aid [but You]! O' Everlasting who will never perish! O' reviver of the dead! O' judge of every soul and what it has done! Judge between me and them, for You are the best of the judges.[166]

Enemy Generals are Bewildered and Unable to Behead al-Hussain (a)

ثم غشي عليه، و بقي ثلاث ساعات من النهار، و القوم في حيرة لا يدرون أهو
حيّ أم ميّت! قال: و بقي الحسين (عليه السلام) مكبوبا على الأرض ملطّخا
بدمه ثلاث ساعات، و هو يقول:

[Al-Hussain (a)] then fell unconscious with the soldiers surrounding him for three hours, not knowing whether he was dead of alive. Al-Hussain (a) remained on laying on the ground for three hours, stained with his own blood. He would say,

صبرا على قضائك، لا إله سواك، يا غياث المستغيثين.

[O' God, grant us] patience with Your judgment! There is no God but You, O' aid of whoever asks [You] for aid!

فابتدر إليه أربعون رجلا كل منهم يريد حزّ نحره الشريف. و عمر بن سعد يقول:
ويلكم عجّلوا عليه. و كان أول من ابتدر إليه (شبث بن ربعي) و بيده السيف،
فدنا منه ليحتزّ رأسه، فرمق الحسين (عليه السلام) بطرفه، فرمى السيف من
يده و ولى هاربا، و هو يقول: ويحك يابن سعد، تريد أن تكون بريئا من قتل
الحسين و إهراق دمه، و أكون أنا مطالب به! معاذ الله أن ألقى الله بدمك يا
حسين.

Forty men approached him, attempting to sever his noble head. All the while, Omar ibn Saad would call out, "Woe to you! Finish him quickly!"

The first to approach [al-Hussain (a)] was Shabath ibn Rib'i carrying a sword. He came close to sever his head, but when al-Hussain (a) opened his eyes, [Shabath] threw down the sword and ran away saying,

"Woe to you, ibn Saad! You wish to claim innocence from the blood and murder of al-Hussain (a), while I would be the one responsible for it! God forbid that I should meet Him with your blood [on my hands], O' Hussain (a)!"

فأقبل (سنان بن أنس) و قال: ثكلتك أمك و عدموك قومك لو رجعت عن قتله. فقال شبث: يا ويلك إنه فتح عينيه في وجهي فأشبهتا عيني رسول الله (صلى الله عليه و آله و سلم) فاستحييت أن أقتل شبيها لرسول الله. فقال له: يا ويلك أعطني السيف فأنا أحقّ منك بقتله.

Sinan ibn Anas stepped forward and said [to Shabath], "May your mother mourn you and your tribe grieve for you if you refuse to kill him!" Sabath replied, "Woe to you! He opened his eyes when I drew near and they looked like the eyes of the Messenger of God (s). Shame did not allow me to kill a man who looked like the Messenger of God (s)." [Sinan] said, "Woe to you! Give me the sword, for I am more deserving [of the honor] to kill him then you!"

فأخذ السيف و همّ أن يعلو رأسه، فنظر إليه الحسين (عليه السلام) فارتعد سنان، و سقط السيف من يده و ولى هاربا، و هو يقول: معاذ الله أن ألقى الله بدمك يا حسين. فأقبل إليه (شمر) و قال: ثكلتك أمك ما أرجعك عن قتله؟. فقال: يا ويلك، إنه فتح في وجهي عينيه، فذكرت شجاعة أبيه، فذهلت عن قتله.

He took the sword, hoping to sever [al-Hussain's (a)] head. But when al-Hussain (a) looked at him, Sinan began to shake. The sword fell from his hand and he ran off, saying, "God forbid that I should meet him with your blood [on my hands], O' Hussain (a)!"

Shimr approached [Sinan] and said, "May your mother mourn you, why have you returned without killing him?" He replied, "Woe to you! He opened his eyes when I drew near, so I remembered the valor of his father and was too overcome to kill him!"[167]

Who Will Finish Off al-Hussain (a)?

و قال سنان لخولي بن يزيد الأصبحي: احتزّ رأسه، فضعف و ارتعدت يداه.
فقال له سنان: فتّ الله عضدك و أبان يدك. فنزل إليه (شمر بن ذي الجوشن)
و كان أبرص، فضربه برجله و ألقاه على قفاه ثم أخذ بلحيته. فقال له الحسين
(عليه السلام):

Sinan [ibn Anas] said to Khawli ibn Yazid al-Asbahi, "Sever his head!"
But he hesitated and his hands shook [in fear]. Sinan said to him, "May
God ruin your arms and sever your hands!"

Then Shimr ibn Thiljawshan, who was a leper, came to al-Hussain (a),
kicked him, threw him on his back, and grabbed his beard. Al-Hussain
(a) said to him,

أنت الكلب الأبقع الّذي رأيته في منامي.

You are the piebald dog I saw in my vision!

قال شمر: أتنشبّهني بالكلاب يابن فاطمة؟. ثم جعل يضرب بسيفه مذبح الحسين
(عليه السلام). و روي أنه جاء إليه شمر بن ذي الجوشن و سنان بن أنس،
و الحسين (عليه السلام) بآخر رمق، يلوك بلسانه من العطش. فرفسه شمر
برجله، و قال: يابن أبي تراب، ألست تزعم أن أباك على حوض النبي يسقي
من أحبه؟. فاصبر حتى تأخذ الماء من يده.

Shimr says, "Do you liken me to a dog, O' son of Fatima (a)?" and
began to strike al-Hussain's (a) neck with his sword.

It is also narrated that al-Hussain (a) was approached by Shimr ibn
Thiljawshan and Sinan ibn Anas while he was taking his last breaths
and chewing his tongue out of thirst. Shirm kicked him and said, "O'

son of Abu Turab, do you not claim that your father stands at the Prophet's (s) Pond [in Paradise], giving water to whomever loves him? So wait until you take a drink from his hand."

ثم قال الشمر لسنان بن أنس: احتزّ رأسه من قفاه. فقال: و الله لا أفعل ذلك، فيكون جده محمّد خصمي. فغضب شمر منه، و جلس على صدر الحسين (عليه السلام) و قبض على لحيته، و همّ بقتله. فضحك الحسين (عليه السلام) و قال له:

Shimr then said to Sinan, "Sever his head from the back!" Sinan replied, "By God I will not do so, for his grandfather Muhammad (s) would be my adversary!" Shimr grew angry, sat on al-Hussain's (a) chest, held on to his bear, and proceeded to finish him. Al-Hussain (a) smiled and said,

أتقتلني! أو لا تعلم من أنا؟

Will you kill me? Do you not know who I am?

قال: أعرفك حق المعرفة؛ أمك فاطمة الزهراء، و أبوك علي المرتضى، و جدك محمّد المصطفى، و خصمك الله العليّ الأعلى، و أقتلك و لا أبالي. و ضربه الشمر بسيفه اثنتي عشرة ضربة، ثم حزّ رأسه الشريف.

Shimr replied, "I know you well. Your mother is Fatima al-Zahraa (a), your father is Ali al-Murtada (a), and your grandfather is Muhammad al-Mustafa (s), but your enemy is God the Most Hight and Sublime! I will kill you without hesitation!" Shimr struck al-Hussain (a) twelve times and then severed his noble head.[168]

Shimr Beheads al-Hussain (a)

فقال الشمر لسنان: يا ويلك إنك لجبان في الحرب، هلمّ إليّ بالسيف فو الله
ما أحد أحقّ مني بدم الحسين. إني لأقتله سواء أشبه المصطفى أو علي المرتضى.
فأخذ السيف من يد سنان و ركب صدر الحسين (عليه السلام) فلم يرهب
منه، و قال: لا تظنّ أني كمن أتاك، فلست أردّ عن قتلك يا حسين! فقال له
الحسين (عليه السلام):

Shimr said to Sinan, "Woe to you! What a coward in the midst of battle.
Give me the sword, for by God no one is more deservant of al-
Hussain's (a) blood then I am. I will kill him whether he is the like of
al-Mustafa (a) or Ali al-Murtada (a)!" He took the sword from Sinan's
hand and sat on al-Hussain's (a) chest. But al-Hussain (a) did not show
fear, so Shimr said, "Do not think that I am like the ones who came to
you before, for I will not hesitate to kill you O' Hussain (a)!" Al-
Hussain (a) said,

من أنت ويلك، فلقد ارتقيت مرتقى صعبا طالما قبّله النبي (صلى الله
عليه و آله و سلم).

Woe to you, who are you? You have surely sat on a great place
which the Prophet (s) would always kiss!

فقال له: أنا الشمر الضبابي. فقال الحسين (عليه السلام):

Shimr [who had masked himself] replied, "I am al-Shimr al-Dababi."
Al-Hussain (a) asked,

أما تعرفني ؟!

Do you not know who I am?

فقال ولد الزنا: بلى، أنت الحسين، و أبوك المرتضى، و أمك الزهرا، و جدك المصطفى، وجدتك خديجة الكبرى. فقال له:

The bastard replied, "Yes, you are al-Hussain (a), your father is al-Murtada (a), your mother is al-Zahraa (a), your grandfather is al-Mustafa (s), and your grandmother is Khadija al-Kubra." Al-Hussain (a) said,

ويحك إذا عرفتني فلم تقتلني ؟

Woe to you, if you know me then why would you kill me?

فقال له: أطلب بقتلك الجائزة من يزيد. فقال له الحسين (عليه السلام):

Shimr replied, "By killing you, I wish to earn the prize of Yazid." Al-Hussain (a) asked,

أيّا أحبّ إليك؛ شفاعة جدي رسول الله (صلى الله عليه و آله و سلم) أم جائزة يزيد ؟

Which is more preferable to you, the intercession of my grandfather the Messenger of God (s) or the prize of Yazid?

فقال: دانق من جائزة يزيد أحب إليّ منك و من شفاعة جدك و أبيك. فقال له الحسين (عليه السلام):

Shimr replied, "A single coin from the prize of Yazid is more preferable to me than the intercession of your father and grandfather!" Al-Hussain (a) said,

إذا كان لا بدّ من قتلي فاسقني شربة من الماء.

If you must kill me, then give me a drink of water first!

فقال: هيهات هيهات، و الله ما تذوق الماء أو تذوق الموت غُصّة بعد غصة و
جرعة بعد جرعة. ثم قال شمر: يابن أبي تراب، ألست تزعم أن أباك على الحوض
يسقي من أحبّ، اصبر قليلا حتى يسقيك أبوك. فقال له (عليه السلام):

Shimr said, "Alas! Alas! You will not taste water until you taste death
[slowly by my hand]! O' son of Abu Turab (a), do you not claim that
your father is at the Pond [of Paradise], quenching the thirst of
whomever he likes? So wait a little until your father gives you a drink!"
Al-Hussain (a) said,

سألتك بالله إلا ما كشفت لي عن لثامك لأنظر إليك.

I ask you by God to lift your mask so that I can see your face!

فكشف له عن لثامه، فإذا هو أبرص أعور، له بوز كبوز الكلب، و شعر كشعر
الخنزير. فقال له الإمام (عليه السلام):

When Shimr lifted his mask, al-Hussain (a) saw that he was a leper and
was blind in one eye, having a long nose like the snout of a dog and
hair like the hair of a pig. Al-Hussain (a) said,

صدق جدي رسول الله (صلى الله عليه و آله و سلم).

Surely, my grandfather the Messenger of God (s) has told the truth!

فقال له الشمر: و ما قال جدك رسول الله (صلى الله عليه و آله و سلم)؟ قال:

Shimr asked, "And what has your grandfather the Messenger of God
(s) said?" Al-Hussain (a) replied,

سمعته يقول لأبي (عليه السلام): يا علي يقتل ولدك هذا أبرص
أعور، له بوز كبوز الكلب، و شعر كشعر الخنزير.

I heard him say to my father, 'O' Ali (a), this son of yours [i.e. al-Hussain (a)] will be killed by a leper who is blind in one eye, having a long nose like the snout of a dog and hair like the hair of a pig.

فقال له شمر: يشبّهني جدك رسول الله بالكلاب، و الله لأذبحنّك من القفا، جزاء لما شبّهني جدك. ثم أكبّه على وجهه، و جعل يحزّ أوداجه بالسيف [...]و كلّما قطع منه عضوا نادى الحسين (عليه السلام):

Shimr said, "Does your grandfather the Messenger of God (s) liken me to a dog! By God, I will slaughter you from the back as punishment for the words of your grandfather!" Shimr then turned al-Hussain (a) on his face and began to slit his veins with the sword [...]. Whenever Shimr severed a part of him, al-Hussain (a) cried out,

وا محمداه وا علياه وا حسناه وا جعفراه وا حمزتاه وا عقيلاه وا عباساه وا قتيلاه وا قلة ناصراه وا غربتاه.

O' Muhammad (s)! O' Ali (a)! O' Hassan (a)! O' Ja'far! O' Hamza! O' Aqeel! O' Abbas! O' the murder! O' how few my supporters are! O' how distant I am from home!

فاحتزّ الشمر رأسه الشريف، و علاه على قناة طويلة .. فكبّر العسكر ثلاث تكبيرات.

Shimr severed al-Hussain's (a) head and hoisted it on a long spear. The army cried out thrice, "*Allah Akbar!*"[169]

The Number of al-Hussain's (a) Wounds

ثم عدّوا ما في جسد الحسين (عليه السلام)، فوجدوه ثلاثا و ثلاثين طعنة
برمح، و أربعا و ثلاثين ضربة بالسيف. و وجدوا في ثيابه مائة و عشرين رمية
بسهم. و هذا مطابق لما أورده الطبري في تاريخه. و في (لواعج الأشجان) للسيد
الأمين، ص 169 ط نجف: وجد في قميص الحسين (عليه السلام) الّذي سلب،
مائة و بضع عشرة؛ ما بين رمية و طعنة و ضربة.

When they counted the number of wounds in al-Hussain's (a) body,
they found 33 spear stabs and 34 sword cuts. They found on his clothes
120 arrow holes. This is in accordance to what al-Tabari mentioned in
his historical account.

Al-Sayyid al-Ameen writes in *Lawa'ij al-Ashjan* (p. 169), "They found in
al-Hussain's (a) shirt over a hundred and ten of tears due to arrows,
stabs, and strikes."

و عن الصادق (عليه السلام): أنه وجد بالحسين (عليه السلام) ثلاث و
ثلاثون طعنة، و أربع و ثلاثون ضربة. و عن الباقر (عليه السلام): أنه وجد
به ثلاثمائة و بضع و عشرون جراحة. و في مخطوطة مصرع الحسين [الموجودة
في مكتبة الأسد بدمشق] قال أبو مخنف: و كان عليه جبّة خزّ دكناء، فوقع
فيها مائة و ثمانون ضربة، فوصل إلى بدنه الشريف اثنان و ستون ضربة و
طعنة.

It is narrated that al-Sadiq (a) said there were 33 stabs and 34 cuts seen
on al-Hussain's (a) body. It is also narrated that al-Baqir (a) said there
were three hundred and twenty some wounds found on al-Hussain's
(a) body.

In the manuscript of *Masra' al-Hussain (a)* [found in the Asad Library in Damascus], Abu Mikhnaf says, "He was wearing a dark woolen cloak which received 180 hits. Some 62 stabs and strikes actually reached his noble body."[170]

Al-Hussain's (a) Horse at the Moment of his Martyrdom

و لما صرع الحسين (عليه السلام) جعل فرسه يحامي عنه، و يثب على الفارس [أي من الأعداء] فيخبطه عن سرجه و يدوسه، حتى قتل الفرس أربعين رجلا، كما في (مدينة المعاجز) عن الجلودي. ثم تمرّغ الفرس في دم الحسين (عليه السلام) و أقبل يركض نحو خيمة النساء و هو يصهل. فسمعت بنات النبي (صلى الله عليه و آله و سلم) صهيله فخرجن، فإذا الفرس بلا راكب، فعرفن أن حسينا (عليه السلام) قد قتل.

When al-Hussain (a) was felled, his horse began to defend him. It would jump at every enemy rider, push him off his saddle, and trample him, until it killed forty men (as narrated by al-Jaloudi in *Madinat al-Ma'ajiz*).

The horse then stained its mane with al-Hussain's (a) blood and galloped toward the camp, neighing loudly. The daughter's of the Prophet (s) heard his neighs and stepped out [to greet al-Hussain (a)]. When they saw that the horse returned without a rider, they knew that al-Hussain (a) was killed.[171]

Lady Zaynab Rushes Toward al-Hussain (a)

لما سقط الحسين (عليه السلام) عن فرسه عفيرا بدمه، رامقا بطرفه إلى السماء، و أمّ جواده إلى الخيام، و سمعت زينب (عليها السلام) صهيله، خرجت لاستقباله، لأنها كانت كلما أقبل أخوها الحسين (عليه السلام) من الحرب تتلقاه و تقع على صدره، و تقبّله و هو يقبّل رأسها. فلما رأت الفرس خالية من راكبها، و عنانها [أي حبل الفرس] يسحب على وجه الأرض، خرّت مغشيّا عليها.

When al-Hussain (a) fell to the ground bloodied and looked upon the heavens, his horse galloped toward the tents. [Lady] Zaynab heard the horse's neighs and rushed out of the tent. Whenever her brother al-Hussain (a) would approach, she used to rush to him, embrace him, and kiss him, and he would kiss her head. But when she saw the horse without a knight and its reigns dragging on the ground, she fainted [out of distress].

فلما أفاقت من غشوتها ركضت إلى نحو المعركة، تنظر يمينا و شمالا، و هي تعثر بأذيالها، و تسقط على وجهها من عظم دهشتها. فرأت أخاها الحسين (عليه السلام) ملقى على وجه الأرض، يقبض يمينا و شمالا، و الدم يسيل من جراحاته كالميزاب، و كان فيه ثلاثمائة و ثمانون جرحا، ما بين ضربة و طعنة؛ فطرحت نفسها على جسده الشريف، و جعلت تنادي و تقول: وا أخاه، وا سيداه، وا أهل بيتاه. ليت السماء أطبقت على الأرض، و ليت الجبال تدكدكت على السهل. و يحك يا عمر بن سعد، أيقتل أبو عبد الله و أنت تنظر إليه؟. فلم يجبها أحد بشيء.

When she woke, she rushed into the battlefield looking right and left, constantly tripping on her robe and falling to her face in her horror. She saw her brother al-Hussain (a) lying on the ground, clinching the sands with his hands. Blood flowed from his wounds; three hundred and eighty of them, between cuts and stabs. She threw herself on his noble body and called out, "O' bother! O' master! O' [martyred] family! Let the sky fall upon the earth! Let the mountains crumble into vallies! Woe to you, Omar ibn Saad! Was Abu Abdullah killed while you looked on?" But no one gave her any answer.

فبينما هي تخاطبه و إذا بالشمر يضربها بالسوط على كتفيها، و قال لها: تنحّي عنه و إلا ألحقتك به! فجذبها عنه قهرا، و ضربها ضربا عنيفا، فرجعت إلى المخيم.

And as she was speaking, Shimr whipped her on her shoulders and said, "Get away from him or I'll send you right after him!" He forcefully pushed her away from [her brother] and began to hit her relentlessly until she returned to the camp.[172]

What did Imam Hussain's (a) Horse say in its Neighs?

عن صاحب (المناقب) و محمد بن أبي طالب: أن الفرس [كان] يصهل و يضرب برأسه الأرض عند الخيمة، حتى مات. قال أمير المؤمنين (عليه السلام) يوم صفين:

The author of *al-Manaqib* and Muhammad ibn Abu Talib say that the horse would neigh and strike its head on the ground near the tent until it died. The Commander of the Faithful (a) said on the day of Siffin,

ولدي هذا يقتل بكربلا عطشانا، و ينفر فرسه و يحمحم، و يقول في حمحمته: الظليمة الظليمة، من أمة قتلت ابن بنت نبيها، و هم يقرؤون القرآن الّذي جاء به إليهم.

This son of mine will be killed thirsty in Karbala. His horse will gallop and neigh. It would say in its neighs, 'The injustice! The injustice! This nation has killed the son of their Prophet's (s) daughter while they read the Quran that [the Prophet (s)] had brought them!'[173]

Why is the Tragedy of Ashura the Greatest Tragedy?

سأل أحدهم الإمام الصادق (عليه السلام) قال: يابن رسول الله كيف صار يوم
عاشوراء يوم مصيبة و غمّ و جزع و بكاء، دون اليوم الّذي قبض فيه رسول
الله (صلى الله عليه و آله و سلم) و اليوم الّذي ماتت فيه فاطمة (عليها السلام)
و اليوم الّذي قتل فيه أمير المؤمنين (عليه السلام) و اليوم الّذي قتل فيه الحسن
(عليه السلام) بالسم؟ فقال:

Someone asked Imam Sadiq (a), "O' son of the Messenger of God (s),
why is it that the day of Ashura has become a day of tragedy, sadness,
mourning, and tears, but the same has not occurred for the day in
which the Messenger of God (s) passed away, or the day in which
[Lady] Fatima (a) died, or the day in which the Commander of the
Faithful (a) was murdered, or the day in which al-Hassan (a) was killed
by poison?" Imam Sadiq (a) replied,

إن يوم الحسين (عليه السلام) أعظم مصيبة من جميع سائر الأيام،
و ذلك أن أصحاب الكساء الذين كانوا أكرم الخلق على الله تعالى،
كانوا خمسة؛ فلما مضى عنهم النبي (صلى الله عليه و آله و سلم) بقي
أمير المؤمنين و فاطمة و الحسن و الحسين (عليهم السلام) فكان
فيهم للناس عزاء و سلوة. فلما مضت فاطمة (عليها السلام) كان في
أمير المؤمنين و الحسن و الحسين (عليهم السلام) عزاء و سلوة.

*The day of al-Hussain (a) [and his martyrdom] is the greatest
tragedy throughout time. That is because the Ashab al-Kisa' - the
People of the Cloak - who were the most honored creation of God*

Almighty, were five. When the Prophet (s) passed away, the Commander of the Faithful (a), [Lady] Fatima (a), al-Hassan (a), and al-Hussain (a) remained as solace and consolation. When [Lady] Fatima (a) passed away, the Commander of the Faithful (a), al-Hassan (a), and al-Hussain (a) remained as solace and consolation.

فلما مضى عنهم أمير المؤمنين (عليه السلام) كان للناس في الحسن و الحسين (عليهما السلام) عزاء و سلوة. فلما مضى الحسن (عليه السلام) كان للناس في الحسين (عليه السلام) عزاء و سلوة. فلما قتل الحسين (عليه السلام) لم يكن بقي من أهل الكساء أحد للناس فيه بعده عزاء و سلوة، فكان ذهابه كذهاب جميعهم، كما كان بقاؤه كبقاء جميعهم. فلذلك صار يومه أعظم مصيبة.

When the Commander of the Faithful (a) passed away, al-Hassan (a) and al-Hussain (a) remained as solace and consolation. When al-Hassan (a) passed away, al-Hussain (a) remained as solace and consolation. When al-Hussain (a) was killed, none of Ahl al-Kisa' remained to be of solace and consolation. Thus, his passing was like the passing of all of them combined, just as his presence was like the presence of all of them combined. That is why his day [i.e. his martyrdom] is the greatest tragedy.[174]

A Caller from the Heavens Warns a Misguided Nation

قال أبو عبد الله الصادق (عليه السلام):

Imam Sadiq (a) said,

لما ضرب الحسين بن علي (عليهما السلام) بالسيف، ثم ابتدر [شمر] ليقطع رأسه، نادى مناد (بعض الملائكة) من قبل الله رب العزّة تبارك و تعالى، من بطنان العرش، فقال: ألا أيتها الأمة المتحيّرة الظالمة الضالّة بعد نبيّها (القاتلة عترة نبيّها)، لا وقّقكم الله (لصوم) و لا فطر و لا أضحى. لا جرم و الله ما وقّقوا و لا يوقّقون أبدا، حتى يقوم ثائر الحسين (عليه السلام).

When al-Hussain ibn Ali (a) was struck with the sword and Shimr approached to sever his head, a caller [an angel] called by the command of God, the Blessed and Almighty Lord of Majesty, from the vicinity of the Throne, 'O' nation that has become confused, oppressive, and deviant after it's Prophet (s), may God never bless you with a fast, a Fitr, or an Adha.' By God, surely they were not blessed nor will they ever be blessed until the rising of the one will seek vengence for al-Hussain (a) [meaning the Awaited Twelfth Imam (a)].[175]

A Caller from the Heavens Mourns al-Hussain (a)

يقول أبو مخنف: إن (الشمر) لما شال الرأس الشريف في رمح طويل، و كبّر العسكر ثلاث تكبيرات؛ زلزلت الأرض، و أظلمت السموات، و قطرت السماء دما. و نادى مناد من السماء: قتل و الله الإمام ابن الإمام أخو الإمام. قتل و الله الهمام بن الهمام، الحسين بن علي بن أبي طالب (عليه السلام). فارتفعت في ذلك الوقت غبرة شديدة سوداء مظلمة، فيها ريح حمراء، لا يرى فيها عين و لا أثر، حتى ظنّ القوم أن العذاب قد جاء. فلبثوا كذلك ساعة ثم انجلت عنهم.

Abu Mikhnaf says that when al-Shimr hoisted the blessed head on a long spear and the enemy called out *Takbir* three times, the earth quaked, the heavens darkened, and the sky rained blood. A caller from the heavens called, "By God, an Imam - the son of an Imam and brother to an Imam - has been killed. By God, a valiant knight - son to a valiant knight - has been killed. He is al-Hussain ibn Ali ibn Abi Talib (a)." Then, a dark dust cloud rose carrying red sand. No thing or movement could be seen in it. People thought that [God's] punishment had befallen them. They were in that state for an hour until [the dust cloud] dissipated.[176]

Savage Crimes Never Seen Before in History

في (مطالب السّؤول) لمحمد بن طلحة الشافعي قال: ثم احتزّوا رأس سبط
رسول الله (صلى الله عليه و آله و سلم) و حبّه الحسين (عليه السلام) بشبا
الحداد، و رفعوه كما ترفع رؤوس ذوي الإلحاد، على رؤوس الصعاد، و اخترقوا
به أرجاء البلاد بين العباد، و استاقوا حرمه و أطفاله أذلاء من الاضطهاد، و
أركبوهم على أخشاب الأقتاب بغير وطاء و لا مهاد. هذا مع علمهم بأنها الذرية
النبوية، المسؤول لها بالمودّة، بصريح القرآن و صحيح الاعتقاد!

Muhammad ibn Talha al-Shafi'i wrote in *Matalib al-Sa'oul*: Then they
severed the head of the beloved grandson of the Messenger of God
(s), al-Hussain (a), with the edges of their swords. They raised his head
[...] on the top of a spear, and paraded it across the land and throught
the nation. They dragged his weakened family and children
oppressively, transporting them on bony camels without any saddle.
This is all despite their knowledge that they are the progeny of the
Prophet (s), whom they were commanded to love in the express verses
of the Holy Quran, [which says, "Say [O' Prophet (s)], 'I do not ask
you any reward for [delivery of the Message] except the love of [my]
relatives.'"][177]

Who Killed al-Hussain (a)?

يجب أن نفرّق عند دراسة هذا التحقيق بين أمرين: الأول: من الّذي ضرب الحسين (عليه السلام) ضربة مميتة حتى صرعه، أي ألقاه على الأرض. و الثاني: من الّذي ذبح الحسين (عليه السلام) و فصل رأسه عن جسده الشريف، و هو ما يسمى بالإجهاز عليه أي الإسراع في قتله و تتميمه. و قد يكون الذبح هو سبب القتل، و قد يكون تعجيلا للقتل، كما حدث للحسين (عليه السلام)، فقد ذبح و به رمق.

When studying this issue we must distinguish between two separate questions. First, who struck al-Hussain (a) with the critical blow that defeated him, felling him to the ground? Second, who is the one who slaughtered him and severed his head? In other words, who finished him off and hastened his death? Note that beheading may be the cause of death, or that it may simply be a hastening of death. The latter was what happened with al-Hussain (a), who was beheaded as he was in his last breaths.

و هذان الأمران مترددان حسب الروايات بين ثلاثة أشخاص هم: شمر - و سنان - و خولي. أما ما يذكر من أن عمر بن سعد قتل الحسين (عليه السلام) فهو من قبيل المجاز، بمعنى أنه هو الآمر لقتله، باعتباره قائد الجيوش التي تولّت قتله، فيكون هو القاتل حكما لا فعلا. و الظاهر من الروايات أن خولي ليس هو القاتل الفعلي، فيكون أمر صرع الحسين (عليه السلام) ثم ذبحه، دائرا بين شمر و سنان. و الذي أرجّحه أن القاتل هو (شمر)، مستدلا بأمور ثلاثة:

The answer to the question revolves, according to historical accounts, between three individuals - Shimr ibn Thiljawshan al-Dababi, Sinan ibn Anas al-Nakha'i, and Khawli ibn Yazid al-Asbahi. As for what is mentioned that Omar ibn Saad is the one who killed al-Hussain (a), that is a matter of metaphor. In other words, he was the one who gave the command to kill al-Hussain (a) and was the commander of the army that murdered him. Thus, Omar ibn Saad was the killer but indirectly.

The historical accounts seem to suggest that Khawli is not the actual killer either. Thus, the question of who delivered the critical blow and who beheaded al-Hussain (a) revolves between Shimr and Sinan.

I believe it is more probable that the killer is Shimr for the following reasons:

أولا، الشهرة التي على ألسن الخطباء، و التي توارثوها أبا عن جدّ؛ أن قاتل الحسين (عليه السلام) هو شمر بن ذي الجوشن. ثانيا، ما صرّحت به الزيارة القائمية، من أن الّذي قتل الحسين (عليه السلام) هو الشمر. ثالثا، أن الثلاثة المذكورين كانوا قساة أجلافا، و لكن الشمر كان أجرأهم على القتل و سفك الدماء. و الذي زاد في حقد الشمر على الحسين (عليه السلام) قول السبط له أنه رأى النبي (صلى الله عليه و آله و سلم) في منامه، فقال له: إن الّذي يتولى قتله رجل أبرص أبقع، له بوز طويل كبوز الكلب. و هذا ينطبق على الشمر. [...].

First, the prominence of the account relayed by lecturers, and which they have passed along for generations, that the killer of al-Hussain (a) is Shimr ibn Thiljawshan. Second, the express words of *Ziyarat al-Nahiya al-Muqaddasa*, stating that al-Hussain's (a) killer is Shimr.

Third, these three individuals were hardhearted brutes, but Shimr was the most audacious and bloodthirsty. Shimr's hatred for al-Hussain (a) was multiplied when al-Hussain (a) told him that he saw the Prophet

(s) in a vision and was told that the individual who would kill him was a piebald leper who had a long snout like a dog. This description applies to Shimr. [...]

لذلك عندما أقبل خولي لقتل الحسين (عليه السلام) فضعف و أرعد، قال له شمر: ثكلتك أمك، ما أرجعك عن قتله؟! و أمامي الآن على الطاولة عشرون رواية، يمكن أن أستخلص منها النتائج التالية:

That is why when Khawli wanted to finish off al-Hussain (a) but hesitated and returned unsuccessful, Shimr said to him, "May your mother mourn you, why have you hesitated in killing him?"

As I write this, I have twenty historical accounts in front of me on the table from which I can deduce the following:

أن الّذي ضرب الحسين (عليه السلام) بسهم فأوقعه عن ظهر جواده صريعا إلى الأرض، هو خولي بن يزيد الأصبحي. و الذي ضرب الحسين (عليه السلام) بالسيف على رأسه (أو بالرمح في حلقه) فصرعه، هو سنان بن أنس النخعي. أما الّذي أجهز على الحسين (عليه السلام) فذبحه و قطع رأسه، فهو شمر بن ذي الجوشن الضبابي. و بعد ذبحه دفع الرأس إلى خولي. فالذين زعموا أن خولي هو الّذي ذبحه، فلأنهم رأوا الرأس في يده، فتوهموا أنه هو الّذي ذبحه. فيكون سنان و شمر قد اشتركا في قتله (عليه السلام).

The one who shot al-Hussain (a) with an arrow, knocking him off his horse and to the ground, was Khawli ibn Yazid al-Asbahi. The one who struck al-Hussain (a) the final critical blow with a sword on his head - or in other accounts with a spear in his jaw - was Sinan ibn Anas al-Nakha'i. The one who beheaded al-Hussain (a) while he was taking his final breaths, hastening his death, was Shimr ibn Thiljawshan al-

Dababi. After he beheaded al-Hussain (a), he gave the head to Khawli to carry.

As for the accounts that asserted that Khawli was the one who beheaded al-Hussain (a), that was a confusion caused by the fact that he hoisted the head on the spear. Thus, we conclude that Sinan and Shimr were actually the two who joined in the killing of al-Hussain (a).[178]

The Martyrdom of Al-Hussain (a) was on a Friday

قال أبو الفرج الاصفهاني في (مقاتل الطالبيين): كان مولده (عليه السلام) لخمس

خلون من شعبان سنة أربع من الهجرة. و قتل يوم الجمعة لعشر خلون من المحرم

سنة إحدى و ستين، و له ست و خمسون سنة و شهور. و قيل: قتل يوم

السبت، و الذي ذكرناه أولا أصح. و أما ما نقله العامة من أنه قتل يوم الاثنين

فباطل، هو شيء قالوه بلا رواية. و كان أول المحرم الّذي قتل فيه (عليه السلام)

يوم الأربعاء. أخرجنا ذلك بالحساب الهندي من سائر الزيجات [أي قوائم

الحسابات الفلكية]، و إذ كان ذلك كذلك، فليس يجوز أن يكون اليوم العاشر

من المحرم يوم الاثنين.

Abu al-Faraj al-Asfahani says in *Maqatil al-Talibiyyin*: He was born on the 5th of Shabaan, 4 AH. He was killed on Friday, the 10th of Muharram, 61 AH, while he was fifty six years and some months old. It is also said that he was killed on a Saturday, but what we mentioned earlier is more accurate. As for what is mentioned by the public that he was killed on a Monday, it is incorrect and relayed without any attribution. The 1st of Muharram in the year of his martyrdom was on a Wednesday, as can be deduced by [astronomical] calculations through several calendars. If that is the case, then the 1oth day cannot be a Monday. This is a clear and obvious truth that can be added to the available narrations.[179]

Notes

1 Beydoun, *Mawsu'at Karbala*, 2:19.

2 Al-Khowarizmi, *Maqtal al-Hussain (a)*, 1:220.

3 Al-A'lami, *Da'erat al-Ma'arif*, 23:194.

4 Chamseddine, *Ansar al-Hussain*, 49.

5 Al-Ameen, *A'yan al-Shia*, 4:143.

6 Al-Khowarizmi, *Maqtal al-Hussain (a)*, 2:171.

7 Al-Darabandi, *Asrar al-Shahada*, 315.

8 Al-Darabandi, *Asrar al-Shahada*, 315.

9 Al-Qummi, *Kamil al-Ziyarat*, 192.

10 Ibn Tawus, *Al-Luhuf*, 43.

11 Al-Shalaq, *Al-Hussain (a) Imam al-Shahideen*, 107.

12 Chamseddine, *Ansar al-Hussain*, 57, 2nd ed.

13 Al-Muqarram, *Maqtal al-Hussain (a)*, 292.

14 Ibn Tawus, *Al-Luhuf*, 42.

15 Al-Qazwini, *Al-Watha'eq al-Rasmiyya*, 162.

16 Al-Khowarizmi, *Maqtal al-Hussain (a)*, 2:9.

17 Al-Qazwini, *Al-Watha'eq al-Rasmiyya*, 168.

18 Al-Khowarizmi, *Maqtal al-Hussain (a)*, 2:14.

19 Al-Muqarram, *Maqtal al-Hussain (a)*, 296.

20 Al-Mufid, *Al-Irshad*, 236.

21 Al-Khowarizmi, *Maqtal al-Hussain (a)*, 2:15.

22 Al-Muqarram, *Maqtal al-Hussain (a)*, 297.

23 Al-Mufid, *Al-Irshad*, 237.

24 Al-Tabari, *Al-Tareekh*, 6:245.

25 Al-Muqarram, *Maqtal al-Hussain (a)*, 297.

26 Beydoun, *Mawsu'at Karbala*, 2:66.

27 Al-Jawahiri, *Mutheer al-Ahzan*, 73.

28 Al-Muqarram, *Maqtal al-Hussain (a)*, 299.

29 Al-Hashimi, *Al-Hussain (a) fi Tareeq al-Shahada*, 147. Al-Mutazili, *Sharh Nahj al-Balagha*, 3:307.

30 Al-Muqarram, *Maqtal al-Hussain (a)*, 300.

31 Al-Khowarizmi, *Maqtal al-Hussain (a)*, 2:11.

32 Beydoun, *Mawsu'at Karbala*, 2:70.

33 Al-Khowarizmi, *Maqtal al-Hussain (a)*, 2:10.

34 Al-Majlisi, *Muqaddimat Mir'aat al-'Uqool*, 2:253.

35 Al-Muqarram, *Maqtal al-Hussain (a)*, 302.

36 Beydoun, *Mawsu'at Karbala*, 2:74.

37 Al-Jaza'eri, *Al-Anwar al-Nu'maniya*, 3:265.

38 Al-Ameen, *Lawa'ij al-Ashjan*, 146.

39 Abu Mikhnaf, *Maqtal al-Hussain (a)*, 64.

40 Al-Majlisi, *Muqaddimat Mir'aat al-'Uqool*, 2:254.

41 Al-Majlisi, *Muqaddimat Mir'aat al-'Uqool*, 2:255.

42 Al-Majlisi, *Muqaddimat Mir'aat al-'Uqool*, 2:255.

43 Al-Ameen, *Lawa'ij al-Ashjan*, 142.

44 Beydoun, *Mawsu'at Karbala*, 2:76.

45 Al-Tabari, *al-Tareekh*, 6:255.

46 Shubbar, *Adab al-Taf*, 81.

47 Al-Mufid, *Al-Irshad*, 238.

48 Al-Khowarizmi, *Maqtal al-Hussain (a)*, 2:17; Abu Mikhnaf, *Maqtal al-Hussain (a)*, 65; Al-Muqarram, *Maqtal al-Hussain (a)*, 301.

49 Al-Muqarram, *Maqtal al-Hussain (a)*, 301.

50 Al-Ameen, *Lawa'ij al-Ashjan*, 141.

51 Beydoun, *Mawsu'at Karbala*, 2:83.

52 Abu Mikhnaf, *Maqtal al-Hussain (a)*, 66.

53 Al-Khowarizmi, *Maqtal al-Hussain (a)*, 2:17.

54 Al-Khowarizmi, *Maqtal al-Hussain (a)*, 2:17.

55 Shubbar, *Adab al-Taf*, 81.

[56] Abu Mikhnaf, *Maqtal al-Hussain (a)*, 67.

[57] Al-Muqarram, *Maqtal al-Hussain (a)*, 305.

[58] Al-Muqarram, *Maqtal al-Hussain (a)*, 305.

[59] Al-Khowarizmi, *Maqtal al-Hussain (a)*, 2:20.

[60] Shubbar, *Adab al-Taf*, 117.

[61] Al-Muqarram, *Maqtal al-Hussain (a)*, 306.

[62] Al-Muqarram, *Maqtal al-Hussain (a)*, 307.

[63] Beydoun, *Mawsu'at Karbala*, 2:91.

[64] Al-Muqarram, *Maqtal al-Hussain (a)*, 312.

[65] Al-Bayan Magazine, Najaf, 2:35-39.

[66] Abu Mikhnaf, *Maqtal al-Hussain (a)*, 138.

[67] Al-Khowarizmi, *Maqtal al-Hussain (a)*, 2:24.

[68] Al-Muqarram, *Maqtal al-Hussain (a)*, 311.

[69] Al-Khowarizmi, *Maqtal al-Hussain (a)*, 2:23.

[70] Beydoun, *Mawsu'at Karbala*, 2:95.

[71] Al-Khowarizmi, *Maqtal al-Hussain (a)*, 2:14.

[72] Al-Khowarizmi, *Maqtal al-Hussain (a)*, 2:14.

[73] Al-Khowarizmi, *Maqtal al-Hussain (a)*, 2:17.

[74] Al-Khowarizmi, *Maqtal al-Hussain (a)*, 2:17.

[75] Al-Khowarizmi, *Maqtal al-Hussain (a)*, 2:18.

[76] Ibn Asakir, *al-Tareekh*, 212.

[77] Al-Muqarram, *Maqtal al-Hussain (a)*, 313.

[78] Al-Zinjani, *Wasilat al-Darain*, 101.

[79] Al-Khowarizmi, *Maqtal al-Hussain (a)*, 2:18.

[80] Al-Khowarizmi, *Maqtal al-Hussain (a)*, 2:19.

[81] Al-Khowarizmi, *Maqtal al-Hussain (a)*, 2:20.

[82] Al-Muqarram, *Maqtal al-Hussain (a)*, 294.

[83] Al-Ameen, *Lawa'ij al-Ashjan*, 146.

[84] Al-Ameen, *Lawa'ij al-Ashjan*, 146.

[85] Al-Khowarizmi, *Maqtal al-Hussain (a)*, 2:21.

[86] Al-Khowarizmi, *Maqtal al-Hussain (a)*, 2:21.

[87] Beydoun, *Mawsu'at Karbala*, 2:103.

[88] Al-Ameen, *A'yan al-Shia*, 4:234.

[89] Al-Muqarram, *Maqtal al-Hussain (a)*, 308.

[90] Al-Ameen, *Lawa'ij al-Ashjan*, 148.

[91] Al-Ameen, *Lawa'ij al-Ashjan*, 147.

[92] Al-Ameen, *Lawa'ij al-Ashjan*, 148.

[93] Al-Ameen, *Lawa'ij al-Ashjan*, 148.

[94] Al-Muqarram, *Maqtal al-Hussain (a)*, 315.

[95] Al-Zinjani, *Wasilat al-Darain*, 149.

[96] Ibn al-Atheer, *al-Kamil*, 3:394.

[97] Al-Khowarizmi, Maqtal al-Hussain (a), 2:25.

[98] Al-Khowarizmi, Maqtal al-Hussain (a), 2:26.

[99] Al-Muqarram, *Maqtal al-Hussain (a)*, 318.

[100] Al-Ha'eri, *Al-Faji'a al-'Uthma*, 138.

[101] Al-Khowarizmi, Maqtal al-Hussain (a), 2:30.

[102] Al-Ha'eri, *Al-Faji'a al-'Uthma*, 137.

[103] Beydoun, *Mawsu'at Karbala*, 2:120.

[104] Beydoun, *Mawsu'at Karbala*, 2:120.

[105] Al-Ameen, *Lawa'ij al-Ashjan*, 152.

[106] Beydoun, *Mawsu'at Karbala*, 2:122.

[107] Al-Ameen, *Lawa'ij al-Ashjan*, 152.

[108] Al-Ameen, *Lawa'ij al-Ashjan*, 174.

[109] Al-Ameen, *Lawa'ij al-Ashjan*, 152.

[110] Beydoun, *Mawsu'at Karbala*, 2:124.

[111] Beydoun, *Mawsu'at Karbala*, 2:124.

[112] Al-Ameen, *Lawa'ij al-Ashjan*, 175.

[113] Al-Muqarram, *Maqtal al-Hussain (a)*, 330.

[114] Al-Ameen, *Lawa'ij al-Ashjan*, 173-4.

[115] Al-Darabandi, *Asrar al-Shahada*, 310.

[116] Al-Mayaniji, *Al-'Uyoon al-'Abra*, 158.

[117] Al-Ameen, *Lawa'ij al-Ashjan*, 178.

[118] Al-Ameen, *Lawa'ij al-Ashjan*, 179.

[119] Al-Muqarram, *Maqtal al-Hussain (a)*, 334.

[120] Al-Ha'eri, *Al-Faji'a al-'Uthma*, 146.

[121] Al-Muqarram, *Maqtal al-Hussain (a)*, 335.

[122] Beydoun, *Mawsu'at Karbala*, 2:138.

[123] Al-Ha'eri, *Al-Faji'a al-'Uthma*, 104.

[124] Al-Zinjani, *Wasilat al-Darain*, 278.

[125] Al-Muqarram, *Maqtal al-Hussain (a)*, 340.

[126] Al-Turaihi, *Al-Muntakhab*, 450.

[127] Abu Mikhnaf, *Maqtal al-Hussain (a)*, 84.

[128] Al-Darabandi, *Asrar al-Shahada*, 423.

[129] Al-Turaihi, *Al-Muntakhab*, 451.

[130] Al-Dhahabi, *Siyar A'lam al-Nubala*, 302.

[131] Al-Muqarram, *Maqtal al-Hussain (a)*, 340.

[132] Al-Darabandi, *Asrar al-Shahada*, 405.

[133] Al-Darabandi, *Asrar al-Shahada*, 406.

[134] Al-Mayaniji, *Al-'Uyoon al-'Abra*, 176.

[135] Al-Qirmani, *Akhbar al-Duwal*, 108.

[136] Al-Muqarram, *Maqtal al-Hussain (a)*, 341.

[137] Beydoun, *Mawsu'at Karbala*, 2:148.

[138] Abu Mikhnaf, *Maqtal al-Hussain (a)*, 84.

[139] Al-Tabari, *Al-Tareekh*, 7:354.

[140] Abu Mikhnaf, *Maqtal al-Hussain (a)*, 86.

[141] Al-Qirmani, *Akhbar al-Duwal*, 107.

[142] Ibn Tawus, *Al-Luhuf*, 66.

[143] Al-Shabrawi, *Al-Ithaf*, 73.

[144] Al-Ha'eri, *Al-Faji'a al-'Uthma*, 105.

[145] Al-Khowarizmi, *Maqtal al-Hussain (a)*, 2:33.

[146] Al-Jawahiri, *Mutheer al-Ahzan*, 86.

[147] Al-Muqarram, *Maqtal al-Hussain (a)*, 348.

[148] Al-Khowarizmi, *Maqtal al-Hussain (a)*, 2:34.

[149] Abu Mikhnaf, *Maqtal al-Hussain (a)*, 89.

[150] Al-Majlisi, *Muqaddimat Mir'aat al-'Uqool*, 2:282.

[151] Al-Majlisi, *Muqaddimat Mir'aat al-'Uqool*, 2:282.

[152] Al-Muqarram, *Maqtal al-Hussain (a)*, 346.

[153] Al-Khowarizmi, *Maqtal al-Hussain (a)*, 2:34.

[154] Al-Khowarizmi, *Maqtal al-Hussain (a)*, 2:35.

[155] Al-Khowarizmi, *Maqtal al-Hussain (a)*, 2:35.

[156] Al-Ha'eri, *Al-Faji'a al-'Uthma*, 167.

[157] Al-Majlisi, *Muqaddimat Mir'aat al-'Uqool*, 2:283.

[158] Al-Muqarram, *Maqtal al-Hussain (a)*, 353.

[159] Al-Muqarram, *Maqtal al-Hussain (a)*, 354.

[160] Al-Mufid, *Al-Irshad*, 242.

[161] Sibt ibn Al-Jawzi, *Tathkirat al-Khawas*, 263.

[162] Ibn Tawus, *Al-Luhuf*, 52.

[163] Al-Muqarram, *Maqtal al-Hussain (a)*, 354.

[164] Al-Hilli, *Mutheer al-Ahzan*, 57.

[165] Al-Muqarram, *Maqtal al-Hussain (a)*, 356.

[166] Al-Muqarram, *Maqtal al-Hussain (a)*, 356.

[167] Abu Mikhnaf, *Maqtal al-Hussain (a)*, 89.

[168] Al-Khowarizmi, *Maqtal al-Hussain (a)*, 2:36.

[169] Abu Mikhnaf, *Maqtal al-Hussain (a)*, 91.

[170] Sibt ibn Al-Jawzi, *Tathkirat al-Khawas*, 253.

[171] Al-Mayaniji, *Al-'Uyoon al-'Abra*, 193.

[172] Al-Ha'eri, *Al-Faji'a al-'Uthma*, 171.

[173] Al-Darabandi, *Asrar al-Shahada*, 435.

[174] Al-Sadouq, *Ilal al-Sharae'*, 1:225.

[175] Al-Nisabouri, *Rawdat al-Wa'edhin*, 193.

[176] Al-Darabandi, *Asrar al-Shahada*, 429.

[177] Al-Mayaniji, *Al-'Uyoon al-'Abra*, 186.

[178] Beydoun, *Mawsu'at Karbala*, 2:184.

[179] Al-Bahrani, *Maqtal al-'Awalim*, 17:327.

Made in the USA
Monee, IL
23 May 2020